Think on Purpose

Dan Green, PhD

Copyright © 2019 Dan Green, PhD
Published by Psyndesis, LLC
www.Psyndesis.com
All rights reserved.

No part of this publication may be reproduced, stored in a retrieval system, or transmitted in any form or by any means, electronic, mechanical, photocopying, recording, scanning, or otherwise, or used in any form or by any means - graphic, electronic or mechanical - except as permitted under Section 107 or 108 of the 1976 United States Copyright Act, without the prior written permission of the Publisher, except in the case of brief quotations, with citation, embodied in critical articles or reviews. Requests to the Publisher for permission should be addressed to the Publications department e-mail: Dan@Psyndesis.com.

Care has been taken to trace ownership of copyrighted material sourced and contained in this book. The publisher will gladly receive any requests to correct references, citations, or credit lines in subsequent editions. This publication is designed to provide truthful and authoritative information in reference to the subject matter covered. This publication is sold with the understanding that the material contained is for academic purposes only and not to be used for professional diagnosis of any conditions presented. Any professional advice should be sought from competent professionals.

The author of this book does not dispense any medical advice or prescribe the use of any technique as a form of treatment for physical, emotional, or medical problems without the advice of a physician, either directly or indirectly. The intent of the author is only to offer information of a general nature to help in your quest for emotional and spiritual well-being. In the event you use any of the information in this book for yourself, the author and the publisher assume no responsibility for your actions.

Publication Data

Green, Dan.

Title: Think on Purpose / Dan Green. Includes bibliographical references and index.

Subjects: 1. Psychology. 2. Personality. 3. Emotional Intelligence. 4. Inner Passivity. 5. Inner Aggression. 6. Locus of Control. 7. Cognitive Distortion. 8. Emotional Distortion.

Production Credits

Cover and Interior Design: Ian Gillespie

Edited by: Ken Wohleking

Printed in the United States of America

FIRST EDITION - ISBN: 9781095544181

BOOK QUOTES

"An important read for anyone who wants to learn how to eliminate anxiety and depression using the power of the human mind."

- Fortune 500 Leader

"For the first time, I know what blocks my ability to think on purpose. Better yet, I now know what to do about it."

- IT Executive

"Green masterfully organizes hundreds of academic studies, psychological perspectives, and philosophical positions into a single masterpiece that shows the reader how to maximize purposeful thinking."

- Psychology Professor

"The Purposeful Cognition Index is truly the first of its kind; an assessment that will be an important building block of this subject matter for years to come."

- Industrial-Organizational Psychologist

Other Books By Dan Green

The Art of Modern War: 21 Applications of the Art of War to Modern Business

The EQ Shinobi: Advanced Applications of Emotional Intelligence to Modern Business

DEDICATION

To Dexter, who showed me the way.

CONTENTS

Table of Contents

INTRODUCTION | THE QUEST FOR PURPOSE 1

Part I 5

CHAPTER 1 | THE SEARCH FOR SANITY 6
    The Emergence of Modern Psychotherapy 8
    The Five Psychological Perspectives 10

CHAPTER 2 | THE INNER DEPTHS OF THE MIND 12
    The Id, The Ego, and the Superego 14
    The Unconscious Controversy 17
    Freud's Contributions 18

CHAPTER 3 | THERE WILL BE CONSEQUENCES 21
    Types of Conditioning 22
    Schedules of Reinforcement 24

CHAPTER 4 | THE THIRD FORCE 27
    Self-Actualization 28
    Hierarchy of Needs 29

CHAPTER 5 | THE REVOLUTION 37
    Memory, Language, and Chunks 39
    Mental Processes 41

CHAPTER 6 | INVESTIGATION OF INHERITANCE 44
    The Brain and the Nervous System 47

CHAPTER 7 | PART I SUMMARY 50

Part II 55

CHAPTER 8 | INNER PASSIVITY 56
    Inner Passivity in Our Relationships 60

Inner Passivity and Our Health	62
Freeing Ourselves from Inner Passivity	67
Generate Self-Awareness of Your Inner Passivity	68
Develop Your Antifragility	68
Aim For Your Average	75

CHAPTER 9 | INNER AGGRESSION 80

Our Inner Critic	80
Self-Defeating Personality Disorder	82
Self-Esteem, the Main Victim of Inner Aggression	85
Freeing Ourselves from Inner Aggression	87
Get in the Zone	88
Tame Your Inner Critic	91
Focus on Building Your Self-Esteem	93

CHAPTER 10 | LOCUS OF CONTROL 100

Locus of Control Versus Inner Passivity	102
Positive Outcomes	103
Develop an Internal Locus of Control	105

CHAPTER 11 | COGNITIVE DISTORTION 110

Cognitive Behavioral Therapy	111
Fight or Flight	114
Emotional Intelligence	116
Bias, Decision Paradoxes, and Heuristics	122
How to Overcome Your Cognitive Distortions	126
Avoid Zahavian Signals	127
Separate Facts and Opinions	130
Summon the Challenger, Bring an Anchor	132

CHAPTER 12 | EMOTIONAL DISTORTION 137

How Memories Are Made	138
The Source of Emotional Distortion	140

How to Overcome Your Emotional Distortions 141
Understand Your Body Map 141
Label Your Emotions 143
Recognize That There Are No Bad Emotions 147

CHAPTER 13 | PART II SUMMARY 151
The Bright Side and the Dark Side 153

Part III 157

CHAPTER 14 | LEADING ON PURPOSE 158
What Leaders Do 161

CHAPTER 15 | RELATING ON PURPOSE 172
Mutually Satisfying Relationships 174
The Social Interaction 178
Symbolic Interactionism 181
The Looking Glass Self 185
Why Marriages Begin 186
Why Marriages Fail 188

CHAPTER 16 | BEING ON PURPOSE 193
Break Free From Inner Passivity 196
Destroy Your Inner Aggression 198
Regain Your Locus of Control 200
Starve Your Cognitive Distortion 201
Know Your Emotional Distortion 203

CHAPTER 17 | PART III SUMMARY 206

CHAPTER 18 | CONCLUSION 208

About the Purposeful Cognition Index 212

References 213

ABOUT THE AUTHOR 227

INDEX 228

Foreword by Kelly Vandersluis Morgan, Ph.D.

I have known Dan, literally, my entire life. We were both born on the same day, in the same hospital, but it took until high school for us to become friends. The young man I knew back then was wise beyond his years, motivated, charismatic. I'm pretty sure you'll recognize that young man's voice in his writing here. Dan has only grown in those qualities.

In this book, Dan will start by telling you the story of psychology - the story of us. We mature and develop through trial and error and, eventually, learning to think on purpose. Though schooling teaches us to think linearly, our brains and emotions don't work that way. When we force ourselves to think linearly, we miss opportunities for creativity and growth.

We are the summation of our experiences, enculturation, and social norms. But, it's not just that. We multiply that by the spark of magic that makes you, you - personality. Further, we continue to mature and grow, and we continue to expand our repertoire of experiences in the world. At any point in our lives, we can take control of our thinking and use it in powerful ways.

This idea that we can be in charge of our own thinking, and, therefore, behavior and lives, is a powerful assumption. In my world, I use these concepts for health behavior change. Often, people try to manipulate behavior alone - missing the key that purposeful cognition is what you do, and behavior is the outcome.

I'm positive that you'll not only find value in this book, but you'll also enjoy it. I encourage you to take the time to examine your beliefs and assumptions as you read. That is part of thinking on purpose.

Kelly Vandersluis Morgan, Ph.D.
Tsirona Health Coaching
George Mason University
www.tsirona.com
Kelly.Morgan@tsirona.com

ACKNOWLEDGMENTS

This book would not be possible without the help of the following:

Erin, Ian, Ken, Caleb, Drake, Dexter, and Peter.

Think on Purpose

Dan Green, PhD

INTRODUCTION | THE QUEST FOR PURPOSE

"Watch your thoughts; they become words;
watch your words; they become actions;
watch your actions; they become habits;
watch your habits; they become character;
watch your character, for it becomes your destiny."

LAO TZU, *sixth century BCE*[1]

This book is about the bright side and the dark side of the human mind and about the psychological nature of passive thinking, the genesis of Inner Aggression, and our sources of intellectual power. Many cultures throughout history contemplated on the nature of the mind, the infinite depths of the psyche, and how our innermost thoughts, both conscious and unconscious, affect our behaviors, well-being, and overall quality of life. Even though the term "psychology" is considered a modern term and was first attributed to German philosopher Rudolf Goclenius[2] in 1590, philosophers, psychologists, and scientists have researched the brain for more than a few thousand years. In Ancient Egypt, the Edwin Smith Papyrus,[3] an early manual of military surgery that describes 48 cases of injury, fractures, wounds, dislocations, and tumors, contained an early description of the brain and its functions. Ancient Greek philosophers, such as Thales, Plato, Pythagoras, and Aristotle developed theories of the *psuchē*,[4] (the term from which the first half of "psychology" is derived), starting around 550 BCE. The Manual of Discipline, an important Jewish historical document from the Dead Sea Scrolls, dated around 21 BCE – 61 AD, mentions a "division of human nature into two opposing spirits of veracity and perversity."[5] Medieval thinkers, such as Ibn Sirin and Al-Farabi, wrote books on topics related to dream interpretation, psychotherapy, consciousness, reaction time, and mind imbalance.[6] A common theme was present within all of this research – the notion that the mind seeks truth, accuracy, and fidelity on one hand, yet has a deliberate desire to behave in unreasonable ways on the other. The mind has a proclivity for the conscious and the unconscious, a penchant for the bright side and the dark side, a tendency to be passive and aggressive, and an affinity for clear and distorted thinking.

In 1637, René Descartes wrote in *Discourse on the Method*, [translated from French] "And as I observed that this truth, I think, therefore I am, was so certain and of such evidence that no ground of doubt, however extravagant, could be alleged by the Sceptics capable of shaking it, I concluded that I might, without scruple, accept it as the first principle of the philosophy of which I was in search." This is summarized by the phrase "I think, therefore I am."[7] The Latin philosophical proposition by Descartes, later appearing in *Principles of Philosophy* as "cogito, ergo sum," is the supreme notion that thinking makes something so. Thinking makes us real. All other knowledge can be a figment of the imagination, a deception, or a mistake, but at a minimum, Descartes realized that his own thinking, even if that thinking is rooted in doubt, is the only thing that proves his own existence (this theory still holds true for those that believe we currently live in an artificial intelligence simulation, like Elon Musk[8] famously claims or as portrayed in the movie series *The Matrix*). As Charles Porterfield Krauth, a leading theologian often credited for the revival of the Lutheran Confessions, later translated, "that cannot doubt which does not think, and that cannot think which does not exist. I doubt, I think, I exist."[9] Another translation articulated by French Poet Antoine Leonard Thomas further expanded upon the translation by deciphering Descartes's full intent; "dubito, ergo cogito, ergo sum," or "I doubt, therefore I think, therefore I am."[10] This concept, often referred to as the cogito,[11] would later become a fundamental element of Western Philosophy.

The psychological concept of competing spirits, a conscious and an unconscious, or a bright side and a dark side, would continue to be expanded upon by researchers, scientists, and philosophers. The concept that our active thoughts, even if those active thoughts are doubts, which prove our existence to be real and shape our theories of existentialism, continue to be foundations of modern philosophical and psychological thinking. The purpose of this book is to explore the levels of the mind, such as the unconscious and the conscious, the passive and the aggressive, and our Cognitive Distortions. I will discuss the relationship of those levels to emotional intelligence and active thinking, and introduce a mechanism for assessing the interconnections of these structures to deliver actionable insights and descriptions of how these relationships affect our lives.

I will dive into many different psychological concepts and philosophical constructs such as: the id, ego, superego, emotional intelligence, Cognitive Distortions, the five psychological perspectives, Locus of Control, cognitive bias, self-fulfilling prophecies, self-actualization, and emotional self-awareness, just to name a few, in order to create a single model that can be used to assess certain aspects of our mental health and psychological well-being.

In my professional career as a Fortune 500 consultant, during my time as a university professor, and by performing thousands of hours as an executive coach that included conversations with top leaders within organizations, managers from every industry, and everyday people who lead everyday lives, I began to notice something. I began to see common themes that were responsible for most of the anxiety, depression, and other destructive cognitive factors that block us from achieving our maximum potential because they destroy our ability to *own our own thoughts and to think on purpose*. Through my research, I have organized these themes into five domains and created an assessment that can measure the level that each of these domains is present within you. The assessment, which will be available to you after you finish the book, is called the Purposeful Cognition Index, or PCI. The five key domains that affect our ability to think on purpose, or put differently, to develop purposeful cognition are:

Inner Passivity
Inner Aggression
Locus of Control
Cognitive Distortion
Emotional Distortion

I hope that by learning about these psychological constructs, in combination with an ability to assess them, will bring about a sense of clarity and mental health that has not yet been previously available. I am a firm believer in Cognitive Behavioral Therapy, or CBT, as a drug-free alternative to many psychological dysfunctions and the goal of the PCI assessment is to further expand the application of targeted cognition as a healing mechanism for the many maladies of the modern mind.

Thinking makes us real. Actively thinking, or thinking on purpose, shapes our existence. If we can enhance our ability to think on purpose, we can improve our performance at work, our relationships with others, and our overall quality of life.

This book is organized into three parts. Part I will cover many of the important historical milestones in psychology that show the progression of how the treatment of mental disorders developed into its modern form. Each chapter in Part I builds upon the previous chapter and highlights important concepts from each of the five major perspectives of psychology. These are important concepts to understand while on your quest for purposeful cognition. Part II will explore the five domains of Inner Passivity, Inner Aggression, Locus of Control, Cognitive Distortion and Emotional Distortion, and provide proven strategies to master them. Part III will show how purposeful cognition will make you a stronger leader, enhance your relationships, and maximize your ability to live in the present.

I am an industrial-organizational psychologist and philosopher of cognition, humanism and positive thinking. I investigate methods that improve employee performance for organizations and seek new ways to help people enhance mental stamina and develop lasting cognitive power. I am also a teacher. I teach organizational leadership and performance psychology to students all over the world, using emotional intelligence, personality, and cognitive psychology. Over the course of thousands of lectures, I began to notice several common ideas that were recurring. Our emotions, our reactions to events, our passive nature and our inner critic, all shape how we see the world, interact with others, and ultimately, whether we achieve success in life. I have used these concepts to help those in dire life circumstances pull themselves from the depths of despair to later learn how to develop a positive outlook on life. Circumstances such as: alcoholism, extreme stress and anxiety, or life-threatening illness. I have personal experience helping others, who have been addicted to drugs and prescription medications, kick these poisons by helping them develop the power of their own mind. I am not against medication or anti-drugs for that matter (I generally take a Libertarian view of drug use) but I do believe that our mind is the most potent source of power we have access to; our most powerful drug available to us. As Shakespeare once said in *Hamlet*, "There is nothing good or bad, but thinking makes it so" or the Buddha once proclaimed, "Our life is the creation of our mind." I believe that we can reshape our lives, no matter what the circumstances are that surround us, by believing in the ineffable power of our thoughts. But that power goes both ways, for good and for evil, because our thoughts are not always our own. We have to work on controlling them, understanding them, and purposely generating the ones we desire. We need to think on purpose. I hope that the historical accounts of previous philosophers and the results of my own research that I present will help you achieve this. That is my goal for this book.

Part I

CHAPTER 1 | THE SEARCH FOR SANITY

"We all go a little mad sometimes."

NORMAN BATES, Alfred Hitchcock's *Psycho*

"You're only given a little spark of madness. You mustn't lose it."

ROBIN WILLIAMS, American comedian

Around 1494, Hieronymus Bosch,[1] a Dutch draftsman and painter, completed a painting called *The Extraction of the Stone of Madness*,[2] an oil on board painting that shows four people sitting around a table in the Dutch countryside. The painting depicts the scene with dry wit and a mordant view of the removal of a "stone of madness." One of the four people, presumably a doctor, is wearing a funnel hat (which happened to be an early symbol of madness) and is shown slicing open the skull of a patient, as onlookers watch with a sense of overwhelming ennui. Considered a work of satire, it portrayed the common practice of trepanation (skull boring) as a means to cure stupidity.

"Extracting the Stone of Madness" by Hieronymus Bosch

Evidence of trepanning[3] has been found in prehistoric human remains. Recently discovered ancient cave paintings indicate that Neolithic[4] people believed that the practice could cure mental disorders, migraines, epilepsy, and a variety of other psychological defects. Considered one of the earliest forms of mental health treatment, trepanation is the surgical process of removing a small part of the skull using a bore or bone saw. Historians date the earliest forms of this practice to over 7000 years ago and posit that it was likely used to relieve migraines, cure various forms of mental illness, or even purge demons.[5] One burial site in France discovered 120 prehistoric skulls that date back to 6500 BCE, of which 40 had trepanation holes. Not only did the skulls possess these holes, but evidence of healing was also present, suggesting that many of these patients survived the surgery for many years after. The consensus at the time was that this surgical method was the only way to relieve pressure beneath the surface that was caused by a small stone inside the brain, a stone that provided safe haven for mental illness to flourish or demonic spirits to reside. People that behaved in abnormal ways due to unconscious factors, or factors outside of their conscious control, needed to have these stones removed.[6]

While this practice continued through the Early Middle Ages,[7] a variant of trepanation started to gain prominence in the Western world beginning in the 1600s. Claudius Galen, a Greek physician and philosopher, drew upon texts from ancient Greek medicine and believed that disease and mental illness came from the imbalance of "humors" within the body.[8] He looked at the body's natural physical response to disease, such as bleeding and vomiting, as evidence that purging through a process called bloodletting could cure countless diseases, such as diabetes, asthma, cancer, depression, anxiety, and other various forms of mental illness. Ancient Greek and Roman physicians believed that an excess of any of the four distinct bodily fluids, known as humors, negatively impacted mental and physical health directly. According to these ancient physicians, the four bodily fluids are: black bile, yellow bile, phlegm, and blood, and each of these fluids corresponds to desired temperaments and the balance of these four fluids are essential for the body to be healthy.[9] So while trepanation sought to relieve the mind of an unexplained unconscious drive that created various abnormal behaviors, bloodletting combined this notion with the concept of bodily balance, suggesting that achieving a state of equilibrium was the key to a healthy life, while also purging elements that affected the inaccessible parts of the mind.

More recently, a Portuguese neurologist named Antonio Egas Moniz drilled a hole into a patient's head to access the brain at a Lisbon hospital in 1935. His surgical operation, then referred to as a leucotomy, involved an incision in the prefrontal lobe that aimed to sever certain nerves in the brain. The procedure was found to mitigate severe symptoms of serious mental illness within his patient, an operation that would later win him the Nobel Prize. The theory behind the leucotomy was that nerves in the prefrontal lobe that were responsible for overthinking or emotional build-up could be severed, curing patient madness. In 1936, psychiatrist Walter Freeman performed the first U.S. based operation, which he later renamed "lobotomy," on a Kansas housewife that was believed to be suffering from mental illness due to an overload of emotions. Freeman believed "that cutting certain nerves in the brain could eliminate excess emotion and stabilize a personality."[10] At a time when insane asylums were overcrowded and people were desperate for treatments to various mental illnesses, Freeman created a more efficient procedure for lobotomies that avoided the use of drilling into a patient's skull. Instead, he created a 10-minute procedure known as the "icepick" lobotomy, which involved using an icepick-like instrument that was inserted just above the patient's eyeballs into the frontal lobes of the brain, and randomly wiggled around until a few things "popped." At his peak, Freeman would perform up to 25 lobotomies in a single day, amassing over 2,500 in his career, on patients as young as 12-years-old. Due to a low success rate and countless patient deaths, lobotomies soon fell out of favor and were eventually banned from practice, as two new treatments for mental illness began their ascent. These two new treatments would mark the end of the barbaric era of mental illness intervention through surgical means, though they would have similar goals of trying to exhume the unconscious and achieve states of emotional and mental balance. These two methods were modern psychotherapy and antipsychotic medications.

The Emergence of Modern Psychotherapy

The emergence of modern psychotherapy, or talk therapy, as a mainstream method to combat mental illness, marked a new era of importance for psychology as a scientific discipline. Today, psychotherapy is more prevalent than ever. Men and women are seeking talk therapy as an alternative to drugs for a variety of issues, from stress and anxiety relief, to overcoming traumatic events. A recent longitudinal study that analyzed data between 1995-2008 from over 8,000 people found that men who saw a psychotherapist saw an increase of 13% in income in the following year, when women saw an increase of 8%, showing that psychotherapy even has an effect on modern labor efficiency.[11] Imagine that - seeing a shrink can make you richer! The term "modern" is used because treatment of emotional or psychological problems can actually be traced back to antiquity. The ancient Greeks were the first to identify mental illness as a medical condition that could be treated, rather than an indication of demonic possession. Even though many of their notions were incorrect about the overall nature of mental illness (as an example they believed that a "wandering uterus" was responsible for hysteria, so the condition only affected women, or that bathing would eliminate depression), they saw the value of verbal counseling and positive encouragement.[12]

The Early Middle Ages brought back a belief that paranormal spirits caused mental illness and that physical means, such as torture, were needed to expel demonic spirits. This "renaissance" paved the way for philosophers and scientists of the time to desperately seek out new methods. Paracelsus, a Swiss physician and alchemist, emphasized the value of observation and investigated the relationship between biology and chemistry (now referred to as toxicology). Often referred to as "the father of toxicology" and a pioneer in several areas of the medical revolution,[13] he advocated for the use of psychotherapy and medication for treatment of the insane.

There are various scattered references of "talk therapy" in historical psychological account. Though in 1853, Walter Cooper Dendy first introduced the term "psycho-therapeia" to refer to how physicians might address mental suffering by creating opposing emotions to promote mental balance.[14] In 1872, Daniel Hack Tuke, an English physician, wrote "psycho-therapeutics," where he proposed creating a science known as animal magnetism.[15] Animal magnetism, also referred to as mesmerism, was considered a presumed intangible or mysterious force that influenced human behavior and was possessed by all living things. Frank Mesmer, an 18th-century German doctor, repeatedly tried to prove that these forces had healing effects, with little to no scientific recognition. He believed that an invisible fluid emanated from the body that was ubiquitous throughout the universe, originating from the stars. Professional "magnetizers" were said to have the power to manipulate magnetic fluid and the practice became popular in Europe and the United States in the 19th century. Even though the practice is completely forgotten about today, hundreds of books were written on the subject between 1766 and 1925,[16] when the practice soared in popularity and even influenced national politics. During the decline of magnetism, traveling stage hypnosis, or hypnosis performed in front of a large audience which produced apparent effects of amnesia, mood alternation, or hallucinations, started to gain prominence due to the swift rise of hypnotism. Using the treatment procedures described by Frank Mesmer in animal magnetism while discarding the notion of an occult force that flowed from the stars, mesmerism (named after its creator Frank Mesmer), attracted widespread interest in the mid 19th century.[17] English physician James Braid studied the phenomena and coined the terms hypnotism and hypnosis, after the Greek god of sleep, Hypnos.[18]

The evolution of talk therapy, from Paracelsus to Frank Mesmer, though riddled with incorrect thinking and ignorant methods, marked a trend of practitioners moving away from physical intervention as a way to treat mental illness toward a conversation-based approach to achieve emotional balance. The development and popularity of hypnosis were widely documented and drew support from many different schools of medicine and interest from many burgeoning young scientists. In 1885, an Austrian neurologist traveled to Paris on a fellowship study with Jean-Martin Charcot, the founder of modern neurology who is best known for his work on hypnosis and hysteria. The Austrian neurologist was impressed by the therapeutic potential of hypnosis for neurotic disorders, specifically the ability of hypnosis to help patients recall disturbing events that had long been forgotten. Using these new techniques, he began to develop his system of psychoanalysis. His name was Sigmund Freud.

The Five Psychological Perspectives

Shortly before Freud began developing his system of psychoanalysis, many psychologists around the world began to investigate the origin of behavior within the human mind. Wilhelm Wundt[19] opened the first psychology lab in 1879 to study psychology as a discipline that was separate from philosophy or biology. Operating out of his research facility at the University of Leipzig, Wundt founded experimental psychology, the process of using experimental methods with human participants to study topics of sensation, perception, memory, cognition, learning, motivation, emotion, developmental processes, social psychology, and many others,[20] and he also pioneered cultural psychology, which is the study of how cultures affect the psychological processes of their members.[21]

Wundt wanted to study the structure of the human mind and he believed that consciousness could be reduced to basic elements which could be studied. His scientific contributions of the psychological research method of experimentation, alongside his reductionist approach to the investigation of the mind, encouraged future scientists to follow the same experimental approach to discover the process of organizing the mind.[22] As psychology progressed, different angles and theories began to develop among researchers as sources for the genesis of our thoughts, feelings, and behaviors.

Today, these different angles are organized into five main approaches that guide modern psychological research and are referred to as the Five Major Perspectives in Psychology. They are the Psychodynamic, Behavioral, Humanistic, Cognitive, and Biological perspectives.

In Sum

- Mental illness has been around since the beginning of time and various methods have been investigated to treat it.
- Early civilizations researched the brain and always looked for new ways to expel demons or eradicate mental illness.
- Treatment used to include barbaric methods, such as trepanation, surgery, lobotomy, and other physical methods.

- Non-physical treatments, such as psychotherapy, started to gain prominence as a rebuke to physical intervention, but this led to many charlatans creating fraudulent methods initially.
- There are five major perspectives in psychology that organize historical thinking and modern research. They are the Psychodynamic, Behavioral, Humanistic, Cognitive and Biological perspectives.

CHAPTER 2 | THE INNER DEPTHS OF THE MIND

"Many a person cannot bear the thought of being completely controlled by the unconscious."

EDMUND BERGLER, *The Writer and Psychoanalysis*

"One does not become enlightened by imagining figures of light, but by making the darkness conscious."

CARL JUNG, referring to the Shadow archetype

In early 1907, a man was seeking professional help for his problems and stumbled upon the writings of Sigmund Freud, who touted psychoanalysis as a treatment method for his inner demons. Going by the pseudonym "Rat Man," the patient eventually approached Freud and complained of obsessive thoughts that would surface for no apparent reason, which mainly centered around obsessively thinking about his own father's death. Before developing his mental condition, Rat Man worked with a military lieutenant who was known to have a proclivity for sadistic torture. Rat Man told Freud how one day, the lieutenant came to him and relayed a particular form of corporal punishment that was one of his favorite forms, which involved placing a container of live rats on a person's stomach who was lying on their back.[1] The lieutenant claimed that the rats would try to escape their captivity by burrowing through the victim's stomach. This idea repulsed him, quickly becoming the center of his obsessive thoughts, and he began to fear that this punishment would happen to his father. Because of this story, the patient, whose real name was later revealed as Ernst Lanzer, would be dubbed Rat Man by Freud in his 1909 case study "Notes upon a Case of Obsessional Neurosis." Freud worked with Rat Man for six months, who recounted numerous events that occurred in childhood that were troubling him in the present. Rat Man described becoming sexually aware at an early age and he recalled a desire to see women whom he knew naked. Freud asserted that the guilt Rat Man felt during this time eventually manifested into these irrational fears later in life. Freud claimed this to be one of the first successful cases of free association and psychoanalysis, asserting that Rat Man was cured of his obsessive thoughts after psychotherapy linked his childhood guilt and repressed memories to his adult neurosis. This outcome would not last long, however, as Freud noted a few years later that Rat Man would be killed in the First World War.[2]

Popularized by Freud's work, the psychodynamic approach includes all of the psychological theories that see human functioning as a relationship between unconscious drives within the mind and different structures of human personality. Psychologists in this school of thought believe that unconscious drives and experiences from early childhood are at the root of our behaviors and that discovering these hidden and often repressed memories are the key to determining current day behavior.[3]

Though Freud's system of psychoanalysis is considered the original psychodynamic theory, other psychologists who later expanded upon his ideas, such as Carl Jung, Alfred Adler, Edmund Bergler, and Erik Erikson are also included. The psychodynamic theory operates under the premise that our behavior and feelings are strongly, if not entirely, affected by the unconscious mind. The idea of an unconscious mind, though popularized by Freud, has actually been postulated by ancient cultures since 2500 BCE. An ancient Hindu text, known as the *Vedas*, described that "pure consciousness is an abstract, silent, completely unified field of consciousness."[4] William Shakespeare explored the role of the unconscious mind in various works, such as *Hamlet, Richard III,* and *Macbeth*, which later influenced Freud's *The Interpretation of Dreams.*[5] Robert Louis Stevenson also explored the unconscious mind in his 19th-century Gothic fiction, *Dr. Jekyll and Mr. Hyde.* Western philosophers, such as Baruch Spinoza (who Albert Einstein claimed most influenced his own world view), Gottfried Leibniz, Arthur Schopenhauer, and Friedrich Wilhelm Nietzsche, developed Western views of the mind that would eventually influence Freud's theories. Schopenhauer drew upon his readings of the Hindu *Vedas* and the *Kabbala*, a collection of Jewish doctrines about God's relationship to creation, to craft the idea that something not conscious contained deeper, hidden truths and esoteric knowledge concerning God, much of which now can be found in the *Torah*.[6]

Freud developed a system of the mind and proposed a hierarchical architecture of human consciousness: the conscious mind, the preconscious mind, and the unconscious mind, in descending order.[7] He believed that the unconscious mind was where all significant events took place that drove all aspects of human behavior and that hidden messages periodically "leaked out," in the forms of Freudian slips (inadvertent slips of the tongue) or dreams, which contained insight into unconscious drives. According to Freud, the conscious mind contains the ego, while the unconscious contains the id and the superego.

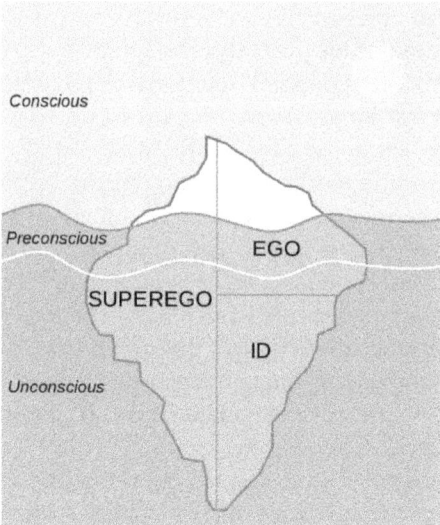

Freud's Model of the Mind

The Id, The Ego, and the Superego

One of Freud's most important contributions to psychology is the concept that human personality has more than one component. He divided the human psyche into three parts known as the id, the ego, and the superego. It is important to note that Freud claimed that all of these parts develop at different stages of our lives and that they are invisible systems, not physical parts of the brain itself.

The id is the primitive part of the psyche that contains our instincts, all of our inherited biological components, our Eros (libido), Thanatos (aggressive death instinct), and our sex instinct. It is a reservoir of feelings, urges, and memories that are inaccessible and outside of our conscious awareness.[8] According to Freud, this is where our major influence of behavior comes from and it includes our hidden memories and secret desires. Born with the id, it remains throughout our lives and does not change with reflection, growth, introspection or experience. The id operates on the pleasure principle alone and is not subject to reason, logic, reality, or conscious self-analysis. The id is selfish and expects its demands to be met immediately, often engaging in irrational or fantasy-oriented primary process thinking.

The ego develops as we age to mediate between the primitive id and the outside world. Operating on reason, our decision-making capability resides within the ego as this part of the psyche works off of the reality principle. The ego is cognizant of cultural norms, social etiquette, and realistic rules as it tries to satisfy the id's demands by discovering and applying realistic methods, but it prefers rationality above all else. However, the ego is weak relative to the id. "Freud made the analogy of the id being a horse while the ego is the rider. The ego is like a man on horseback, who has to hold in check the superior strength of the horse."[9] Similar to Plato's Chariot Allegory (a metaphor where a charioteer is controlling two winged horses), which he described in his dialogue *Phaedrus*[10] to explain his view of the human soul and of divine madness, this metaphor conveys that the ego is more knowledgeable than the id, but in a battle of wits or brute strength, the horse would win over the rider. We will see a similar concept in chapter 12 when we look at psychologist Jonathan Haidt's metaphor of the elephant and the rider.

The superego integrates the values and morals of a society that are learned from parents, teachers, and others. Developing around 3-years-old, the superego's main function is to control the impulses of the id, especially impulses that could be deemed immoral or forbidden by societal norms. The superego uses the concept of the ideal self to punish the ego if the ego gives in to the id's demands, by producing feelings of guilt, shame, or anxiety. Conversely, the superego can also reward the ego when it deems that we behave in a proper manner that is not subservient to the id.

Freud believed that the conscious mind was the tip of the iceberg and that the unconscious mind made up for the majority of the iceberg underneath the water surface. The unconscious mind retained painful, shameful, embarrassing, or distressing thoughts and memories from childhood that were out of reach from the conscious mind. Only through the interpretation of dreams, free association, and psychoanalysis could one access these repressed memories, and then determine how these memories affected our current day behavior. His theories of the structure of the mind would later influence many future psychoanalysts. Two are important to recognize as they specifically helped further the practice of psychoanalysis toward applications of mental health. They are Carl Jung and Edmund Bergler.

Carl Gustav Jung was a Swiss psychiatrist who expanded upon Freudian theories of the unconscious. He agreed with Freud that the unconscious mind was a major determinant of personality, but he proposed that the unconscious was composed of two layers: the personal unconscious and the collective unconscious. Similar to Freud's view, Jung believed that the personal unconscious was a reservoir of material that has been suppressed, but the collective unconscious contained all of the inherited material of your ancestors, suggesting that your genetic code contains all of the spiritual heritage and biological information for every human that came before you in your lineage. Jung famously claimed that "every person shares the collective unconscious with the entire human species, born anew in the brain structure of every individual."[11] This is a central theory behind the phenomena where people claim that they experience a past or former life, remember people they knew, locations they lived, or other various details and memories that have no direct linkage to their current life or time period.

Jung's theories would soon influence the creation of one of the most famous personality assessments in the world – The Myers-Briggs Type Indicator, or MBTI. Jung developed major concepts within analytical psychology that emphasized the importance of the individual psyche and believed that psychological "types" could be determined for each individual through methods of observation, self-examination, and anecdote. Jung's typology theories developed a sequence of four cognitive functions. They are as follows:

- Thinking, which is a function of intellectual cognition
- Feeling, which is a function of subjectivity of experience
- Sensation, which is a function of our sense organs
- Intuition, which is a function of unconscious perception

Each of these has a polar orientation of Extraversion or Introversion and comprise eight psychological types or temperaments, which are:

1. The extraverted thinking type
2. The introverted thinking type
3. The extraverted feeling type
4. The introverted feeling type
5. The extraverted sensation type
6. The introverted sensation type
7. The extraverted intuitive type
8. The introverted intuitive type

The use of personality assessments using type-based principles based on Jung's theories is still widespread today, with many executive coaches and organizational psychologists using them as their gateway to client development. Jung's theories were some of the first to further expand the theories of psychoanalysis to personality assessment and mental health.

Edmund Bergler, an Austrian and American psychoanalyst, is most widely known for his psychoanalytic views on homosexuality in the 1950s and his theories on basic neurosis. Bergler posited that the human psyche constantly defends against the darkest aspects of our human nature and that every individual has a deep emotional connection to unresolved negative emotions.[12] He wrote in 1958 "I can only reiterate my opinion that the superego is the real master of the personality, that psychic masochism constitutes the most dangerous countermeasure of the unconscious ego against the superego's tyranny, that psychic masochism is 'the life-blood of neurosis' and is in fact the basic neurosis. I still subscribe to my dictum,

'Man's inhumanity to man is equaled only by man's inhumanity to himself.'"[13] In 1956, he authored a book called *Homosexuality: Disease or a Way of Life?* where he argued that homosexuality was a curable illness. While these views (which are outdated and nonsensical looking through today's lens) balkanized the scientific community in the 1950s, it is important to mention because he was one of the first to suggest that humans were not merely victims of their genetic material and locked into our behavioral patterns forever. Bergler advocated new clinical solutions, such as talking to patients at great length about issues in order to counteract viewpoints through talk therapy. He believed that through his clinical methods, he could get patients to realize that we were our own worst enemy because of a concept he dubbed as "psychic masochism." Bergler argued that we purposely seek out psychic pain to varying levels. Psychic masochism is found in its most extreme form in alcoholics, drug addicts, and gamblers, and is produced by many interrelated factors, such as dependency, guilt, aggression, narcissism, perceived persecution, need for control, a joy from losing, or self-seeking martyrdom.[14] Bergler was the first to stumble upon an unconscious neurotic aggression that humans possess which promotes self-damage, even if his views on homosexuality, childhood development and marriage would be considered wildly outdated and preposterous today. Much like Freud, he was a sign of his times and while many of his ideas are no longer considered valid, his concept of psychic masochism would eventually serve an important role in mental health.

The Unconscious Controversy

Despite the dynamism of the modern psychodynamic movement and all of the scientific breakthroughs of Wundt and Freud that ushered psychology into a new era, the idea of unseeable, untouchable, and unmeasurable part of the brain never sat well with many 19th-century philosophers and the idea continues fomenting psychological and philosophical debate to this day.

The unconscious mind has never actually been proven to exist and it continues to be heavily disputed. There are still major fundamental disagreements within psychology about the nature of the unconscious mind. Many critics, opponents, and scientists have provided antithetical views to Freud's theories of the unconscious mind.

The primary issue with Freud's concepts today is that his theories, even though they appear insightful and to be rooted in common sense, have very little empirical evidence to support them. Modern psychologists, researchers, and scientists have produced little to no evidence that substantiates any of his claims of the amorphous structure of the human mind. The idea of an unconscious primitive powerhouse that sublimates deep, dark desires into socially acceptable behaviors has yet to be validated by any social or scientific experiment to date and is anathema to many modern psychologists. Many critics deride some of his most famous work. For example, there is no scientific evidence to support the idea that an Oedipus complex exists (the term used by Freud to describe a child's feelings of desire for his mother and anger toward the father). Freud was completely wrong about gender, suggesting that young girls distance themselves from their mothers between the ages of three and five because they hold their mothers responsible for their own lack of a penis and have what he referred to as "penis envy."[15] Despite Freud's assiduous development of his structure of the mind, there is no proof that the id, ego, or superego exist, or that human development follows the oral, anal, phallic, and genital stages that he famously promulgated. He theorized that homosexuality was a failure of the individual to reconcile during the anal phase and that women who could only climax via clitoral stimulation (as opposed to "mature" women who could orgasm from vaginal sex) were somehow stuck in an undeveloped or latent phase. We know today that these views are nonsensical and an affront to modern philosophy and overall society.[16]

Freud's Contributions

So you may be asking yourself, if many of Freud's theories have been debunked, rebuked, or deflated, then what does his work have to do with purposeful cognition? If many researchers repudiate his theories, why is he an essential figure to the modern psychology movement? What does the unconscious mind, seemingly an antipode to purposeful thinking, have to do with our quest for mental health? It's because Freud actually stumbled onto something very significant, even if he didn't realize it at the time.

Even though Freud's theories have been criticized for over a century, with many believing that his virulent notions of human sexuality are ludicrous and that credit for the unconscious mental model should be wiped from his heritage,[17] his work is still considered to be some of the most important psychological discovery of all time. Many argue that modern scientists shouldn't look back on Freud's work and deem them to be fallacies, but rather general guidelines that should be expanded upon.

Freud's work was revolutionary in many ways because he was the first to organize the psychodynamic model and popularize the practice of addressing mental health through talk therapy, rather than a physical intervention that mimicked torture. He was correct in his assertion that we are not masters of our own mind and that irrational factors outside of our control were responsible for our behavior. He was correct in his view that our adult behavior is a combination of our nature and our nurture.[18] He was also correct in proposing that much of our thinking is automatic or implicit. While he referred to this as unconscious thinking and his proposed notion that the genesis for this thinking resides within a mystical, invisible psyche rather than somatic parts of the physical brain has never been proved, many modern researchers and scientists have been able to definitively prove that most of our thinking is truly automatic due to how electrical signals flow through our brains. Modern researchers have also proved that thinking can be harnessed through techniques such as emotional intelligence and Cognitive Behavioral Therapy, which is discussed later in this book. He was correct about the premise, just wrong about the mechanics.

Lastly, Freud's most significant contribution to the field of mental health lies within his research into the unconscious that has led future researchers, like Edmund Bergler, to uncover a realm within our psyche that has a direct influence over our emotional states and overall well-being. This unconscious realm rooted within psychic masochism, factors into hundreds of symptoms within human thinking, including anxiety, fear, anger, addictions, compulsions, and depression. That unconscious realm is called our Inner Passivity, which is explored in depth in chapter 8. Next, we will take a look at the behavioral perspective of psychology, which suggests that psychosocial dynamics, environmental factors, upbringing, social norms, and external influences are the causes of human behavior.

In Sum
According to the psychodynamic approach:

- Our unconscious mind contains mental processes that dictate our feelings, thoughts, and subsequent behaviors, and is not accessible to our conscious mind.[19]
- The unconscious mind is the primary source of human behavior.
- Feelings, thoughts and our decision-making are stored in the unconscious, which is most directly linked to our past experiences, specifically our experiences from childhood.
- Our childhood experiences shape our personality as adults and are at the root of all of our psychological problems and dysfunctions.
- Conflicts in childhood alter personality drives that solidify as adults.
- All behaviors are caused by unconscious factors that we do not have control over.
- Transference of unconscious thoughts and feelings to the conscious mind occur in the form of "parapraxes," or slips of the tongue, or Freudian slips.

- Even Freudian slips are significant because all behavior is determined and not accidental.
- Our personality is made up of three parts; the id, the ego, and the superego. The id is the primitive drive of personality and contains all of our inherited components (nature). The ego develops over time and mediates between the id and the real world. The superego contains our societal morals and values that are learned from our parents (nurture).
- Dysfunction comes from a constant conflict between the id, ego, and superego.

Psychodynamic contributions to purposeful cognition:

- Carl Jung's theories would influence how these principles could be applied to individual assessment.
- Bergler's psychic masochism is found in its most extreme form in alcoholics, drug addicts, and gamblers, and is produced by a number of interrelated factors, such as dependency, guilt, aggression, narcissism, perceived persecution, need for control, a joy of losing, or self-seeking martyrdom. It resides within the realm of Inner Passivity.
- Freud helped frame the concept of unconscious and conscious thinking, that serve as the basis for modern psychological research around automatic and manual thinking.
- This approach helped usher talk therapy into the modern era.

CHAPTER 3 | THERE WILL BE CONSEQUENCES

"I did not direct my life. I didn't design it. I never made decisions. Things always came up and made them for me. That's what life is."

B.F. SKINNER, American behaviorist, philosopher, scientist

"We all claim to be self-made, yet we all have accents."

UNKNOWN, behaviorism proverb

Little Albert was first presented with a small white rat. As the rat approached him, crawled all over and meandered all around him, Albert showed scant interest in the tiny creature. While the rat was crawling around the play space, other white objects, such as a white rabbit, a white dog, white masks, and other white things were presented to little Albert. Having never experienced any of these before, Albert showed no signs of fear, but growing interest as time passed by.

All of the white items would be taken from Albert for a short while, only to be presented again. But this time, each new object that was offered was also accompanied by a loud clang, made by slamming a hammer into a pipe. The loud noise would startle Albert, and he would begin to cry. After a few times of presenting Albert with the items and combining them with a loud bang, Albert eventually began to cry at just the sight of the rat alone, even when a loud noise did not follow. The researcher, Dr. John B. Watson, believed that he created an emotionally conditioned response within Albert where the baby now expected the stimuli (the rat) to also accompany something frightening. Being the first of its kind, this experiment would forever be known as the little Albert experiment.

A controversial experiment at the time that would not be replicable today due to ethics and health concerns, the little Albert experiment was a bold step away from psychodynamics, harnessing the guidelines that Ivan Pavlov used to condition dogs. In one of the most famous experiments of modern psychology, Pavlov used food to condition dogs, pairing the food with the sound of a bell, which conditioned the dogs to associate the food with the sound of the bell ringing. Each time the dogs were fed, they would salivate, while also hearing the tone of a ringing bell. Eventually, the dogs would salivate when the bell rung and no food was presented. In one of the first examples of classical conditioning, Pavlov showed that a neutral stimulus (the bell), which would not normally create a response like salivation within a dog, could be paired with a non-neutral stimulus (the food), in order to create the response even when the non-neutral stimulus was not present. Pavlov and Watson showed with their experiments that behaviors could be learned by associating an environmental stimulus with a naturally occurring stimulus. Even though Watson's experiment remains controversial to this day, not only for the ethical implications and the fact that modern researchers frequently cite that the study was replete with validity concerns, it marked the beginning of a new way to explain why humans behave the way that we do.

Even though his experiments were many years after Pavlov, Watson is considered to be the father of behaviorism. An influential American psychologist, Watson thought that the study of consciousness was flawed, claiming that objective analysis of the mind was impossible.[1] Watson's seminal 1913 paper, "Psychology as the Behaviorist Views It," formally established behaviorism and can be succinctly summed up with the following quote:

> Give me a dozen healthy infants, well-formed, and my own specified world to bring them up in and I'll guarantee to take any one at random and train him to become any type of specialist I might select-doctor, lawyer, artist, merchant-chief and, yes, even beggar-man and thief, regardless of his talents, penchants, tendencies, abilities, vocations, and race of his ancestors.[2]

Types of Conditioning

Psychologists of the behavioral approach believe that external environmental stimuli influence your behavior and that individuals can be led to act in a certain way if the environment promoted it. Behavioral psychologists believe that you learn through a system of reinforcements and punishment and that free will does not exist since our behavior is a consequence of environment and conditioning. Behaviorism is the theory of learning based on the notion that all behaviors are acquired through the process of conditioning, which can be studied through systematic and observable methods. Behaviorists posit that *only observable behavior is valid and that emotions, conscious and unconscious thinking, and feelings are not only subjective, but also unimportant*. Essentially, behaviorists believe that all behaviors are a result of experience and that anyone, regardless of background or genetics, could be trained to act a certain way if given the right conditioning. There are two major types of conditioning:

- Classical conditioning – A technique where a neutral stimulus is associated with a naturally occurring stimulus. Eventually, the subject is conditioned to produce the same response to the neutral stimulus when the naturally occurring stimulus is removed. Classical conditioning involves involuntary responses.
- Operant conditioning – A technique where an association is made between a behavior and a consequence for that behavior, often referred to as reinforcement and punishment. Operant conditioning involves voluntary responses.

Behaviorism dramatically altered the psychological landscape in the early 20th century as a growing desire to establish psychology as an objective and measurable science led to the rejection of historical theories, such as the existence of the conscious and unconscious mind. Behaviorism sought to shape psychology as a strict discipline that only focused on observable behavior. Watson later wrote in his classic 1924 book *Behaviorism*, that:

> Behaviorism...holds that the subject matter of human psychology is the *behavior of the human being.* Behaviorism claims that consciousness is neither a definite nor a usable concept. The behaviorist, who has been trained always as an experimentalist, holds, further, that belief in the existence of consciousness goes back to the ancient days of superstition and magic.[3]

Behaviorism dominated experimental psychology for half a century and led psychologists like B.F. Skinner to further develop behavior association concepts such as operant conditioning, which demonstrated the effect of punishment and reinforcement on behavior. Skinner, an American psychologist who was also prominent in the behaviorist movement, researched the relationship of behavior and consequence. He investigated the process by which the consequences of our behavior affect the future probability of its recurrence given particular antecedent conditions. In other words, Skinner believed that behaviors which are reinforced and recur more often in the future are "selected" by those consequences.[4]

He studied how to modify behavior based on punishment and reinforcement, creating a device known as an operant conditioning chamber, or later known as a Skinner box. The Skinner box isolates a subject (common subjects included rats, pigeons, and even primates) from the external world and has a behavior indicator such as a lever or a button. When the subject pushes the button, the box delivers a positive reinforcement such as food, a negative punishment such as a loud noise, or a neutral response. When a positive response was paired with the behavior indicator, the subjects would quickly learn to go straight for the button after only a few times of being put in the box and would repeat the action over and over. The opposite would hold true when the button would create a negative punishment, such as an electric shock. The subject would quickly learn to avoid the button in order to elude punishment.

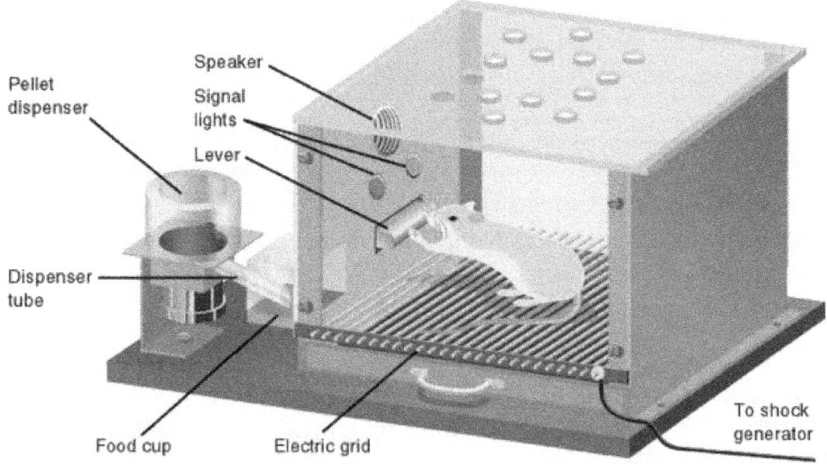

The Skinner Box

Schedules of Reinforcement

Skinner's work led to a significant discovery called "schedules of reinforcement." He discovered that different patterns had different effects on the speed of learning and behavior extinction. Imagine the effect on behavior if the rat in the Skinner box didn't receive food immediately after the button was pushed and then eventually gave up after several attempts. The behavior would eventually extinguish. Skinner[5] investigated different patterns and the effect on response rate, which is the rate at which the rat pressed the lever (how hard the rat worked), and extinction rate, which is the rate at which lever pressing dies out (how soon the rat gave up).[6] Skinner classified five main schedules of reinforcement, which are:

- Continuous – the subject is positively reinforced every time a specific behavior occurs. An example would be every time the button was pushed, food would be delivered.

- Fixed Ratio – the subject is positively reinforced at a fixed ratio. An example would be where reinforcement is given after every 5th button push or a child is given candy after five correct answers on a quiz.
- Fixed Internal – the subject is positively reinforced after a fixed time after pushing the button. An example would be getting paid by the hour.
- Variable Ratio – the subject is positively reinforced after an unpredictable number of times. An example would be fishing or gambling.
- Variable Interval – the subject is positively reinforced after a correct response is given and a random amount of time has passed. An example of this would be someone that is paid at unpredictable times, like a commission salesperson.

Skinner found that the schedule of reinforcement that had the slowest rate of extinction, or the schedule where subjects would go on continuing the behavior for the longest amount of time without any positive reinforcement is the variable-ratio reinforcement (this explains why people continue to fish without catching anything or buy lottery tickets without winning anything). The schedule of reinforcement which had the quickest rate of behavior extinction is continuous reinforcement[7] (for example, how long would you continue to go to work if your bi-weekly paycheck, which you were used to for years, suddenly stopped?). These findings would eventually serve to become the basis of behavior modification and behavior therapies that are still in use today. Behavior modification is used in the classroom for skill development and helps children overcome maladaptive or malevolent behaviors by conditioning students to associate certain behaviors with various forms of punishment. Behaviorism also led to a focus on researching environmental influences on behavior and how the timing of rewards encouraged desired behaviors. Much of behaviorism is responsible for developing modern drivers of employee engagement, such as workplace perks or the timing of bonuses.

Even though behaviorism would start to lose its supremacy in the mid 20th-century, it led to many psychological treatments that are still used today, such as Cognitive Behavioral Therapy (which is discussed in chapter 11). Psychologists eventually became uncomfortable with the pessimism and determinism of the psychoanalytic and behavioral perspectives, developing a growing aversion to the simplistic, reductionist nature of behaviorism. Psychologists began to reject the fatalistic ideas of behaviorism and began to emphasize personal control, developing ideas that aligned with free will. A return to focusing on conscious experience and self-actualization led to the birth of the humanistic perspective of psychology.

In Sum

According to the behavioral approach:

- Psychology should be seen as a science that is measured by observable behavior.
- Emotion and internal events are irrelevant.
- Nurture is dominant over nature.
- Our environment shapes our behavior through consequence via processes of classical and operant conditioning.
- The schedule of reinforcement has a large impact on the continuation or extinction of behaviors.

Behaviorism contributions to purposeful cognition:

- Learning can occur and subsequent behavior can be influenced through how we view the external environment and its effect on us.
- Environment, or external factors, shape human behavior via compliments, affirmation, and task outcomes.
- External elements affect internal human factors, such as motivation, resilience, and task encouragement, which ultimately influence our self-view.

CHAPTER 4 | THE THIRD FORCE

"Every living organism is fulfilled when it follows the right path for its own nature."

MARCUS AURELIUS, *Meditations*

"What is necessary to change a person is to change his awareness of himself."

ABRAHAM MASLOW, American psychologist, professor

Life on the American frontier in the early 19th century represented a time of promise and fortune which led many to travel west in search of a better life. However, it required hours of back-breaking work, rough travel, disease, danger, and drudgery. In 1816, a young boy and his family were forced out of their family home, a farm near the Ohio River in Kentucky. Thomas, the father of the family, eventually settled down in Indiana, where the seven-year-old boy had to work to support his family to avoid financial ruin. When the young boy was nearly nine, his mother would die in 1818 of milk sickness, a disease that occurs when humans eat meat affected by a toxic alcohol that comes from cattle eating white snakeroot. The boy would spend his teenage years on the farm, helping where he could, until he eventually left home in search of life's meaning. Taking a flatboat with his cousin John Hanks to New Orleans, he would travel many miles in search of work to eventually find employment in a general store that quickly failed due to the poor business skills of the owner. Still searching for his true purpose, the young man would experience a plethora of failures. He would run for state legislature in 1832 and lose, apply to law school but be denied acceptance, and eventually go into heavy debt in 1833, a debt that would take many years to pay off. Things seemed to brighten up when he met his first love in 1835 and was engaged to be married. Tragedy struck again when his sweetheart died and he would have a total nervous breakdown in 1836, never leaving his bed, lying in a near catatonic state. By 1838, he was able to pick himself up and venture into the world again. He would run for state legislature in Illinois but would be defeated. He would suffer additional political losses in 1843 during a run for Congress, 1848 in another run for Congress, 1849 in a bid to become a land officer, in 1854 in a run to become a United States Senator, in 1856 to become his party's Vice-Presidential nominee, and in 1858 for another run for the U.S. Senate. He pushed himself through the perennial failures, knowing that his potential was not yet realized and with persistence and positive thinking, he could achieve all of the great things he desired. Through perseverance and self-actualization, despite all of the failures and hardships of his life until this point, Abraham Lincoln was elected the 16th President of the United States in 1860.[1]

Self-Actualization

If Lincoln followed a behaviorist view of psychology, the multiple punishments and negative reinforcements dealt to him from life would have crushed him early on. He was able to persevere through with grit, positive thinking, and a skill called self-actualization. Self-actualization is a core skill within emotional intelligence and refers to the drive one has to pursue meaning in life or maximize one's talents and potentialities. Reuven Bar-On, the creator of one of the major models of emotional and social intelligence, defines self-actualization as "the willingness to persistently try to improve oneself and engage in the pursuit of personally relevant and meaningful objectives that lead to a rich and enjoyable life."[2]

Essentially, self-actualization is the process of looking fate in the eye and emphatically demonstrating that you have other plans. It is the motivation to pull yourself from the depths of despair and try to better your station in life. Many famous people have failed multiple times or been victims of extreme circumstances, yet overcome them to be wildly successful. Oprah Winfrey was born to a poor, single mother, lived in poverty, and was sexually abused on multiple occasions, yet became one of the most influential and wealthiest women in the world. Stephen King's first novel, *Carrie*, would be rejected 30 times and he would eventually throw it in the trash. Luckily his wife fished it out of the bin and resubmitted it, leading to it being published and giving the world one of the best horror writers of all time. J.K. Rowling, author of *Harry Potter,* would suffer abuse, divorce, the death of her mother, and the rejection of the book by all major British publishing houses, until one reluctantly said "yes," giving us the 15-billion-dollar *Harry Potter* franchise we have today. Bethany Hamilton, the famous surfer who won her division of the NSSA National Championship, had her arm bitten off by a shark when she was 13-years-old and was back on a surfboard only a month later. Comedian Jim Carrey dropped out of school to support his family as they lived in a van, going to comedy clubs for years before he was finally recognized as a great comedic talent. Walt Disney was fired from a newspaper job early in life because his boss said he lacked imagination (this particular one is my favorite due to the irony). Marilyn Monroe was advised early on that she didn't have what it took to become a successful model and that she should perhaps pursue being a secretary instead. There are many more various stories of grit and perseverance, but they all have one thing in common; they didn't take the hand that life dealt, they didn't let external events condition their behavior, and they believed in themselves when seemingly no one else did. These are elements of those that subscribe to the humanistic perspective of psychology.

Commonly referred to as the "third force" in psychology, (after psychoanalysts looked at unconscious impulses and behaviorists focused on environmental factors) humanism shattered paradigms of historical psychological thinking and emphasized concepts of free will, self-efficacy, and self-actualization. Humanist thinkers did not accept the findings of previous psychological researchers as a fait accompli. Influenced by schools of thought that looked at the human mind and behavior as a whole (often referred to as Gestalt psychology, the philosophy that posits that "the whole is greater than the sum of its parts") humanist thinkers sought to find ways for people to fulfill their potential and amplify well-being as opposed to concentrating on dysfunction and negativity.[3] Humanist thinkers felt that earlier psychological perspectives were too pessimistic and instead operated under the principle belief that humans were innately good and that people possess the power to motivate themselves to thrive, despite environmental punishments or genetic setbacks. Humanistic psychologists believe that all humans are essentially good and that each is motivated to realize his or her full potential. Feeling good about yourself is merely a function of fulfilling your needs and goals, or at the very least, constantly aspiring to do so. The humanistic approach works on individual empowerment and humanistic psychologists believe in the good of humankind and emphasize the individual's inherent drive towards self-actualization and creativity. With this approach, the sole focus is on strengths.[4]

Hierarchy of Needs

Early humanistic psychology was heavily influenced by two key theorists, Abraham Maslow and Carl Rogers. Abraham Maslow is most famously known for creating Maslow's Hierarchy of Needs, which describes human needs as ordered in a prepotent hierarchy, where lower-level needs require satisfaction before higher-level needs can be addressed.[5] Maslow observed and studied those that he believed were highly self-actualized people, such as Albert Einstein and Henry David Thoreau, and based his theory on assumptions of human potentiality. Often represented by a pyramid, the model shows more basic needs at the bottom, providing a foundation that can only support higher-level needs if the foundational elements are met.

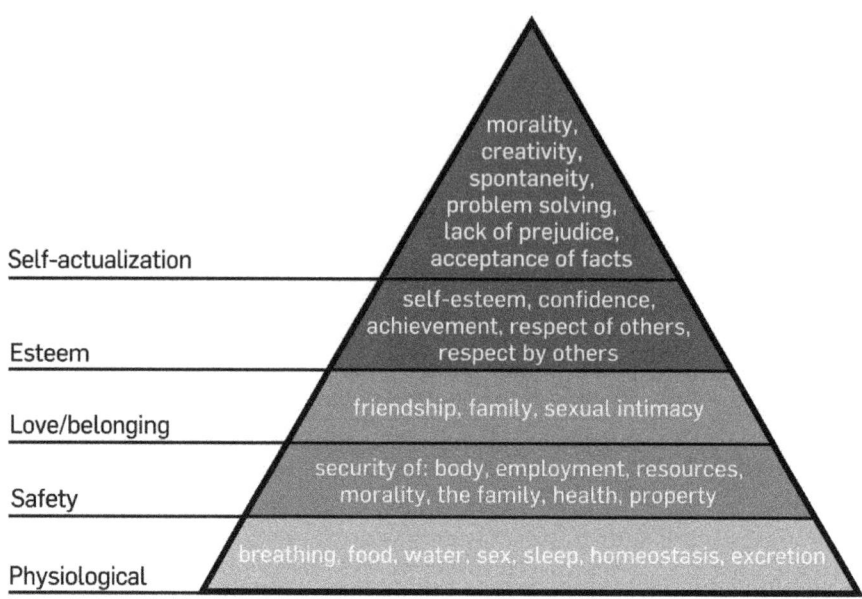

Maslow's Hierarchy of Needs

Maslow's hierarchy shows how humans must first meet physiological needs, such as food, water, sex, and sleep. Only after those needs are met, can one seek out safety needs such as security, property, and employment, or other needs that are important to the physical survival of the person. Love and belonging are psychological needs that can be sought only after one takes care of himself/herself physically, such as friendship or intimacy. When people feel comfortable that the preceding needs have been met, they can then seek esteem, which are needs associated with being recognized for successes or status. Only when all of these needs are met, can one engage in self-actualization, where people are free to maximize their potential. In 1970, Maslow identified 15 characteristics of a self-actualized person:[6]

1. They perceive reality efficiently and can tolerate uncertainty;

2. Accept themselves and others for what they are;

3. Spontaneous in thought and action;

4. Problem-centered (not self-centered);

5. Unusual sense of humor;

6. Able to look at life objectively;

7. Highly creative;

8. Resistant to enculturation, but not purposely unconventional;

9. Concerned for the welfare of humanity;

10. Capable of deep appreciation of basic life-experience;

11. Establish deep, satisfying interpersonal relationships with a few people;

12. Peak experiences;

13. Need for privacy;

14. Democratic attitudes;

15. Strong moral/ethical standards.

Carl Rogers was an American psychologist who is considered one of the founders of the humanistic school of thought. In his 1951 seminal publication, *Client-centered therapy: Its current practice, implications and theory*, Rogers published 19 propositions describing his approach to understanding human personality, relationships, and behavior:[7]

1. All individuals (organisms) exist in a continually changing world of experience (phenomenal field) of which they are the center.

2. The organism reacts to the field as it is experienced and perceived. This perceptual field is "reality" for the individual.

3. The organism reacts as an organized whole to this phenomenal field.

4. A portion of the total perceptual field gradually becomes differentiated as the self.

5. As a result of interaction with the environment, and particularly as a result of evaluational interaction with others, the structure of the self is formed - an

organized, fluid but consistent conceptual pattern of perceptions of characteristics and relationships of the "I" or the "me," together with values attached to these concepts.

6. The organism has one basic tendency and striving - to actualize, maintain and enhance the experiencing organism.

7. The best vantage point for understanding behavior is from the internal frame of reference of the individual.

8. Behavior is basically the goal-directed attempt of the organism to satisfy its needs as experienced, in the field as perceived.

9. Emotion accompanies, and in general facilitates, such goal-directed behavior, the kind of emotion being related to the perceived significance of the behavior for the maintenance and enhancement of the organism.

10. The values attached to experiences, and the values that are a part of the self-structure, in some instances, are values experienced directly by the organism, and in some instances are values introjected or taken over from others, but perceived in distorted fashion, as if they had been experienced directly.

11. As experiences occur in the life of the individual, they are either, a) symbolized, perceived and organized into some relation to the self, b) ignored because there is no perceived relationship to the self-structure, c) denied symbolization or given distorted symbolization because the experience is inconsistent with the structure of the self.

12. Most of the ways of behaving that are adopted by the organism are those that are consistent with the concept of self.

13. In some instances, behavior may be brought about by organic experiences and needs which have not

been symbolized. Such behavior may be inconsistent with the structure of the self but in such instances the behavior is not "owned" by the individual (e.g. underlying needs or experiences that one denies, distorts, or fails to make sense of, leak through into behaviors).

14. Psychological adjustment exists when the concept of the self is such that all the sensory and visceral experiences of the organism are, or may be, assimilated on a symbolic level into a consistent relationship with the concept of self.

15. Psychological maladjustment exists when the organism denies awareness of significant sensory and visceral experiences, which consequently are not symbolized and organized into the gestalt of the self-structure. When this situation exists, there is a basic or potential psychological tension (e.g. tension is created when one is disconnected from their authentic self).

16. Any experience which is inconsistent with the organization of the structure of the self may be perceived as a threat, and the more of these perceptions there are, the more rigidly the self-structure is organized to maintain itself.

17. Under certain conditions, involving primarily complete absence of threat to the self-structure, experiences which are inconsistent with it may be perceived and examined, and the structure of self-revised to assimilate and include such experiences (e.g. when one feels safe enough, one can examine experiences that might have previously been too threatening).

18. When the individual perceives and accepts into one consistent and integrated system all his sensory and visceral experiences, then he is necessarily more understanding of others and is more accepting of others as separate individuals (e.g. higher awareness generates more understanding and tolerance).

19. As the individual perceives and accepts into his self-structure more of his organic experiences, he finds that he is replacing his present value system - based extensively on introjections which have been distortedly symbolized - with a continuing organismic valuing process (e.g. by including denied experiences one can reshape their world view).

Rogers heavily stressed the importance of the phenomenological theory of the "self" and feelings about the self, more commonly known as self-esteem. According to Rogers, humans have a natural tendency to maintain and enhance the self, driving toward self-actualization while preserving self-esteem. His work was instrumental in establishing the concept of person-centered approaches to therapy and it continues to heavily influence the modern therapist's methods of counseling and treatment. Many major ideas and concepts emerged from the humanistic perspective that continue to serve as pillars of modern-day psychological theory and mental health, such as self-concept, the hierarchy of needs, positive regard, free will, client-centered therapy, self-actualization, and peak experiences. Many versions of humanism exist today, such as positive psychology and transpersonal psychology, and the humanistic movement led to the beginnings of the cognitive psychological perspective, which serves as the basis for the Purposeful Cognition Index. The humanistic perspective is summarized by five core principles that were first documented in 1965 by James Bugental, an early advocate of the Existential-Humanistic Therapy movement, in the *Journal of Humanistic Psychology*:[8]

1. Human beings, as human, supersede the sum of their parts. They cannot be reduced to components.

2. Human beings have their existence in a uniquely human context, as well as in a cosmic ecology.

3. Human beings are aware and are aware of being aware - i.e., they are conscious. Human consciousness always includes an awareness of oneself in the context of other people.

4. Human beings have the ability to make choices and therefore have responsibility.

5. Human beings are intentional, aim at goals, are aware that they cause future events, and seek meaning, value, and creativity.

These humanistic principles would serve as a harbinger for the coming cognitive revolution, which was an intellectual movement in the 1950s that gave birth to many of the modern fields of science we have today, such as cognitive psychology, artificial intelligence, computer science, and neuroscience.

In Sum

According to the humanistic approach:

- Traits and environment are secondary to self-actualization when it comes to shaping the human experience.
- Free will is dominant over determinism or fatalism.
- An optimistic approach to therapy is more powerful than the pessimistic approaches of psychoanalysts and behaviorists.
- Human beings are motivated by a hierarchy of needs.
- Needs are organized in a hierarchy of prepotency in which more basic needs must be more or less met (rather than all or none) prior to higher needs.
- Most behavior is simultaneously determined by more than one basic need, referred to as multi-motivated.
- Maslow considers these to be characteristics of self-actualizers: perceive reality efficiently and can tolerate uncertainty; accept themselves and others for what they are; are spontaneous in thought and action; are problem-centered (not self-centered); have an unusual sense of humor; are able to look at life objectively; are highly creative; are resistant to enculturation, but not purposely unconventional; are concerned for the welfare of humanity; are capable of deep appreciation of basic life-experience; establish deep satisfying interpersonal relationships with a few people; seek out peak experiences; have a need for privacy; possess democratic attitudes; and possess strong moral/ethical standards.

Humanism contributions to purposeful cognition:

- Humans can visualize a different future for themselves, one that is in contrast to genetic makeup or environmental circumstance.

- Grit, perseverance and determination are major determinants of life success.
- Focusing on optimism drives positive outcomes, even in dire circumstances.

CHAPTER 5 | THE REVOLUTION

"People are not disturbed by things, but by the view we take of them. We create our emotions, positive and negative, through our interpretations."

EPICTETUS, Greek Stoic philosopher

"Such as are your habitual thoughts, such also will be the character of your mind; for the soul is dyed by the thoughts."

MARCUS AURELIUS, Roman Emperor, philosopher

In 1976, participants were invited into a laboratory where they were instructed to wait in a reception area. The receptionist, who was seated nearby, excused herself, leaving the participants alone while they were waiting for the researchers to arrive. The participants were divided into two groups. The first group overheard a conversation in the laboratory next door about equipment that was failing which would be needed to run the eventual experiment. A door opens, and the individual who was having the conversation with the scientist walks into the waiting area, hands covered in grease while holding onto a writing pen. The second group had a different experience. They overheard a heated exchange between the individual and the scientist, followed by a sound of glass breaking and thrashing chairs. The same individual who walked into the waiting area with greasy hands and a pen in the first scenario, came sprinting through the room where the participants anxiously waited, holding a letter opener that was soaked in blood, leaving spatter on the floor as he darted away.

Both groups were then shown 50 photographs and asked to identify the person who left the laboratory through the waiting room. Those who had witnessed the man holding the pen identified the individual 49% of the time, compared to those who witnessed the man fleeing with a bloodied weapon identified the individual 33% of the time. The researchers claimed that the group who witnessed the argument and apparent assault had higher levels of anxiety and were more likely to focus on the letter opener rather than the target's face. This phenomenon, known as the weapon focus effect, would serve as the basis for studying eye witness testimony, false memory, and recall cognition for many years to come.[1] This was one of the first studies to show that a scenario experienced by multiple people at the same time, generated different mental processes which were unique to each individual and subsequently affected memory recall and eventual behavior differently for each participant.

What effect does emotion have on our ability to think and on our perception of experiences? In the early 1950s, researchers started to build on humanistic psychology and began to look at the mind and its processes. Behaviorism started to fall out of favor because philosophers started to see the importance of memories, goals, and emotions – all concepts that were shunned in the behaviorist movement. Advances in artificial intelligence and computational technology gave researchers a new metaphor to shape thinking around the human mind, such as its ability to process information and receive feedback. Dubbed the cognitive revolution, a radical shift in the psychological landscape began to take shape, which focused on the study of mental processes, such as memory, emotion, perception, and creativity, and their effects on human behavior. This revolution would create a wave of cognitive psychologists who began to study mental processes in controlled lab settings.

Cognitive psychologists believe that your behavior is determined by your thoughts and emotions. How you act is based upon internal processes and cognitive psychology combines behavioral outcomes with self-insight about negative or self-limiting thoughts. Essentially, your thoughts create self-fulfilling prophecies about outcomes and behavior. A quote by Henry Ford that illustrates this approach is "whether you think you can, or you think you can't, you're right." Essentially, humans are information processors and our outputs (behaviors) are a result of our inputs (stimuli) and our mental processes that analyze them (emotions, memories, etc.). There were three major influences that arose during this time that began to solidify cognitive psychology as a formal school of thought.

The development of new technology during the Second World War created a greater need to understand human performance, especially in relation to manipulating advancing technology. Researchers began to investigate how to best train new soldiers and how behavior changed when subjected to stressful conditions, such as gunfire or battlefield explosions. Behaviorism provided little to no insight in these areas since it became evident that soldiers would all respond differently to similar stimuli.[2]

Developments in computer science would start to provide researchers with a new lens to view human thought. Researchers began to see how computers functioned – a series of inputs, computations, and then outputs – as a parallel to how the human mind could also operate. These parallels would guide researchers toward investigating how computers handled functions such as memory storage and retrieval, which then led to laboratory experiments with humans that sought to investigate any similarities between man and machine learning.[3]

The third factor was a group of four Harvard scholars who sought to truly establish behavior as a science of the mind. George Miller, Noam Chomsky, Jerome Bruner, and Roger Brown, published landmark articles to officially launch the cognitive revolution.

Memory, Language, and Chunks

One of the most frequently cited papers in psychology is George Miller's 1956 article "The Magic Number Seven, Plus or Minus Two." First published in *Psychological Review,* Miller's research concludes that the average human can hold in working memory seven distinct items, plus or minus two (this would eventually come to be known as Miller's law). Miller observed that people could recall with 100% accuracy a string of five random numbers if given the numbers and then asked to repeat them back. Accuracy would drastically start to fall off as more numbers were added.[4] Miller also recognized that the memory span wasn't limited to single numbers themselves, but rather centered around chunks of information. For example, when recalling a random string such as 12162017, it might be difficult for some to repeat the number back since it represents seven individual numbers. Now break it apart into chunks, such as 12, 16, 2017. We can easily create a mnemonic (in this case resembling a date), where it now represents three distinct chunks, making memory recall easier for most. Essentially, a chunk represents the largest meaningful unit in the material that is presented that a person can easily or automatically recognize.[5] This also means that chunks are different for each person since each person has a different interpretation of what the largest meaningful unit within the presented material is. Not only was this study an important maiden voyage into the sea of cognition, it also showed how humans could respond differently to similar stimuli. This shattered the major paradigm of the behavioral perspective which posited that all behavior was a generalized product in response to external stimuli since it started to show that human rationality and the subsequent behavior were uniquely due to the cognitive processes of the *individual.*

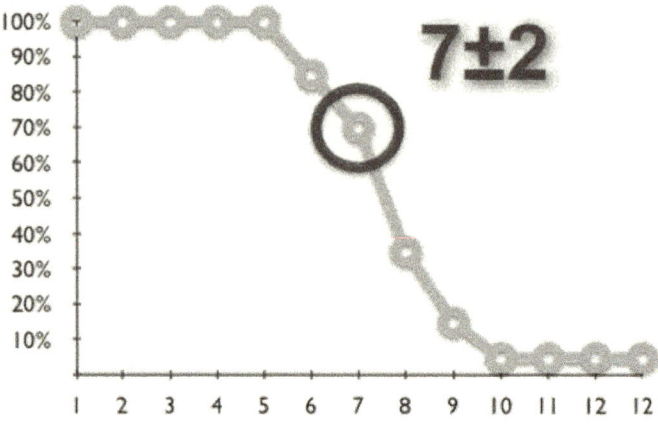
Memory Recall vs. Chunks of Information Presented

Linguist Noam Chomsky rejected the behaviorist approach in his 1959 review of B.F. Skinner's *Verbal Behavior*. He claimed that Skinner's book was no more than an untested hypothesis, that Skinner's technical vocabulary was a paraphrase of traditional terms, and that speech requires complex neurological theory to understand.[6] Essentially, he argued that the burden of proof was on Skinner to show how his theories could be tested, further pushing psychology into the laboratory and establishing the case for the discipline to be considered a hard science.

Jerome Bruner co-authored a paper in 1956 named "A Study of Thinking," which viewed people as constructive problem solvers who achieve a measure of rationality in spite of imposed bias, external stimuli, attention and memory deficits. This work still holds as one of the major contributions of our understanding of the human mind. It was used to formally initiate the study of cognitive psychology at Harvard and found the Harvard Center of Cognitive Studies.

Bruner's colleague, Roger Brown, studied the developing language of pre-school children, and how that language ultimately would permit them to understand themselves and the world around them. His core findings, which he published in *A First Language,* showed that he developed five stages of linguistic development that children go through during their speech development.[7] Ultimately, his work focused on the nature and development of knowledge, further ushering cognitive psychology into a discipline that mirrored epistemology, which is a branch in philosophy concerned with the theory of knowledge. His work started to develop an important theoretical sequence in regard to human behavior. Humans learn language at different rates. That linguistic capacity then determines how humans perceive and remember events, then how perception and memory of those events (which is packaged mentally within language and knowledge) uniquely affect the human experience and eventual behavior. This is a major reason why humans cannot remember anything in our infant years – we lack the linguistic capacity to code events into our memory.

Mental Processes

The main focus of psychologists within the cognitive perspective is to study how mental processes affect behavior. There are many mental processes which scientists have studied since the start of the cognitive revolution, but the main ones are attention, memory, perception, language, and metacognition.

Attention is a major mental process that is constantly studied within this perspective. The American Psychological Association defines attention as "a state of focused awareness on a subset of the available perceptual information."[8] The key component of attention is being able to identify irrelevant information, filter it out, and assign information correctly to stimuli. The accuracy of attention dramatically affects how we perceive situations, people, and events, and continues to be a major focus of cognitive psychology research today.

Memory, which is often divided into two subjects of short-term and long-term memory, is also considered a core cognitive process. In "The Magic Number Seven, Plus or Minus Two," researchers were investigating working memory, which is a combination of short and long-term memory in the face of distractions. Cognitive psychologists have long been interested in how memory affects behavior because some memory is considered conscious while other memory is unconscious. As an example, procedural memory, which is the memory for the performance of particular types of action, is considered subconscious because it requires minimal effort since it is activated through association with particular routines. An example would be driving a vehicle, which is a behavior that has drastic consequences if performed in certain ways, and one that our mental processes respond to automatically. Semantic memory, which is the factual knowledge a person possesses, refers to the recall of facts, figures, pictures, and other information from our past, such as what our sixth-grade teacher's name was or what the Washington Monument looks like. This recall is conscious and can take varying degrees of effort. Episodic memory, or our autobiography of events which we can linguistically describe, contains all of the memories that are temporal in nature, such as when the last time we ate breakfast or where we were on September 11, 2001. Episodic memory requires the deepest level of conscious thinking since it combines semantic memory with temporal information to encapsulate our entire memory.[9]

Perception is the cognitive process that takes information delivered to us from all of our physical senses (sight, hearing, taste, touch, and smell) and interprets them, producing our understanding of the world around us. All perception is the organization and interpretation of electrical signals that pass through our nervous system and it is considered the processing of sensory input or the processing which is connected to selective mechanisms that influence perception, such as knowledge or attention. After the cognitive revolution, many disciplines have launched to further explore how perception affects human behavior, such as psychophysics, which studies the relationships between physical qualities of sensory input, and sensory neuroscience, which studies the neural mechanisms that underpin human perception. Perception is at the core of how humans experience reality.

Language, in reference to cognitive psychology, is a mental process that was first studied in the 1870s, when Carl Wernicke proposed a model for how our brains process language. His research was among the first to localize brain function of speech. Wernicke's aphasia is the eponymous term for when a person has an inability to understand or produce meaningful speech due to damage to the language epicenter of the brain. Cognitive psychologists used these early mental models to research how language acquisition and formation affects behavior and how language is used in the altering of human moods.[10] As you will see in the chapters ahead, language plays a vital role in our ability to think on purpose, specifically within our verbal cortex.

Metacognition is simply defined as the thoughts a person has about their own thoughts. Metacognition contributes to detrimental self-rumination, how powerful our inner critic is, how effective we are at monitoring our own performance, our self-awareness around our own capabilities, and the ability to apply cognitive strategies in our battle against distorted thinking. As you will see in chapter 11 about emotional intelligence, metacognition, or self-awareness, is a foundational element of our ability to think on purpose. Cognitive psychologists study the application of metacognitive abilities and the impact on learning and behavior. Self-actualization, a core component of the humanistic movement which is defined as our ability to set goals, is an example of improving one's metacognitive abilities. The concept of thinking about our own thinking is unique to the cognitive perspective of psychology.

The cognitive revolution romanticized the allure of free will. Humans were slowly abandoning the concepts of determinism/fatalism and simply accepting their lives as a consequence of whatever random event life dealt them. Instead, humans began to believe that they could create their own destiny and pave their own futures through a process of investigating thoughts, mental processes, and how our brains work. This paved the way for the biological perspective of psychology, which expanded upon how genetics, physical characteristics, and brain chemistry affect our mental processes and ultimately our behavior.

In Sum

According to the cognitive approach:

- Humans are information processors, much like computers.
- How you act is based upon internal processes. Cognitive psychology combines behavioral outcomes with self-insight about negative or self-limiting thoughts. Essentially, your thoughts create self-fulfilling prophecies about outcomes and behavior.
- Mental processes, such as attention, memory, perception, language, and metacognition, are core focus areas within the study of cognitive psychology.
- There were three major influences that arose during this time that began to solidify cognitive psychology as a formal school of thought. The development of new technology during the Second World War which created a greater need to understand human performance, developments in computer science and a group of four Harvard scholars who published landmark articles to officially launch the cognitive revolution.
- Studies of memory recall and perception queues that affected behavior shattered behavioral psychology principles and paved the way for the cognitive revolution.

Cognitive contributions to purposeful cognition:

- Our mental processes, such as perception, language, and memory shape our worldview.
- Self-awareness in combination with self-actualization is an important cornerstone of our ability to think on purpose.
- We are not passive participants who are powerless victims of our environments. We have the ability to analyze our thinking, change our thinking, and change our futures.

CHAPTER 6 | INVESTIGATION OF INHERITANCE

"The connection between psychology, mythology, and literature is as important as the connection between psychology and biology and the hard sciences."

DR. JORDAN B. PETERSON, author of *12 Rules for Life*

"Most intellectuals today have a phobia of any explanation of the mind that invokes genetics."

STEVEN PINKER, evolutionary psychologist

On September 13, 1848, a 25-year-old foreman was preparing a railroad bed in Cavendish, Vermont. Using an iron rod to pack blasting powder, the explosives detonated, sending a 43-inch pole upward, piercing his left cheek and tearing through his brain. Despite massive head and brain trauma, he survived the initial injury and was able to travel upright to a nearby doctor in town to verbally explain what happened. Known as the famous case of Phineas Gage, it would mark one of the earliest and most important cases of neuroscience, providing evidence that the frontal lobe was involved in personality. Gage would live for another 13 years after the accident, but friends and family would note that he was an entirely different person, often citing that he was "no longer Gage." He was prone to outbursts and unable to hold a steady job. Eventually, a series of seizures would claim his life on May 20, 1860. In 1994, researchers used neuroimaging to reconstruct Gage's skull and research his injuries further. They found that the brain damage significantly impacted the brain regions associated with emotional processing and decision-making. Further research found that 11 percent of the white matter in Gage's frontal lobe and 4 percent of his cerebral cortex were decimated by the iron rod.[1]

Phineas Gage and the Iron Rod

It is only within recent human history that people have developed an agreed upon understanding of the location of the human mind. Many early philosophers subscribed to the theory of mind-body duality, which posits that mental aspects and phenomena are non-physical, meaning that the mind and the body are two separate and distinct entities. For example, Aristotle thought that our feelings generated from the heart. Leonardo da Vinci and René Descartes introduced theories of the nervous system that would later be proven wrong. Da Vinci undertook his research with the broad goal of providing physical explanations of how the brain processed visual and other sensory input and he believed they integrated that information via the soul.[2] Descartes believed that the mind was nonphysical – that inputs are passed on by the sensory organs to the epiphysis in the brain and from there to the immaterial spirit.[3] Cases like Phineas Gage, the philosophical movement away from dualism, and psychological and technological advancements from the cognitive revolution, led to the development of the biological perspective of human psychology.

This perspective builds upon the early work done by cognitive psychologists to establish disciplines such as neuroscience. Psychologists who take the biological approach look at how your nervous system, hormones and genetic makeup affect your behavior. Biological psychologists seek relationships between your mental states, your brain, and hormones, and how those relate to actions. For the biological approach, you are the sum of all of your parts. Your actions and thoughts are a function of your brain chemistry and physiological needs, meaning that all of your actions are based on physical needs and internal characteristics. The biological perspective stresses the importance of nature over nurture.

Also referred to as biopsychology, it contains other related disciplines such as biology, neurology, genetics, and physiology. Advances in science and a pivot towards the biological approach would start to threaten the psychodynamic hegemony during the rise of Charles Darwin. It was Darwin who first introduced the notion of evolution and natural selection, positing that natural selection preferences that were passed down to us were the drivers of our behavioral patterns. Let's take a behavior, such as hostility, and view it through both a psychodynamic and biological lens. Someone who addresses the hostile behaviors of another individual using the psychoanalytic approach may believe that the root cause of this behavior is due to unconscious urges and negative experiences from childhood. Someone who analyzes these behaviors through a biological lens would infer that genetic information or brain trauma was the culprit. Big difference between the two perspectives!

Recent research by Antonio Damasio, a neurologist at the University of Iowa College of Medicine, shows that early thinking by Descartes was incorrect on views of dualism. Appropriately named *Descartes' Error*, he published a series of research findings on patients that had prefrontal lobe damage due to stroke, tumors, or head trauma. They also had difficulty with emotions and reasoning and reported that they "felt nothing." They could speak clearly and make logical arguments, but couldn't make any decisions or participate in a discussion that involved reasoning. He helped discover the neurological connections between reason and emotion, positing that "reason, like almost all mental processes, is 'embodied,' that is, based in the human being's physical self. Emotions and other states that are rooted in physicality profoundly influence not only what people reason about, but how they reason. Without them, people either can't make decisions or they make self-defeating ones."[4] Essentially, he established a physical link between human rationality and emotionality.

Biopsychologists study many of the same things that other psychologists do but instead are interested in looking at how biological factors drive human behavior and decision making. Some topics that a psychologist might explore using this perspective include:

- How brain trauma influences behavior
- How degenerative brain diseases impact behavior
- How genetic factors influence such things as anger
- How genetics and brain trauma are linked to mental disorders

This perspective has grown significantly in recent years as the technology used to study the brain and nervous system has advanced dramatically. Today, scientists can use tools such as PET and MRI scans to investigate how brain development, drugs, disease, and brain damage impact behavior and cognitive functioning.[5] Since those early influences, researchers have continued to make significant discoveries about the inner workings of the brain and the biological underpinnings of human behavior. Research on the localization of brain functions, brain neurons, and neurotransmitters have advanced our comprehension of how biological processes impact thoughts, emotions, and behaviors. The three specific mechanisms that are important to understand in relation to how biology and behavior are related are the brain, the nervous system, and neurotransmitters.[6]

The Brain and the Nervous System

The portion of the brain that is responsible for functioning in cognition, sensation, motor skills, and certain emotions is referred to as the cerebral cortex, which is the outermost part of the brain. The brain is composed of four lobes:

1. Frontal Lobe: Involved in overall motor skills, higher-level cognition, and expressive language.
2. Occipital Lobe: Involved in interpreting visual stimuli and information.
3. Parietal Lobe: Responsible for the processing of tactile sensory information such as pressure, touch, and pain. (This shapes a majority of our human experience with the outside world).
4. Temporal Lobe: Responsible for the interpretation of the sounds and language we hear, memory processing, as well as other functions.

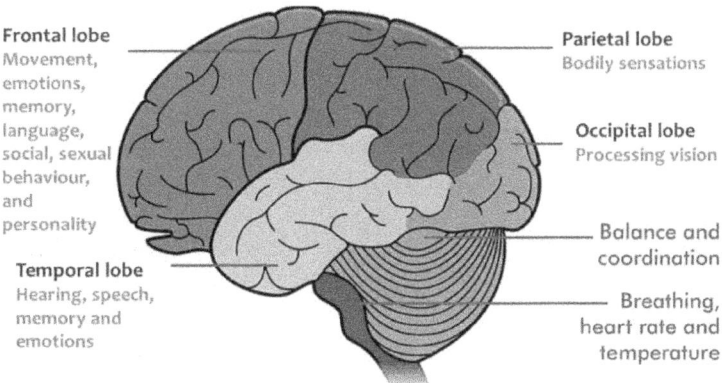

The 4 Lobes of the Brain

An important part of the nervous system is the peripheral nervous system, consisting of two parts:[7]

1. The motor (efferent) division connects the central nervous system to the muscles. The efferent nerve fibers of motor neurons are involved in muscle control, both skeletal and smooth muscle.
2. The sensory (afferent) division carries all types of sensory information to the central nervous system, referring to axonal projections that arrive at a particular region.

Another component of the nervous system that regulates automatic processes such as heart rate, breathing, and blood pressure, is known as the autonomic nervous system, which consists of two parts:

1. The sympathetic nervous system, which controls the "fight or flight" response.
2. The parasympathetic nervous system, which works to bring your body back to a state of rest.[8]

Neurotransmitters are responsible for carrying information between neurons and allowing chemical messages to be sent from various senses, organs, and systems, to the brain and back. Neurotransmitters affect the body in many different ways. For example, dopamine is a neurotransmitter that is involved in learning reinforcement and reward. It helps with motivation because it produces pleasure and helps us focus on tasks. While it sounds like a wonderful neurotransmitter to produce, dopamine has a sinister side as well. Excessive amounts have been associated with psychological disorders such as schizophrenia, while too little amounts are associated with Parkinson's disease.[9] The high that people feel when they are addicted to drugs like cocaine, nicotine, or heroine is from massive amounts of dopamine spikes being produced. This means that a biological function (dopamine) is responsible for certain behaviors (addiction) and the subsequent psychological well-being (anxiety, despair) that is associated with those actions (drug use). Knowing what we know now, due to the overall body of current knowledge of biology, it is easy to see how biological factors, such as genetics, physical sensations, brain chemicals, brain trauma, nerves, heartbeat, breathing, and other physiological factors, produce certain externalized behaviors and psychological states associated with those behaviors.

On the scientific research side of the biological perspective, psychologists within this approach gave rise to the practice of analyzing psychological problems using scientific and empirical methods that produced valid and reliable results. While this approach fails to account for societal factors that drive behavior (as we see in the behavioral perspective of psychology) biological research has helped yield useful medical treatments for a variety of psychological disorders, such as autism, attention-deficit disorder, bipolar disorder, mania, depression, anxiety, and post-traumatic stress disorder, to name a few. While the debate of nature versus nurture continues to be a byzantine psychological debate today, the biological perspective took abstract concepts such as the collective unconscious and mind-body dualism and used demonstrable scientific methods to elucidate origins of behavioral outcomes that exist within our physical bodies.

In Sum

According to the biological approach:

- Heavy focus on natural selection, adaptation, genetics, nomothetic psychology (the study of general scientific laws), and reductionism.
- Psychology should be seen as a science and studied as such.
- Behavior can largely be explained by biology, genes, hormones.
- Genes have adapted over millions of years and behavior is evolutionary.
- High focus on objective measurement and experiments.
- Highly applicable in determining IQ, gender role, relationships, response to stress, and disorders caused by genetics or brain damage.
- Aligns with determinism, meaning there is little to no free will.

Biological contributions to purposeful cognition:

- An understanding that behaviors create real chemical reactions in the brain which produce desired feelings. These feelings lead to our mood and other eventual behaviors.
- Humans make rational decisions through emotionality and there is a physical link between reasoning and emotions, which subsequently produce behaviors.
- Language expression, visual stimuli, and interpretation of others' language affect our Locus of Control and Inner Passivity.
- "Real" components, such as brain chemistry, genetics, brain damage, and body composition drive behavior, as opposed to invisible constructs such as the id, ego, and superego.

CHAPTER 7 | PART I SUMMARY

"Every new beginning comes from some other beginning's end."

SENECA, Roman Imperial Period philosopher

"Whatever good things we build end up building us."

JIM ROHN, American philosopher, entrepreneur

In Part I, you went on a crash course of important events in human psychological history, showing you how approaches to mental health treatment have progressed from the beginning of recorded time until now. It is important to note that any one of the psychological perspectives by themselves could be its own series of books. These progressions and scientific discoveries took many years, many experiments and various publications by men and women who were considered the most intellectual scientists of their era to alter the zeitgeist of their perspective times and attack the hegemony of the psychological school of thought that preceded them. Freud battled the establishment "healers" who perpetuated physical intervention; B.F. Skinner fought against the dominance of an invisible and unmeasurable construct called the human mind; Maslow and Rogers fought to revivify harmony and peak experiences in a world filled with conditioned pessimism; George Miller, Noam Chomsky, Jerome Bruner, and Roger Brown would unite nascent fields of artificial intelligence, computer science, and neuroscience with the domains of psychology, anthropology and linguistics to start a revolution; brain researchers like Damasio would use the nomothetic approach to establish general laws about the brain and how it physically affected mental processes and ultimately human behavior.

Even though each psychological perspective and the scientists within them fought against historical dicta and ancient aphorisms to create new explanations for human behavior, it is important to view each new theory, approach, and method, not as a replacement of the antecedent theory, but as an addition to them. Each psychological perspective contained axioms that should be viewed as starting points, or even launching pads, for the researchers that would come after them looking to add to the burgeoning continua of knowledge. As an example, some of Freud's theories would be considered asinine today, but you can still extrapolate key general concepts from those theories that universally apply to modern psychology.

Each of the perspectives presented provides key contributions to purposeful cognition and to the model we will use to assess the five major domains that affect our ability to think on purpose. Those domains are:

Inner Passivity
Inner Aggression
Locus of Control
Cognitive Distortion
Emotional Distortion

Part II will explore these five domains in depth, providing insight into how they erode our well-being and deteriorate our mental health. Mastering these five domains and understanding how they uniquely affect every one of us is the beginning of your journey toward developing an ability to think on purpose. Here are the key concepts that you should retain as you venture into Part II:

Nonphysical treatment for mental illness is a relatively new concept. Mental illness has been around since the beginning of time and various methods have been investigated to treat it. Early civilizations researched the brain and always looked for new ways to expel demons or eradicate mental illness. These treatments used to include barbaric methods, such as trepanation, surgery, lobotomy, and other physical methods. Nonphysical treatments, such as psychotherapy, started to gain prominence as a rebuke to physical intervention, but this led to many charlatans creating fraudulent methods initially. Psychotherapy gave rise to using psychological methods as the treatment vehicle of choice, which eventually spawned five major psychological perspectives, each differing in their approach to mental illness treatment and looking for the origin of human behavior. The five major perspectives are the Psychodynamic, Behavioral, Humanistic, Cognitive and Biological perspectives.

The human mind contains two modes of thinking, the conscious and the unconscious. The psychodynamic perspective established the modern concept of an unconscious mind. According to this perspective, our unconscious mind contains mental processes that dictate our feelings, thoughts, and subsequent behaviors, and is not accessible to our conscious mind. The unconscious mind is the primary source of human behavior. Feelings, thoughts and our decision-making are stored in the unconscious, which is most directly linked to our past experiences, specifically our experiences from childhood. Psychologists within this perspective believe that our childhood experiences shape our personality as adults and are at the root of all of our psychological problems and dysfunctions. Conflicts in childhood alter personality drives that solidify as adults and all behaviors are caused by unconscious factors that we do not have control over. Transference of unconscious thoughts and feelings to the conscious mind occur in the form of "parapraxes," or slips of the tongue, or Freudian slips and are significant because all behavior is determined and not accidental. Freud and other psychodynamic researchers believe that our personality is made up of three parts: the id, the ego, and the superego. The id is the primitive drive of personality and contains all of our inherited components (nature). The ego develops over time and mediates between the id and the real world. The superego contains our societal morals and values that are learned from our parents (nurture). Dysfunction comes from a constant conflict between the id, ego, and superego.

The psychodynamic perspective provides many key contributions to purposeful cognition. Freud helped frame the concept of unconscious and conscious thinking, which serve as the basis for modern psychological research around automatic and manual thinking. This approach helped move talk therapy into the modern era. Carl Jung's theories were some of the first to influence how psychodynamic principles could be applied to individual psychometric assessment. Bergler's psychic masochism is found in its most extreme form in alcoholics, drug addicts, and gamblers, and is produced by a number of interrelated factors, such as dependency, guilt, aggression, narcissism, perceived persecution, need for control, a joy of losing, or self-seeking martyrdom. *It resides within the domain of Inner Passivity.*

Our environment plays a major role in our behavior. The behavioral perspective took various concepts from the psychodynamic approach but stressed an emphasis on visible, measurable behavior. According to behaviorists, psychology should be seen as a science that is measured by observable behavior, meaning that emotion and internal events are irrelevant. Stressing the importance of nurture over nature, behaviorists believe that our environment shapes our behavior through consequence via processes of classical and operant conditioning. Researchers like B.F. Skinner learned that the schedule of reinforcement, or the timing of rewards in relation to the behavior, has a large impact on the continuation or extinction of behaviors.

The behavioral perspective provides many key contributions to thinking on purpose. This perspective illuminated the fact that learning can occur and subsequent behavior can be influenced by how we view the external environment and its effect on us. Environment, or external factors, shape human behavior via compliments, affirmation, and task outcomes. These external elements affect internal human factors, such as motivation, resilience, and task encouragement, which ultimately influence our self-view. *This is an important concept within the domain of Locus of Control.*

Humans can visualize a different future for themselves, one that is in contrast to genetic makeup or environmental circumstance. The optimistic thinkers within the humanistic approach believe that traits and environment are secondary to self-actualization when it comes to shaping the human experience. An important distinction from the behaviorists is that humanists believe that free will is dominant over determinism or fatalism. Having an optimistic approach to therapy is more powerful than the pessimistic approaches of psychoanalysts and behaviorists because human beings are motivated by a hierarchy of needs. Those needs are organized in a hierarchy of prepotency in which more basic needs must be more or less met (rather than all or none) prior to higher needs. As opposed to purely environmental factors or unconscious drives, humanists believe that most behavior is simultaneously determined by more than one basic need, referred to as multi-motivated.

The humanistic perspective provides many key contributions to purposeful cognition. The notion that humans can visualize a different future for themselves, one that is in contrast to genetic makeup or environmental circumstance, is an important milestone in the history of mental health treatment. This means that something that is not real (a future version of ourselves) can be used to develop key attributes that guide our lives. Attributes such as grit, perseverance and determination, which are major determinants of life success. *This is an important concept within Emotional Intelligence, which can be used to battle Inner Aggression, Inner Passivity, and Cognitive Distortion.*

Our thoughts are the ultimate determinant of our behavior. Even though the environment plays a role in our behavior, our thoughts shape our mental processes, which create self-fulfilling prophecies about our futures. Psychologists within the cognitive approach researched how mental processes, such as attention, memory, perception, language, and metacognition, affected subsequent behavior. According to the cognitive perspective, humans are information processors, much like computers. The cognitive perspective provides may key contributions to purposeful cognition. Generating self-awareness in combination with self-actualization are important cornerstones of our ability to think on purpose. This perspective gave rise to the notion that as humans, we are not passive participants who are powerless victims of our environments. We have the ability to analyze our thinking, change our thinking, and change our futures. *This is an important concept within Emotional Intelligence, which can be used to battle Inner Aggression, Inner Passivity, and Cognitive Distortion.*

Even though our thoughts ultimately determine our behavior, our nature matters too. There is an ongoing debate on whether nature or nurture is responsible for human behavior, but the truth is that it is both. Our environment plays a major role as it shapes our experiences and memories, but our genetics affect our physiology and hormones. Within the biological perspective, there is a heavy focus on natural selection, adaptation, genetics, nomothetic psychology (the study of general scientific laws), and reductionism. Psychology should be seen as a science and studied as such. Psychologists within this perspective believe that behavior can largely be explained by biology, genes, and hormones, because our genetics have adapted over millions of years, meaning that behavior is evolutionary.

The biological perspective provides many key contributions to purposeful cognition. We now have an understanding that behaviors create real chemical reactions in the brain which produce desired feelings. These feelings lead to our mood and eventual behaviors. Thanks to research on the brain, we also now understand that humans make rational decisions through emotionality and there is a physical link between reasoning and emotions, which subsequently produce behaviors. Language expression, visual stimuli, and interpretation of others' language affect our Locus of Control and Inner Passivity. *This is an important concept within Emotional Intelligence, which can be used to battle Inner Aggression, Inner Passivity, Cognitive and Emotional Distortion.*

As you move into Part II, think about what it is in your life that affects your ability to self-actualize. Are you overly anxious? Do you battle depression? Are you terrified at the thought of leading a team? Do you feel that you aren't in control of your own life? Our ability to think on purpose affects everything, such as our abilities to lead others, have meaningful interpersonal relationships, achieve mental clarity, reduce anxiety, eliminate depression, realize life goals, have high self-esteem, and be in control of our thoughts and behaviors. When we succumb to automatic or distorted thinking, yield to our inner critic, dwell in our Inner Passivity or believe that life happens to us and we are submissive passengers, we fail to self-actualize and we waste our chance to maximize our full potential in this ephemeral life. Part II is all about the five domains that hinder our ability to think on purpose. Those domains are our Inner Passivity, Inner Aggression, Locus of Control, Cognitive Distortion, and Emotional Distortion.

Part II

CHAPTER 8 | INNER PASSIVITY

"It is not in the stars to hold our destiny but in ourselves."

WILLIAM SHAKESPEARE, Playwright 1564-1616

"Passivity is fatal to us. Our goal is to make the enemy passive."

MAO ZEDONG, Chinese Communist Party leader 1935-1976

Inner passivity is the first domain within the Purposeful Cognition Index. Rooted in psychoanalytic theory, it is an important element of our unconscious that affects many aspects of our quality of life. Much of the work done by predecessors of the psychoanalytic model has led to the concept of Inner Passivity.

Inner Passivity is defined as an unconscious emotional element that limits the flow of our creativity or hinders our self-expression. It refers to the "manner in which we hold on to negative emotions and create our own self-misery and doubt."[1] Inner Passivity is often experienced as a lack of inertia or as a lack of foresight or vision. It is also the inclination to view what you are actively doing as if it were being done to you, without your consent. Essentially, Inner Passivity is the notion that things happen to you and that you are a victim of things occurring outside of your control. This is a mental predisposition to experience life as if it were happening to us. Considered a mental and emotional perspective, Inner Passivity prevents us from shaping our own destiny and puts us in the passenger seat of our lives, experiencing life as if we have no control over the direction or outcomes. It is the condition of accepting one's fate rather than believing we can craft our own path.[2] Viewed as a self-defeating emotional attachment that *we are often not aware of*, it is important to note that *we can only be aware of the symptoms* of Inner Passivity since it resides within the unconscious. "Inner passivity is almost invisible in the psyche and can be best approached and identified through its symptoms. Like subliminal advertising or carbon monoxide, it influences us strongly even as we are oblivious to its presence."[3] Below are some examples of how Inner Passivity is acted out and can be recognized (taken directly from *The Phantom of the Psyche*, by Peter Michaelson).[4]

1 - Depression, panic attacks, and phobias often are symptoms of underlying passivity, where the individual is caught in an emotional tangle from which he feels unable to extricate himself. Problems with procrastination, fatigue, and lack of motivation can cover up passivity, as does evasion and avoiding direct answers.

2 - Many of us have fears and anxiety about being unable to take care of ourselves physically or financially as we get older. Through passivity, we are preoccupied about the future because we are ready to live through the feeling that we won't be able to take care of ourselves or be supported by others and by life. It feels that we need someone else to protect us, guide us, and make decisions for us.

3 - Passivity can accentuate the fear of dying. Through passivity, the unconscious wish is to feel: "I am too weak and feeble to survive my own death in any form. Nothing will be left of me. I will be completely annihilated." Even for a dying person who believes in God and an afterlife, the presence of passivity can create various irrational fears.

4 - In passivity, we often make statements to others or to ourselves to the effect of, "There's nothing I can do about it;" "Oh, I don't know;" "Who knows;" "Well, anyway;" "If only things had been different;" "Whatever;"

"What difference does it make;" "It's up to you;" and "This isn't going to work." Deep and frequent sighs are another indicator, as is repeated use of the expression, "Everything is fine." Even the common statement on the telephone, "Okay, I'll let you go now," assumes to represent power but has a passive underbelly.

5 - Body language and facial expression such as rolling one's eyes, looking goofy, stumbling or moving awkwardly, shrugging, raised shoulders, and locked knees when standing also are indicators.

6 - Daydreams and fantasies of being reduced to poverty and being at the mercy of others and of life, of being homeless and abandoned, are indicators, too. Included are fears of being diminished, vanquished, and annihilated.

7 - Under the influence of passivity, members of an audience can be held spellbound by a dynamic speaker, while the truth of what he or she says or represents is secondary. Truth is associated with the emotional impact such a speaker has on us: we believe what's said because he or she said it so convincingly.

8 - Conversely, it can feel that one has to withhold oneself in order to avoid being overpowered or "swallowed up" by some other person. Teenagers can react negatively to parents as they try to break away from parental influence and establish their own sense of autonomy. The feeling of having to give up one's reality to accommodate someone else and is often associated with guilt and shame. Initially, this feeling can be experienced with a parent, while later in life it is transferred onto others. Such a person may often avoid others, feeling that he or she needs separation in order to feel whole or complete.

9 - A related indicator is an individual's feeling that he can't avoid being unhappy if his partner or a family member is unhappy. Or vice-versa—if others are happy, now he can be happy. It's the feeling of having no choice but to be under the influence of the mood or energy of others, rather than choosing and maintaining the quality of one's own mood or experience. It's also the feeling of slipping into a bad mood, whether others are present or not, without the hope of regulating oneself or the notion that it is possible to do so.

10 - Common to passivity is the experience of becoming emotionally distraught, or "puffed up," fearful or angry, simply to state one's needs. With passivity, it is difficult to say something to the effect, "Sorry, I can't do it now. I have things I have to do." It also feels that if we make a simple request or express a need, the other person will object. There is a tendency to avoid confrontation or, conversely, to be inappropriately harsh or demanding when confronting someone. Another symptom is to avoid asking for help or for money one is due.

11 - Railing and complaining about people, events, or a situation over which one has no control or influence is a sign of passivity. Complaining is the defense, covering up

how much we are secretly "into" the feeling of being helplessly enmeshed and hopelessly at the mercy of what we are complaining about.

12 - Indoctrination of our children to a subscribed mentality, particularly any dogma, reflects an unconscious compulsion to condition them to submit passively to what we acquiesced to as children. Or the reverse applies: also to the detriment of the child, a passive parent abdicates his responsibility to set boundaries, impose reprimands, and offer moral or spiritual guidance.

13 - Men often resist the development of the soft, intuitive, compassionate (feminine) side of their nature because they associate it with passivity. Normally the development of feminine qualities is a plus for men. Men who criticize or attack gay men are projecting and thus denying, not necessarily homosexual inclinations, but their own passivity, which unconsciously they associate with weakness, humiliation, and femininity.

14 - Acting out of habit is passivity based. We claim that a bad habit is hard to break, that it enslaves us. But the inability to break a harmful habit is founded in passivity, as is the pattern of forgetting inner resolutions or failing to complete projects.

15 - Tuning out or spacing out, absent-mindedness, or incessant daydreaming also indicates the influence of passivity. The practice, for instance, of retreating into the living room to read journals or newspapers and shutting others out, or reacting to their overtures with an absent-minded "Uh huh," is a prime example, as well as a daily occurrence in many homes. One client said of her father when he did this, "I am amazed at how deep he went into that place."

16 - The chronic need for excitement or stimulation—whether as a gambler, sports fanatic, daredevil, or "party-goer"—can be the consequence of a "dead-zone" within oneself that blocks access to life's little pleasures, a zone created in part by inner passivity.

Psychotherapist Peter Michaelson coined the term Inner Passivity through his life's work of researching Bergler's "basic neurosis." Michaelson claims that "Inner Passivity is an aspect of the unconscious mind that induces people to experience themselves through inner conflict, as well as through self-doubt and self-alienation."[5] Inner Passivity is a hidden psychological aspect that is inextricably linked to our ability to think clearly because it is rooted in self-doubt and indecision and it creates emotional weakness, Cognitive Distortion, and inner conflict. Inner Passivity cuts us off from our authentic self and our sense of legitimate authority. Being a negative emotional construct, it creates a virulent lack of enthusiasm for life if left unchecked. Inner Passivity has also been correlated to emotional instability and emotional unpredictability because we lack an ability to surpass oneself, creating a selfish dynamic that requires us to introspect inefficiently while simultaneously ignoring the outside world and other people. A subset within Inner Passivity, Passive Externalization is described as the "the tendency to experience one's emotions as if they were coming from the outside, originating perhaps with other people"[6] Examples of Inner Passivity and Passive Externalization can be seen in the following statements:

Passive: You make me angry.
Active: I am angry at you.

Passive: My inner critic is harassing me.
Active: I am criticizing myself.

Passive: That beautiful sunset inspires me.
Active: I'm looking at that beautiful sunset and feeling inspired.[7]

Michaelson sums up Inner Passivity as being responsible for much of our self-doubt, self-criticism, indecision, procrastination, defensiveness, confusion, loneliness, depression, emptiness, and addictions, as well as feelings of being unworthy and trapped.[8] According to research by Michaelson, Inner Passivity affects two major areas of our well-being: our relationships with others and our overall health. Let's first look at how it affects our interpersonal relationships with others.

Inner Passivity in Our Relationships

Passive elements can inhibit growth within relationships and research has shown that a few prominent patterns often arise. Those who are passive may feel it is his obligation to constantly acquiesce to his partner; go along with all requests, agree on all opinions, provide all that she wants, and even silently provide tacit approval for negative behaviors, all to avoid a confrontation or argument.[9]

Those who are passive may believe that her independent feelings, thoughts, or behaviors may make her partner leave, which leads to a lack of speaking up or a lack of self-defense when her partner criticizes her. This creates a condition where she fails to be assertive, letting Inner Passivity vanquish her self-esteem and confidence while also making her question if her thoughts and feelings are valid, worthy, or even real.

Passivity in relationships also rears its head in the form of ultra-dependency. Those who are passive may feel that he could not live on his own without his partner, so he allows himself to be completely emotionally and financially dependent on his partner. This creates a situation where he is hesitant to provide any substantial opinion on financial matters or candid feedback on daily household related conversations. How many of us have said to ourselves, "I don't really care what decorations, paint colors, or drapes you want to put up honey" when deep down, you actually do care. We rationalize in our minds that an argument over the decorations is worse than simply letting our partner do what they want, even if it's at odds with our own taste. When in our minds, the argument itself is worse than not getting our way, we have high levels of Inner Passivity.[10]

Needing permission to be ourselves or to express our needs is another pattern of passivity in relationships. When we feel guilty, anxious, or intimidated to have conversations about our needs; when we feel that we are forced to explain our behavior or defend our positions when we communicated a particular stance, we are being overly passive. This leads to a condition where our passivity increases how suggestible we are, leading us to distrust our own ideas and perceptions, and in some of the most extreme cases, gaslighting from our partners (gaslighting is a tactic where a person makes another person question their own sanity through psychological manipulation). Gaslighting is a manipulation tactic that is used to gain power. Common techniques of gaslighters include:[11] they tell blatant lies, they deny things they have said even in the face of solid proof, they wear you down over time, their actions do not match their words, they align people against you, or they tell others you are crazy. While these sound like obvious ploys when you read about them, those that have high levels of Inner Passivity are highly susceptible to these techniques within toxic relationships.

Inter-relationship decision making is also an area where Inner Passivity can dramatically affect our well-being. When we allow our partner to make all of the decisions and then resent him for it, we create conditions where we wait for our partner to fix situations that arise or we refrain from making decisions until we have our partner's approval. There is a major difference between discussing things with your partner and obtaining a consensus as a unit before acting versus not feeling comfortable with your own position unless your partner approves it. This can lead to blaming our partner for lack of progress in life, lack of achieving shared life goals or criticizing him behind his back.[12] Now, let's take a look at Inner Passivity and how it affects our health.

Inner Passivity and Our Health

Psychoneuroimmunology, or PNI, is the study which looks at the intersections between psychological processes and the body's immune system. PNI seeks to identify the links between the mental and the physical. In 1911, a Harvard University professor named Walter Cannon published findings in a book named *The Mechanical Factors of Digestion,* where he describes his research into homeostasis, or the internal conditions maintained by living things. Cannon discovered in research with animals that a change in emotional condition, such as anxiety, anger, or stress would be accompanied by an interruption of physical movements within the stomach.[13] This began research into the relationship between emotional states and the nervous system, specifically how stress affects immune function. PNI research into how the immune system and the brain communicate through a complex maze of signaling pathways is referred to as the immune-brain loop. The hypothalamic-pituitary-adrenal axis or HPA axis, is the body's primary stress management system. Essentially, when the mind senses fear, the body produces cortisol, which raises stress levels, and the HPA axis responds by trying to maintain homeostasis through cortisol regulation, hence the immune-brain loop. When stress is limited in duration, researchers have found that emotional manifestations such as anxiety, fear, anger or sadness, can yield beneficial effects from the physiological changes that occur, such as increased heart rate, sweating, or blood pressure rising/lowering.[14] It is when the stress is prolonged that the body struggles to maintain equilibrium or homeostasis and physical manifestations such as indigestion or high blood pressure develop.

Related to PNI, psychosomatic disorders are diseases or physical conditions that involve both mind (psyche) and body (soma). Some physical diseases are thought to be made worse by mental factors and some diseases are thought to be caused by mental factors entirely. There is strong evidence which shows psychosomatic links between negative emotional states and physical conditions, such as hypochondria, hypertension, addictions, compulsions, eating disorders, migraines, constipation, skin problems, obesity, impaired intelligence, attention-deficit disorder, stuttering, herpes, lupus, chronic fatigue, insomnia, hyperactivity, frigidity, impotence, and premature ejaculation.[15] As an example, the powerful emotion of anxiety has been proven to cause physical symptoms such as a fast heart rate, heart palpitations, nausea, tremors, sweating, dry mouth, chest pain, headaches, stomach knots, and fast breathing. The National Social Anxiety Center (NSAC), which is a national organization dedicated to the promotion of treatment for social anxiety, claims that mental therapy can be used to treat a wide variety of disorders, including, but not limited to:

- Panic Disorder
- Agoraphobia
- Social Anxiety Disorder
- Generalized Anxiety Disorder
- Obsessive Compulsive Disorder
- Phobias
- Health Anxiety
- Post-Traumatic Stress Disorders
- Mood Disorders
- Depression
- Bipolar Disorder
- Phase of Life Adjustment Anxiety
- Hoarding
- Insomnia
- Separation Anxiety
- Childhood Anxiety
- Grief/Loss
- Psychosomatic Disorders
- Stress Disorders
- Sexual Dysfunction
- Substance Abuse/Alcohol Abuse
- ADD/ADHD
- Eating Disorders
- Menopausal Anxiety

Meditations, mindfulness, and Cognitive Behavioral Therapy are powerful psychotherapy methods used to treat these various disorders because they attempt to lower or eliminate anxiety through practices of striving for mental clarity, grounding fantastical or magical thinking, or overcoming social anxiety. But oftentimes, these psychosomatic elements that erode our lives are created by our high levels of Inner Passivity.

Our inner emotional conflict may produce feelings that we do not deserve health or happiness, or that we are not worthy of the successes of life. Inner Passivity often manifests itself in a concept referred to as "selected sadness."[16] Researchers have investigated how depressed people regulate their emotions and have found that many who are depressed often engage in maladaptive strategies that reinforce their depression, rather than seeking ways to diminish it. Original theories around depression reinforcement centered on the stimuli selection strategy itself, or the notion that happy people simply had better strategies and mechanisms to create happiness for themselves when depressed people lacked the skills or tools to do so. In a few experiments performed for the *Journal of Psychological Science*, researchers asked depressed and healthy subjects to choose between looking at sad, neutral, or happy pictures. By doing so, all of the subjects used the same stimuli selection strategy (looking at pictures to alter their mood). The researchers discovered that happy people picked more of the happy pictures and sad people picked more of the sad pictures. A later study replicated the findings using music instead of photographs. Even when the study was performed a third time, with subjects hearing about the positive effects of choosing happy imagery when in a depressed state before being shown the pictures, many of the depressed subjects still chose sad photographs.[17] The researchers published their findings, concluding that depressed individuals did not lack the strategies to generate happiness, but *chose* to regulate their emotions in a way that was likely to maintain their sadness. Further qualitative research with depressed individuals found that depressed people often use emotional regulation to verify their emotional selves, and since feeling depressed was more familiar to depressed people, they were more motivated to reinforce their experiences of sadness to reaffirm who they are. Essentially, depressed people believe they deserve their bad feelings.[18]

There is additional research to suggest that humans can become addicted to unhappiness. It would seem intuitive to believe that people only seek pleasure and strive to avoid pain, but if that was the case, why are there so many that wallow in misery, constantly complain about their lives or others, or consistently express dissatisfaction? There is some preliminary research on the theory of people that like negative feelings, which suggests a few reasons why some may be addicted to unhappiness.[19] Unhappiness addiction occurs when:[20] people have deep-rooted insecurity and feel they are undeserving of happiness, are more comfortable with sadness than any other state so they unconsciously seek it out, feel guilty about past events and choose to punish themselves for it, believe that dissatisfaction is a motivator to work harder, or make it their personal mission to take on the world's problems, increasing the size of their cross to bear. All of these feelings that we do not deserve to be happy or our addiction to sadness are a result of psychic masochism, which is a component of Inner Passivity.

Remember back in chapter 2 where I briefly mentioned the concept of psychic masochism, which was Edmund Bergler's idea of how humans have a deep connection to negative emotions. Bergler posited that the human psyche constantly defends against the darkest aspects of our human nature and that every individual has a deep emotional connection to unresolved negative emotions.[21] He wrote in 1958:

> I can only reiterate my opinion that the superego is the real master of the personality, that psychic masochism constitutes the most dangerous countermeasure of the unconscious ego against the superego's tyranny, that psychic masochism is 'the life-blood of neurosis' and is in fact the basic neurosis. I still subscribe to my dictum, 'Man's inhumanity to man is equaled only by man's inhumanity to himself.[22]

He believed that through his clinical methods, he could get patients to realize that we were our own worst enemy because of psychic masochism. Bergler argued that we purposely seek out psychic pain to varying levels. This may seem illogical, a notion that humans seek pain instead of pleasure, but the whole concept of Inner Passivity is that we are allowing emotions and mental states to control us, which leads us to seek comfortable and familiar experiences, even if those experiences are rooted in depression and sadness. Let's take a look at a modern day example of psychic masochism - why humans enjoy scary movies.

Aristotle believed in the notion of catharsis, which is the process of releasing strong or repressed emotions to provide relief from them (Jung and Freud followed in these footsteps in their psychoanalytic approaches as well). Many researchers believe that watching horror films is a modern path to catharsis. In a 2004 paper in the *Journal of Media Psychology*,[23] researchers published data on the primary factors within horror films that made them so alluring to the average movie watcher. In the paper, researchers cite an experiment with college students done in the mid-1990s where the students were exposed to documentaries which depicted cows being killed, live monkeys' brains being eaten for dessert, and a child's facial skin being peeled back to prep for surgery. Ninety percent of the students turned off the videos, suggesting that they viewed the images as abhorrent and repulsive.[24] However, many of those same students would watch an entire horror movie that showed much more gore and blood than was present in the documentaries. The researchers discovered that the students were not repulsed by the horror film, as they were with the documentaries, because with the horror film, the fictional nature of the film gave students a sense of control because they would imagine all of the different ways the story could end. Within the documentaries, these gory scenes "already happened," so there was no control over the outcome. With the horror movies, the events were "fictional," meaning they haven't happened, producing a sense of control among the viewers. Control itself was the pivoting factor to where students willingly engaged in activities that produced negative emotions (and enjoyed them) or avoided those activities altogether.

Psychic masochism works in the same manner. We believe that if we ourselves generate the sadness or constantly seek out experiences that reinforce our sadness, we are in control of it and it does not affect us nearly as much. It is the same concept of self-deprecating humor; if I make fun of myself first then others insulting me won't have nearly as much effect than if someone beats me to the punch. Almost like we are inoculating ourselves with lower levels of sadness, in an attempt to unconsciously protect ourselves from higher levels of sadness. As long as we feel we are in control of the negative things in our lives, it makes it palatable. This creates a dangerous compounding effect where we further engage with psychic masochism as our coping mechanism if we believe that we will experience sadness and pain no matter what, so we should be the ones to do it to ourselves first. This eventually leads to the psychological effects of homophily and contagion. Homophily[25] is when we are attracted to people and situations that reflect our current moods and views. Contagion refers to the notion that people are affected by the emotions of others in real time. When engaged in psychic masochism, negativity seeks out other negativity, where it compounds upon itself in an endless spiral of "comfort" and deleterious reinforcement.

Other research has also shown that another reason humans enjoy scary movies is that watching them creates powerful emotions, even if those emotions are negative (scared, angry, or terrified).[26][27] Powerful emotions, especially negative ones, can produce potent physiological responses, such as rushes of adrenaline or dopamine hits. So, in a strange sense, humans *prefer negative emotions to no emotions at all*. As Alfred Lord Tennyson once said, "it is better to have loved and lost than never to have loved at all." Humans favor emotionality, even if it is negative, because it connects us with primitive regions of our brain that our verbal cortexes do not have access to, such as the basal ganglia (more on this later). It is much easier for humans to create powerful negative emotions instead of powerful positive emotions since we tend to ruminate and worry about things that cannot be changed. As an example, depression generally comes from thinking about past events, where anxiety generally comes from thinking about future events. Neither of these events is changeable in the present moment, however it is easier for us to harvest the negative emotions that ruminating about them produces. Those with a developed sense of emotional intelligence, specifically optimism, can combat this by creating positive emotions when thinking about the future, but humans are evolutionarily wired to scan for threats, think of what can go wrong, have contingency plans, and think about failure. Essentially, it is much easier for us to create negative emotions with our minds than positive ones, so we willingly, albeit sometimes unconsciously, engage in psychic masochism.[28]

Humans may also prefer to generate negative emotions because it makes eventual positive emotions much stronger if those positive emotions quickly follow the negative ones. Excitation Transfer Theory (ETT) states that "Negative feelings created by horror movies actually intensify the positive feelings when the hero triumphs in the end."[29] But what about movies where the hero doesn't triumph, or the boy doesn't end up with the girl? What if the positive emotion never comes? Those who purposely generate negative emotions, with the hope to intensify future positive emotions under ETT are essentially making a physiological arousal gamble, where the two possible outcomes are extreme highs (generated from an external source) or extreme lows (self-generated). As with most gambles, the house always wins and the better is left holding the bag. In this case, those who partake in this gamble are normally left feeling extreme lows more often than extreme highs.

Freeing Ourselves from Inner Passivity

The most important concept to understand about Inner Passivity is that it is unconscious. We are passive and we are not aware of it. "Our default state is to be passive; watch TV, surf the internet, listen to music, sleep, space out. Instead of overcoming Inner Passivity, we become personifications of it."[30] It resides deep within the psyche (hence why you find this within the discipline of depth psychology, the study of unconscious mental processes and motives) and it can be difficult to recognize because it manifests itself on the surface by producing hundreds of various symptoms. Like the creatures at the bottom of the ocean that live their whole lives in darkness, the only way for us to understand them is to shine a light onto them. Inner Passivity operates in the same manner, it maneuvers in the shadows and we first need to illuminate it. While it can never be fully eliminated, it can be managed and sidelined so that it does not negatively affect our lives any longer. This passivity leads to a superfluity of manifested emotional states, behaviors and mental processes. High levels of Inner Passivity lead to sadness, anger, psychic masochism, anxiety, Cognitive Distortion, and a surfeit of other factors that affect our abilities to think on purpose. This is why Inner Passivity is one of the five domains of the Purposeful Cognition Index – freeing ourselves from it is imperative. Does our Inner Passivity cause us to complain on social media constantly? Is it creating jealously, contempt or sadness in our interpersonal relationships? Is it causing us to let life pass us by? Inner Passivity is at the root of many of our anxiety and mood disorders, and while there are many ways to address the surface-level manifestations and behaviors caused by Inner Passivity, it is important to also shine a light on our passivity itself. The three main ways to battle Inner Passivity are to generate self-awareness, develop your anti-fragility, and aim for your average.

Generate Self-Awareness of Your Inner Passivity

The first way we free ourselves from Inner Passivity is to first become aware of it within us and to understand which behaviors it is creating within us. There are two main ways to achieve this:

1. *Talk to a psychotherapist* - A psychotherapist in your area is trained in how to apply the psychodynamic theory that aims to treat mental disorders by investigating the interaction of your conscious and unconscious elements within your psyche. Dream interpretation, free association, or discovering repressed fears could be tactics used. Be sure to check for licensure, reviews from other patients, and other sources before trusting your psyche to someone new. Good news is that most insurance companies have all of this information for you.
2. *Take an assessment* – You are in luck because an assessment is available to you after you complete this book that can illuminate your levels of Inner Passivity. Currently, the Purposeful Cognition Index is the only assessment in the world that can do so.

Develop Your Antifragility

The second way to free ourselves from Inner Passivity is to develop our antifragility. Michaelson sums up Inner Passivity by stating that:[31]

> Inner Passivity, according to depth psychology, produces our defensiveness, which is a psychological maneuver, often used unconsciously or instinctively, intended to mislead us. Whether expressed inwardly to ourselves or outwardly to others, defensiveness is a ploy used to protect us in a variety of ways, often from inner fear associated with challenges to our *fragile* sense of self.

Humans have an extremely fragile sense of self. Our sense of self is the way we think about our traits, beliefs, and purpose in this world. It is a complex construct that encompasses everything we now understand from the five psychological perspectives; from our biology, to our thoughts, to our unconscious drives, to our environment. This sense of self is constantly changing as technology, social media, politics, and other socioeconomic factors change the world around us and what is important to us. Our sense of self changes as we watch our families grow, see loved ones die, achieve important life goals, and start or end life adventures. With so many moving parts, no wonder why our idea about the type of person we are is so delicate. Inner Passivity plays on this fragility.

Antifragility is a concept developed by Nassim Taleb, a professor who has researched systems that increase capability and resilience in response to stress or failure. There is an entire class of things, systems, and ideas that do not simply resist stress but grow, strengthen, and gain from the unwelcome stimuli.[32] Even though Taleb describes antifragility as a concept that affects mathematics, business, economics, and philosophy, there is a psychological component as well.[33] There is an important distinction between resilience and antifragile. One who is resilient can resist stress, shocks, or failure. One who is antifragile grows stronger from them. This distinction is important in regards to Inner Passivity and psychic masochism – we do not simply want to find ways to better cope with their negative effects, we want to grow stronger in spite of them. As an example, bones within a healthy human will grow stronger under increased external load, a concept called Wolff's law.[34] Muscles get bigger when subjected to heavy weights. Within molecular cell growth, some organisms exhibit a favorable biphasic response that results in growth when being exposed to low levels of toxins, a process called hormesis. These are not examples of resilience, where one develops a stronger *ability to cope* with the stressor, these are examples of antifragility, where one *strengthens from being exposed* to the stressor. It is very important to understand the difference.[35] Within my own research, I have found two ways to increase psychological antifragility.

Embrace the chaos, do not attempt to eliminate it. How often do we say to ourselves "if I can just get rid of this or remove that from my life, things will be much better," or conversely "if I just achieve this or purchase that, things will be much better?" Chances are you did get rid of that old car in your driveway taking up space or buy that new house with the bigger yard, and things may have gotten better for a brief moment, but how long was it until something else started to give you similar levels of anxiety? We are attempting to remove stressors which create chaos in our lives. How narcissistic to think we can control the chaos! The key isn't to attempt to control the chaos (despite what our psychic masochism is teaching us), the key is to embrace it and build our antifragility so that the chaos makes us stronger.

Chaos theory is a branch within mathematics which focuses on the behavior of dynamic systems when exposed to small changes which create an infinite number of possibilities. For example, the butterfly effect is a metaphorical example of how a butterfly flapping its wings in one part of the world could create a tornado in another part of the world several weeks later, describing how a small event could create a massive one elsewhere. Even in closed systems, such as a pinball machine that is governed by precise laws of gravitational rolling and elastic collisions that we can fully understand, each game is considered unique and the final outcome is considered to be completely random and unpredictable. A game of billiards is the same way –

closed system, clear rules of physics, yet no two games played have ever been the same mathematically.[36] In psychology, chaos refers to the infinite number of possible outcomes that can occur during a human's life. If the outcomes are infinite, how can we possibly know what to remove or add to create our desired outcomes? Short answer, we don't! We have no way of knowing if a potty training incident when you were two-years-old somehow manifested into social anxiety in public restrooms when you were 37. The key here is that we do not know what events, especially those as small as a butterfly's wings changing the air, affect future outcomes, so aiming to control those outcomes is futile. As noted earlier with the scary movie research, we have a proclivity for control because it somehow makes negativity desirable, but this does not help us embrace the chaos. Based on my research and thousands of executive coaching conversations on this subject, here are some methods one can employ to embrace the chaos and preserve a sense of self:

- *Never multi-task.* There is a multitude of evidence that conveys the harm of multi-tasking. It has been linked to harm in our brains,[37] memory problems,[38] increased distractibility,[39] lower academic grades,[40] relationship issues, chronic stress, increased depression and anxiety, and less productivity and efficiency.[41] A study on the elderly found that multitasking leads to more broken bones and falling.[42] Another study found that multitasking leads people to walk into traffic (look at videos online of people walking into fountains, walls, holes in the ground, or cars, and they are all distracted by something else, like a cell phone). Most importantly, multi-tasking means you are not present. You are ruminating about other events, that are not present, which leads to depression (past events) or anxiety (future events). You can embrace chaos as long as you are fully immersed in the present state of the chaos. One task, right now. Period.
- *Be OK with uncertainty, let go of control.* When we are obsessed with control, that which we cannot control produces immense fear within us. That is the irony of trying to exhibit control is that we end up giving dominating power to the things we cannot control because they produce paralyzing fear. It is natural to fail, it is natural that some will dislike you, and it is natural that things will not go your way. If we try and control those things and they eventually occur, our fear paralyzes us. If we embrace the chaos and understand that these are natural events in our infinite system of chaos, they will make us stronger.
- *Embrace the "principle of charity."* The principle of charity is the notion that we should try to interpret others' statements in the best possible light. In philosophy, it is the idea that we should

consider the best possible interpretation of one's arguments, so that we can debate the validity behind those arguments, rather than debate flaws in the way the argument was presented.[43] For example, when you see two people debating about politics online, you will inevitably see one person comment on the grammar of the other person's written responses, rather than comment on the validity of their actual argument, in an attempt to make the initial person lose credibility. It may prove to be a funny online quip, but it derails the trajectory of the argument and does nothing to further the debate toward resolution. (Example - Person 1: You're president has a bad track record of fiscal responsibility. Person 2: I think you mean "your." See how this doesn't accomplish anything?) In psychology, this principle applies in the same way. Accept people for who they are and assume they have the best intentions when interacting with you. Assume they are doing their best and enjoy your finite time you have with this person, rather than trying to surmise hidden motives that do not exist. Unfortunately, social media and politics have risen to such a boiling point now that many people assume the worst in another if the viewpoint differs, especially politically. Many clients of mine will seethe an entire day because of something they read online that was from an opposing political viewpoint, simply because it was from the "other side," so it must be evil! This constant smoldering of rage makes you extremely irritable, irascible, and peevish, ultimately increasing your fragility. If you engage in the principle of charity, there is no "other side," allowing you to engage in a common humanity ethos,[44] which will increase your antifragility.

- *Shorten your to-do list.* Ever notice how your to-do list never gets any smaller? It's because of the concept we talked about earlier that checking off boxes in an attempt to control the chaos doesn't control the chaos; it's just replaced with other things. Notice I didn't suggest to *eliminate* your to-do list; we all have things we need to do to feed our families, keep clean houses, and live fruitful lives, but how many of these things on our lists are unnecessary? For every one of my executive coaching clients that carps about time management, I always have them show me their to-do list. Every time, half of the things on there can be removed. Reduce your commitments by saying no to certain people, streamline your tasks that you have to complete, prioritize them in order of importance and duration, and tackle the overwhelming stuff first. That way, anxiety isn't being produced from ruminating about the hard tasks you are putting off.

Shortening your to-do list will help reduce rumination about past and future events.

Decrease your downside. The other way I have found through my research as a way to increase psychological antifragility is to engage in a concept called "via negativa." Via negativa is a Latin phrase used in Apophatic (negative) theology as an attempt to describe God by negation, or by focusing on what he is not. Via negativa is a recurring theme in Taleb's book[45] as he describes the best way for a person or organization to become antifragile by decreasing and also eliminating downside risk. Downside risk from an individual standpoint would be a vulnerability to volatility. Essentially, think of downside risk as the risk associated with loss.

An example of this would be accumulating debt. An American habit is to increase our monthly debt and spending to match levels of increased income we receive. We get a raise of $1,000 a month and we go buy a car that costs $989 a month. This expenditure is obviously not an issue *while you have the income flowing in*, but the downside risk is that *as soon as you lose your job*, that debt becomes a big problem, because your income has vanished but your payment remains. Even if you remove volatility from the equation, that $989 a month being spent on the new car can be used for a variety of other things, like paying down current debt, starting a business, or financing your retirement (go calculate how much that $1,000 would be worth in 30 years if invested in an index fund and left untouched, that is how much you are 'taking' from your future retired self). Essentially, downside risk increases your risk during volatility and reduces your options in life. Sensitivity to risk combined with reduced options is a recipe for fragility. Think about it, with every new purchase that accumulates debt for your family, how much of your mental bandwidth does it take up each month? How much additional anxiety does it produce? It works in the other direction as well. Reduction of debt has been shown to be one of the biggest ways to decrease anxiety.

Materialism has been linked to many mental health problems such as anxiety and depression. A recent study from the University of Illinois at Chicago, written in the *Journal of Positive Psychology,* has shown that materialism has been shown to interfere with overall emotional function, increase mental health issues, and threaten mental development in kids.[46] Materialism within millennials is at an all-time high level. This is especially concerning when this data is superimposed with research done by Jonathan Haidt in *The Coddling of the American Mind* which shows that teen self-harm and suicide rates are at an all-time high, rising 300% since 2010.[47] The Chicago study concludes by finding that there is a strong inverse connection between gratitude and materialism, suggesting that the more materials one has, the less gratitude they have and subsequently express. Through my research, I have found that materialism is also inversely related to antifragility, or put more simply, the more stuff you have, the more fragile you are. A study at the University of

Illinois at Urbana-Champaign documented that materialism has negative effects on a person's well-being, makes bad events even worse, and is shown to increase when one has insecurity, or fragility, in one's life. Essentially, materialism increases fragility and vice versa.[48] This aligns with Buddhist ideals and philosophical principles which posit that freedom comes from getting rid of material possessions, or put another way, reducing your downside via negativa. Now, there are obvious things we need that cost a lot of money, like our homes, food, and cars, so the suggestion isn't to get rid of all of your earthly possessions (or even your vices) and live in a tent in the woods in the quest for mental clarity. I like nice stuff just as much as anyone else, but *not if the purchase creates more anxiety than benefit*. There is a simple mental calculation you can perform when trying to determine what to do with some free cash. If you are looking to purchase something you *need*, as opposed to something you *want*, research[49] has shown that you can take on additional volatility and not incur additional anxiety, *if the purchase fulfills a greater personal or familial need*, such as a house or food. Let's say you now have an extra $1,000 a month from a salary raise and you are trying to decide what to do with it. If it is a new purchase you are considering, like a new vehicle, first plot on a scale of 0-10 how much you truly need the item, with 10 being the highest amount of need. You will have to be honest with yourself to distinguish between a want and a need when doing this exercise and only plot based on need. You can refer to Maslow's Hierarchy of Needs as a quick reference if needed.

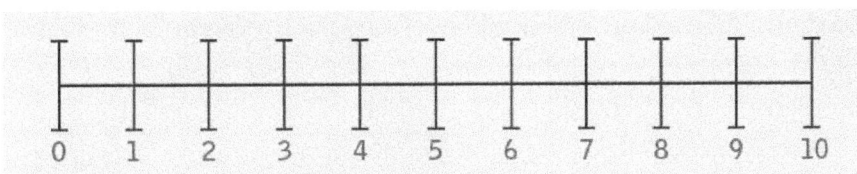

How Much Do I Need This?

Next, plot how much additional anxiety this new purchase will produce (for example, this new car will give me a $989 payment for the next 72 months, so you will worry about when the payment is due, what you will have to sacrifice if you are short cash each month, etc.).

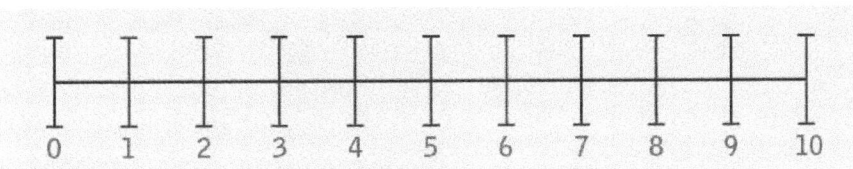

How Much Anxiety Will this Additional Volatility Produce?

If the need score is higher than the anxiety score, go for it. This would most likely be the case if you were finally able to purchase that much-needed minivan to provide adequate space for your family on road trips. If the anxiety score is higher than the need score, which would be the case if you were purchasing a 2-seater sports car instead, then use the cash to pay down existing anxiety, such as current debt. Reduce your downside. As Zac Brown Band sings, "there's no dollar sign on a peace of mind."

Disclaimer – the following section is not based in any science, just random musings of my mind that I wanted to share. An interesting tangential concept that is not based on any scientific data I have reviewed but merely interesting to mention is the concept of energy or spiritual transfer onto possessions, or essentially, how some houses or things can be haunted. Ever get the sense that some old antiques you recently purchased have the spiritual energy of previous owners? Now let's apply some association fallacy (the irrelevant association that if A is to B and A is also to C that all Bs are Cs) to tie this back to fragility. If we take the first law of thermodynamics and believe that matter cannot be created or destroyed, then we can assume that spirit energy transfer from owner to possession means the owner loses a piece of her spirit and more of her spirit cannot be regenerated. The more possessions she has, the more of her spirit she loses. The more of her spirit she loses, the more fragmented her spirit becomes, ultimately leading to a more fragile person. Another example of how material items lead to fragility! *End of random musings.*

Another tactic of via negativa is to avoid losing. Ever hear the phrase "offense wins games, but defense wins championships?" This is rooted in the idea of "not losing" versus trying to win. Taleb mentions, "In practice it is the negative that's used by the pros, those selected by evolution: chess grandmasters usually win by not losing; people become rich by not going bust (particularly when others do); religions are mostly about interdicts; the learning of life is about what to avoid. You reduce most of your personal risks of accident thanks to a small number of measures."[50] Charlie Munger, Vice-Charmain of Berkshire Hathaway said "It is remarkable how much long-term advantage people like us have gotten by trying to be consistently not stupid, instead of trying to be very intelligent." In the end, you can be wildly successful by not losing, or focusing on what you do not want to become. This will also bolster your antifragility.

The concept of via negativa posits that you can be successful by not doing things, by not adding things, and by asking yourself what you do "not" want to be. Reduce your downside, pay down those bills, avoid materialism and anxiety will reduce. You become more antifragile through subtraction, or via negativa, and preserve your sense of self (and maybe retain more of your spirit! OK, I digress.)

These are some of the tactics that will develop your antifragility. These tactics will help you become more present, ruminate less about past and future, and enable you to embrace the chaos that is chipping away at your armor. Do not settle for developing resilience, but embrace activities that will make you stronger as things get more chaotic. Does it matter how chaotic a task is if it is the only one you are focusing on? If your to-do list is reduced to the critical tasks, will the swirling chaos affect those tasks? If we assume everyone is interacting with us in the best possible light, how can we not enjoy their company? If we decrease our downside and material items, what future options will that open for us? These tactics will ensure that as your personal chaos swirls, you will become more powerful along with it, thus reducing your unhealthy dependency on psychic masochism. This will, in turn, reduce your Inner Passivity, bolstering your sense of self in the process.

Aim For Your Average

The third way to free ourselves from Inner Passivity is to aim for our average. An adage about a metaphorical journey states: "In a journey of a thousand miles, the first step is the hardest." Getting started is the most difficult for a variety of reasons, mainly because humans prefer to be passive, lazy, and maintain a body at rest. Inner Passivity certainly plays into this. In my own research, I have seen that the failure to launch for some, whether it is a home improvement project, a work deliverable, or a larger life goal, is rooted in the notion that perfection, or even excellence within the task, is so hard to reach because the psychological distance from zero to a perfectly completed mission is demotivating. Essentially, when you haven't started yet, thinking of a perfectly crafted home project seems extremely "far away." Luckily, thanks to Aristotle, we know that shooting for the average, not perfection, is the best method for success, or more specifically, getting started. Adam Grant, an organizational psychologist and professor at Wharton, published an article in 2011 in *Perspectives on Psychological Science*. In this article, titled "Too Much of a Good Thing : The Challenge and Opportunity of the Inverted U," he and coauthor Barry Schwartz draw upon the teachings of Aristotle where the philosopher claimed that happiness and success in life are maximized when we cultivate virtues as the mean between the extremes of deficiency and excess.

> Both excessive and defective exercise destroys the strength, and similarly drink or food which is above or below a certain amount destroys the health, while that which is proportionate both produces and increases and preserves it. So too is it, then, in the case of temperance and courage and the other virtues. For the man who flies from and fears everything and does not stand his ground against anything becomes a coward, and the man who fears nothing at all but

> goes to meet every danger becomes rash; and similarly the man who indulges in every pleasure and abstains from none becomes self-indulgent, while the man who shuns every pleasure, as boors do, becomes in a way insensible; temperance and courage, then, are destroyed by excess and defect, and preserved by the mean. - Aristotle (trans. 1999)[51]

Simply put, doing nothing is obviously detrimental, but you can also have too much of a good thing. The authors refer to this concept as the Inverted-U, highlighting that Aristotle's viewpoint on the effects of well-being and effectiveness should be nonmonotonic (meaning that they increase or decrease on different intervals). This means that positive phenomena or virtues reach an inflection point at which the effects start to turn negative.[52] See the graph below for a visual representation:

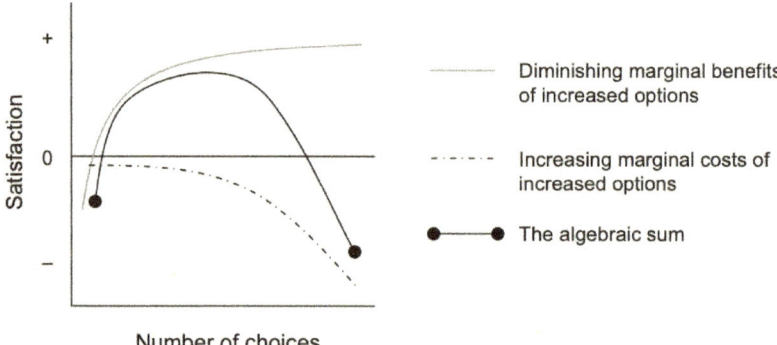

Illustrating the Inverted-U shape relationship between the number of choices and satisfaction, taken from Grant, A. (2011).

In psychology, this is extrapolated to emotions and analyzed to determine what virtue, or behavior, the emotion would exhibit at deficiency, at excess, and at the mean.[53] See table below from Grant's article:

Table 1. Aristotelian Virtues

Domain	Deficiency	Excess	Virtue at the mean
Fear	Cowardice	Recklessness	Courage
Pleasure	Prudence	Self-indulgence	Temperance
Giving and taking small sums of money	Meanness	Prodigality	Generosity
Giving and taking large sums of money	Stinginess	Tastelessness	Magnificence
Great honor	Humility	Vanity	Pride
Anger	Spinelessness	Irascibility	Good temper
Self-presentation	Self-deprecation	Boastfulness	Honesty
Giving amusement	Boorishness	Buffoonery	Wittiness
Pleasing others	Surliness	Obsequiousness	Friendliness

You can see how the virtue, or behavior, at the mean is the sweet spot. Too little (deficiency) or too much (excess) creates undesired behaviors and virtues. Grant goes on to cite other research to show other virtues that demonstrate nonmonotonic inverted-U shaped relationships, such as courage, optimism, self-efficacy, self-esteem, love, justice, and self-control. These can easily be applied to everyday situations. Some examples Grant provides:

- On-the-job learning is considered good and necessary in today's environment, but if people become too focused on learning everything or striving to be perfect, it can take away from job performance, waste valuable resources or distract himself or others from the key priorities of the task.
- Generosity is normally considered good, but too much generosity can lead to tastelessness or prodigality, consuming too much time and energy and reducing the charitable effects that are intended. The article mentions research that suggests volunteering 100 to 800 hours a year is ideal.
- Attention to detail is important within my jobs, but perfectionism can lead to wasting of resources, diminishing returns, and failure to see the big picture.

The concept of a sweet spot that lies between deficiency and excess is also prevalent in emotional intelligence. As you will see in more detail in chapter

11, emotional intelligence skills can be "overused." Emotional intelligence skills such as self-regard, self-actualization, and emotional self-awareness are important skills to develop, but in excess they can create feelings of overconfidence or goal achievement blindness (where you only focus on achieving your goals and nothing else). Other skills, such as empathy, assertiveness, and reality testing are important to develop, but too much empathy can lead to someone never being able to deliver bad news, being too assertive can lead to a lack of communication ability or strong leadership, and being too grounded in reality can affect creative thought processes.

Aristotle did also famously advocate that there was a "priority of the particular." He suggested that the mean between excess and deficiency is not computable by formula, varies from person to person, and can change from one context to another. Your idea of perfection (excess) will vary from your neighbors on the same task. As Grant states: "From this viewpoint, the mean or right amount of a virtue varies by context, and imposing precise boundaries for distinguishing between vice and virtue is a relatively arbitrary choice that involves making categorical judgments along fuzzy continua."[54] In essence, each of us needs to find our Aristotelian mean, or golden mean, which is considered to be where more moral behavior resides between the two extremes.

Finding your average is a surefire way to defeat Inner Passivity and get going. We fail to get going when we strive for perfection in our minds before we even get started. Excess, or perfectionism, feeds our Inner Passivity because it leads to procrastination. Research has also linked perfectionism (excess) to procrastination. Travis Bradberry, an emotional intelligence author, states:[55]

> Perfectionism and fear of failure go hand in hand. This combination leads to procrastination because even mundane tasks are intimidating when they must be completed perfectly. Most writers spend countless hours brainstorming characters and plot, and they even write page after page that they know they'll never include in the book. They do this because they know that ideas need time to develop. We tend to freeze up when it's time to get started because we know that our ideas aren't perfect and what we produce might not be any good. However, how can you ever produce something great if you don't get started and give your ideas time to evolve? Author Jodi Picoult summarized the importance of avoiding perfectionism perfectly: "You can edit a bad page, but you can't edit a blank page." Also, you're afraid to take risks. With the fear of failure comes the fear of taking risks.

Inner Passivity is the only completely unconscious domain that affects our ability to think on purpose. Determining how passive we are, understanding the behaviors and conscious emotions that manifest from it, and implementing strategies that increase our antifragility and decrease our procrastination are all paths toward purposeful cognition. Next, we look at the domain which can be considered the obverse of Inner Passivity. This domain is constantly at war with our Inner Passivity, but not as a benevolent defense, more for its own sinister dominance over our mental processes. The domain is called our Inner Aggression.

In Sum

- Inner Passivity is rooted in psychoanalytic theory and it is an important element of our unconscious that affects many aspects of our quality of life. Inner Passivity is defined as an unconscious emotional element that limits the flow of our creativity or hinders our self-expression. We are only aware of the surface level symptoms of Inner Passivity.
- Inner Passivity can inhibit growth within relationships because it affects interrelationship decision making, creates confrontation avoidance, lessons assertiveness, and produces feelings of guilt and anxiety.
- Inner Passivity has been linked to psychosomatic disorders and has been shown to create physical symptoms and disorders.
- Research has shown that humans can be addicted to unhappiness, due to psychic masochism and preferring negative emotionality to no emotionality.
- We can free ourselves from Inner Passivity by generating awareness of the passivity, developing antifragility, and aiming for our average.

CHAPTER 9 | INNER AGGRESSION

"In the inner courtroom of my mind, mine is the only judgment that counts."

NATHANIEL BRANDEN, author of *Six Pillars of Self-Esteem*

"You've been criticizing yourself for years and it hasn't worked. Try approving of yourself and see what happens."

LOUISE HAY, author of *You Can Heal Your Life*

Inner Aggression is the second domain within the Purposeful Cognition Index. Much like our Inner Passivity, our Inner Aggression is an unconscious force within us that creates many self-defeating thoughts and behaviors on the conscious level. However, the fact that they both begin as unconscious is where the similarities end. Inner Passivity is considered a fully unconscious, static state of the mind and is defined as an unconscious emotional element that limits the flow of our creativity or hinders our self-expression. Inner Aggression, however, is dynamic and represents a mental operating system that is constantly critical, defeating, and judgmental. Similar to how we identify Inner Passivity through the surface level manifestations that it creates, Inner Aggression is also identified in the same manner. Common conscious manifestations of Inner Aggression include an inner critic, self-defeating personality disorder, negative self-talk, lack of self-esteem and self-acceptance, and a variety of other self-destructive behaviors.

Our Inner Critic

Our inner critic, or critical inner voice, or negative self-talk, refers to a subpersonality within humans that judges and demeans the person and is usually experienced as an inner voice that promotes feelings of shame, guilt, worthlessness, inadequacy, or failure.[1] As you can imagine, a persistent voice in the back of your head producing feelings of shame could lead to constant self-doubt and depression. The tiny voice has a knack for playing off of our greatest anxieties. For many people, the voice is different. It can be a specific voice from the past, such as a parent who was overly harsh or a boss who fired you. It could be a voice from the present, impersonating a stranger who made an offhand remark about you recently or a friend who makes passive-aggressive comments about you. Either way, the inner critic has a predilection for teasing mimicry. While the inner critic is considered a psychological construct, there is recent evidence to suggest a neurological component as well. In a study published in the *Journal of Neuroscience,* psychologists wanted to study our ability to learn with an electric "thinking cap." Essentially, scientists wanted to see if it was possible to selectively manipulate learning ability and speed through the application of mild electrical shocks given to certain areas of the brain, specifically the medial-frontal cortex. The medial-frontal cortex is believed to be where our 'Oops!' is localized in the brain. Previous studies have shown that a spike of negative voltage originates from this area nanoseconds after a mistake is made. What the researchers found was that by sending electrical signals to this portion of the brain, they could manipulate how cautious, error-prone, or adaptable a person was to a new learning situation.[2] The subjects of the study who were given real electrical pulses made fewer mistakes and learned more quickly from mistakes than the subjects who were given fake placebo pulses. The researchers concluded, "we wanted to reach into your brain and causally control your inner critic."

Other research performed at the University of Michigan[3] scanned the brains of twelve healthy participants and asked them to perform tasks that required them to push buttons as fast as they could when presented with a string of certain letters. To start the study, each participant received 10 dollars in credit. If the participants reacted too slowly or pressed the button at the wrong time, they would either miss out on a cash reward or incur a cash penalty. The researchers used brain scan results to identify the part of the brain that activates when humans make costly mistakes. It is called the rostral anterior cingulate cortex, or rACC, which is located in the medial-frontal cortex, same as our 'Oops!' center. The rACC was shown to be much more active when participants incurred a cash penalty, as opposed to missing out on a reward, suggesting that the brain responded much more harshly to a mistake that cost them money rather than missing out on a reward. This region of the frontal lobe is also associated with some emotional function, so researchers hypothesize that feelings of critical error create powerful brain activity in the rACC, which in turn create negative emotions. Remember from chapter 8, humans would rather feel negative emotions than no emotions at all. This is one of the theories behind our addiction to our inner critic – we can create powerful, negative emotionality by feeding our inner critic, activating a powerful portion of our brain that connects mistakes and emotions.

Studies investigating Obsessive Compulsive Disorder, or OCD, sufferers found that this region of the brain triggered even when no mistakes or penalties occurred, suggesting that this region was hyperactive in those with OCD. The study found that "Both OCD patients and healthy subjects demonstrated dorsal ACC activation during error commission. The OCD patients exhibited significantly greater error-related activation of the rostral ACC than comparison subjects. Activity in this region was positively correlated with symptom severity in the patients."[4] The study goes on to conclude that "error-processing abnormalities within the rostral anterior cingulate occur in the absence of symptom expression in patients with OCD." What this means is that OCD sufferers were able to spark up this region of the brain *even when no mistakes were present*. They could create powerful, neural brain function, simply by thinking about mistakes that did not exist. Remember, this portion of the brain does not activate when we miss out on rewards, only when we make critical errors, or *when we think about making critical errors*. All of these studies show that costly mistakes (not rewards missed) light up a portion of the brain that creates powerful electrical surges which are tied to emotionality, and that humans can do this in the absence of real mistakes, simply by thinking it so. We cannot activate the rACC by thinking about rewards missed; we can only activate it through critical rumination. This is the very essence of our inner critic, which we now know has a real, neurological genesis.

Self-Defeating Personality Disorder

Self-defeating personality disorder, or SDPD, is another conscious manifestation of our Inner Aggression. Self-defeating personality disorder[5] is a pattern of self-defeating behavior that is rooted in our Inner Aggression as well as our psychic masochism. Thought to begin in early adulthood, this manifestation of Inner Aggression is recognizable in a variety of ways. A person may avoid pleasurable experiences, may be drawn to relationships in which there is great suffering, or refuse help from others even when it is clearly needed. When the disorder was proposed to the *Diagnostic and Statistical Manual of Mental Disorders 3rd edition* in 1987, psychologists suggested that suffers of SDPD exhibited five or more of the following:[6]

1. chooses people and situations that lead to disappointment, failure, or maltreatment even when better options are clearly available
2. rejects or renders ineffective the attempts of others to help them
3. following positive personal events (e.g., new achievement), the person responds with depression, guilt, or a behavior that produces pain (e.g., an accident)

4. incites angry or rejecting responses from others and then feels hurt, defeated, or humiliated (e.g., makes fun of spouse in public, provoking an angry retort, then feels devastated)
5. rejects opportunities for pleasure, or is reluctant to acknowledge enjoying themselves (despite having adequate social skills and the capacity for pleasure)
6. fails to accomplish tasks crucial to their personal objectives despite having demonstrated the ability to do so (e.g., helps fellow students write papers, but is unable to write their own)
7. is uninterested in or rejects people who consistently treat them well
8. engages in excessive self-sacrifice that is unsolicited by the intended recipients of the sacrifice

Researchers at the University of Granada looked at the relationship of a specific destructive behavior, self-defeating humor, and psychological well-being. What they found was quite interesting. The study states the following:[7]

> The UGR group's findings, recently published in the international Journal *Personality and Individual Differences*, contradict some of the research carried out to date in the psychology of humour. Up until now, a significant deal of the research literature has suggested that self-defeating humour is exclusively associated with negative psychological effects among individuals who regularly employ this style of humour. UGR researchers from the Mind, Brain and Behaviour Research Centre (CIMCYC) have established that individuals who frequently use self-defeating humour -- aimed at gaining the approval of others through self-mockery -- exhibit greater levels of psychological well-being.

Self-defeating humor led to *greater psychological well-being* in the study. The researchers discovered that adaptive styles of humor, specifically self-defeating, could strengthen social relationships and remove stress from charged situations. They also found that there was a linear correlation between self-defeating humor and kindness and honesty. So, wait a minute, are all self-defeating behaviors actually good then? Let's take a deeper look. The researchers go on to state:[8]

> Nonetheless, the researchers are also quick to point out that certain styles of humour may be employed to conceal negative intentions and feelings. As Navarro-Carrillo notes [the] results suggest that humour, even when presented as benign or well-intentioned, *can also represent a strategy for*

masking negative intentions...the use of self-enhancing humour, is typically found among people who manage anger more effectively, as well as among those with lower tendencies to exhibit angry feelings or reactions... by contrast, *people who tend to use aggressive or self-defeating humour do not manage anger or rage as well.* In particular, aggressive humour is mainly associated with the expression of anger towards others and a *greater propensity to experience anger in everyday life.* By using aggressive humour, individuals may express negative feelings (for example, anger, superiority, hate, etc.) less explicitly than they would through physical or verbal abuse, since they can allude to the humorous nature of the comments they make in order to justify them.

Essentially, the study concludes that for those that were already psychologically healthy, using self-defeating humor bolstered that well-being, but for many others, self-defeating humor was linked to a greater tendency to suppress anger. Those that engage in self-defeating personality disorder behaviors turn their anger inward, feeding the Inner Aggression beast, bolstering a sense of misplaced masochistic comfort. The psychologically healthy use that type of humor to enhance well-being, while others used it as a maladaptive anger suppression strategy. Research is even more alarming for children that engage in this type of humor. A study performed at Keele University found that there is a clear link between children's use of self-defeating humor, such as self-deprecating language, putting themselves down to make others laugh, etc., and bullying. Those who engaged in self-defeating humor were more likely to be bullied by their peers.[9]

Other research in the *Journal of Biological Psychiatry* found an interesting link between self-defeating behaviors and certain neural processes. Researchers studied which brain regions activate when people engage in depressive rumination, and found that two sections, the subgenual prefrontal cortex (sgPFC) and a brain network involved in reflection, sometimes called the default mode network (DMN), activated.[10]

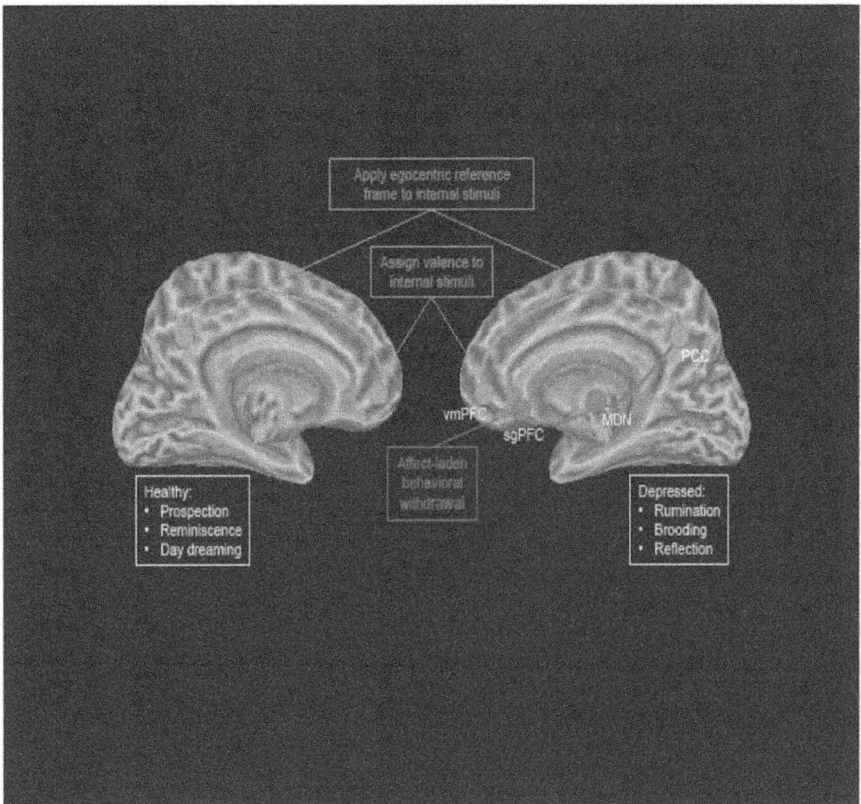

Graphical rendering of our DMN-sgPFC functional integration model of depressive rumination, taken from "Depressive Rumination, the Default-Mode Network, and the Dark Matter of Clinical Neuroscience."

These are also the same two regions that activate when a brain's task circuits are not engaged, or put differently, when the hands and brain go idle during self-referential thought. The researchers concluded from metanalyses of other studies that this is the same portion of the brain that activates when performing self-defeating behaviors. Essentially, engaging in self-defeating behaviors and ruminating in a depressed state activate the same region of the brain that fires when sitting idle.[11] This adds meaning to the adage "Idle hands are the Devil's playground."

Self-Esteem, the Main Victim of Inner Aggression

Self-esteem is normally the main target of our Inner Aggression. Self-esteem is defined as an individual's overall evaluation of their own self-worth. This subjective analysis is considered an emotional evaluation of the self and has roots all the way back to the Platonic Soul – Plato's theory of the soul where he proposed that the psyche consisted of three parts: reason, spirit, and appetite (self-esteem resides within spirit). Self-esteem is the subject of thousands of research articles, psychological constructs, and various experiments. The Core Self-Evaluations assessment (discussed in chapter 10), uses self-esteem as one of its four major dimensions, with Locus of Control, neuroticism, and self-efficacy as the others.[12] Self-esteem is a sexy psychological concept because it has been established as a predictor variable in numerous studies, showing correlations to academic achievement,[13] happiness,[14] satisfaction in marriage and relationships,[15] and criminal behavior.[16]

Nathaniel Branden, the author of *The Six Pillars of Self-Esteem* and a pioneer in the field of self-esteem application, views self-esteem as the most important concept in psychological well-being. He states:

> Apart from disturbance whose roots are biological, I cannot think of a single psychological problem—from anxiety and depression, to underachievement at school or at work, to fear of intimacy, happiness, or success, to alcohol or drug abuse, to spouse battering or child molestation, to co-dependency and sexual disorders, to passivity and chronic aimlessness, to suicide and crimes of violence—that is not traceable, at least in part, to the problem of deficient self-esteem. Of all the judgments we pass in life, none is as important as the one we pass on ourselves.

His Six Pillars of Self-Esteem represent what he refers to as core truths that need to be realized to develop and sustain self-esteem. Those six pillars are:

1. The Practice of Living Consciously
2. The Practice of Self-Acceptance
3. The Practice of Self-Responsibility
4. The Practice of Self-Assertiveness
5. The Practice of Living Purposefully
6. The Practice of Personal Integrity

Many of these pillars have similar themes to developing the ability to think on purpose. The Practice of Living Consciously is similar to the notion of thinking on purpose as a means toward better psychological well-being. In the Practice of Self-Acceptance pillar, Branden writes in the book:

> We can run not only from our dark side but also from our bright side — from anything that threatens to make us stand out or stand alone, or that calls for the awakening of the

hero within us, or that asks that we break through to a higher level of consciousness and reach a higher ground of integrity. The greatest crime we commit against ourselves is not that we may deny or disown our shortcomings, but that we deny and disown our greatness — because it frightens us.

Again, here we see the concept of the bright side and the dark side. The Practice of Self-Responsibility discusses the notion that we should have an internal Locus of Control (which you will learn about in the next chapter) and believe that we are responsible for our choices and actions. The Practice of Self-Assertiveness is an emotional intelligence concept that advocates for the individual to strive for authenticity. The Practice of Living Purposely aligns to the emotional intelligence skill of self-actualization, which is the willingness to improve oneself and pursue meaningful goals. Lastly, the Practice of Personal Integrity pushes us to live according to our morals, ideals, and values, and avoid self-defeating behaviors or masochistic thoughts that could damage us.

Inner Aggression attacks self-esteem because it seeks to damage many of these pillars described by Branden. Knowing that high self-esteem is considered one of the most important psychological goals to achieve and that Inner Aggression attacks it in so many ways, it is vital that we do not let this domain run amok and erode our self-esteem.

Freeing Ourselves from Inner Aggression

Much like Inner Passivity, Inner Aggression is unconscious and only recognizable through the conscious manifestations. To free ourselves from Inner Aggression is to break the shackles of our biggest critic, our loudest detractor, and our strongest denigrator. The private conversations you have with yourself should be a stepping stone towards self-actualization, not a major roadblock that rejoices in your failure and erodes your self-esteem. If you tend to be overly critical of yourself, know that you are not alone. Many people suffer from an inner voice that insults, undercuts, or attacks, keeping us from becoming our authentic selves. Even though everyone can relate to having an inner critic or engaging in negative self-talk, the origin of where the inner voice comes from is still up for debate. Sidney Blatt, a former professor of psychology at Yale and psychoanalyst, believed that self-criticism was an aspect of personality and passed down genetically.[17] Aaron Beck, a psychiatrist who is regarded as the father of cognitive therapy, believes that self-criticism is how individuals preserve and increase independence, mobility, and personal rights, while holding themselves accountable for past failures, and is rooted in our mental processes.[18] Other theories postulate that Inner Aggression develops in childhood through negative experiences, such as rigid parenting, tough sports coaching, or abuse and maltreatment. Regardless of the origin, functional magnetic resonance imaging, or fMRIs, has shown that self-criticism activates areas of the brain that are responsible for processing error detection and correction.[19] As a way to prepare for future events, humans evaluate past performance or engage in pessimistic defense mechanisms through the inner critic because it is activated in the same portion of the brain as event forecasting and course correction. This is why Inner Aggression is one of the five domains of the Purposeful Cognition Index – freeing ourselves from it is imperative. Does your Inner Aggression cause you to miss out on life's opportunities? Is it blocking you from achieving that next life goal, telling you that you won't make it? Is it destroying your self-esteem? Inner Aggression is at the root of many of our depressive disorders, and while there are many ways to address the surface level manifestations and behaviors caused by Inner Aggression, it is important to also shine a light on our aggression itself. Here are the three main ways to do so:

Get in the Zone

Throughout my research exploring self-defeating behaviors and having coaching conversations with leaders who engage in negative self-talk, a common theme arose whenever the topic of a lofty goal came up. Some people are terrified at attempting goals that cannot be immediately satisfied, or in essence, long-term goals. Long-term goals, such as achieving a graduate-level degree that takes a few years or even shorter-term goals, such as custom building a house that takes six months, can seem daunting and difficult. Not impossible, but challenging. Rather than rationally deciding not to pursue the goal (because this would make the person appear to be unambitious or unaspiring) people start to develop reasons why they "cannot" achieve those goals which are "out of their control." "I would love to pursue a graduate degree, but I do not have the time, I don't have the work ethic, and would probably fail out in the first semester, wasting a lot of time and money," says his inner critic. The inner critic starts to defeat his dreams and give him a way out of ever embarking on the journey in the first place. This inner process rarely happens when the goals are immediately realizable or if goal attainment is near. So, what gives? What I have found is that the greater the psychological distance between the start and the attainment of the goal, the more likely an inner critic will engage. Essentially, we are scared of the distance, so we talk ourselves out of it. It seems like too much work. We allow our inner critic to convince us we *can't* do it so that we don't have to decide we *won't* do it. Luckily, there is a way to silence the inner critic by "Getting in the Zone."

Similar to the Inner Passivity strategy of "Aiming For Your Average" where you apply the concepts of the Aristotelian U to start the first step of your long journey, you can use the strategy of "Getting in the Zone" to silence that deleterious inner voice that may be preventing you from achieving lofty goals. Within sports, "she's in the zone" refers to a subjective measurement of heightened performance to dictate that "she is on fire," "she can't miss," "she can't be stopped," and a variety of other phrases that embody short-term sports dominance. A lessor known fact is where that phrase originated. Originally, "in the zone" was a term used to describe when someone was in the zone of proximal development.

The zone of proximal development, or ZPD, is defined as the difference between what a learner can do without help, and what they can't do.[20] Lev Vygotsky, a psychologist who developed the concept in the 1930s, studied how children mimicked adults when learning new tasks and documented the exact moment when those new tasks could be performed by the child without assistance. According to Vygotsky, tasks essentially fall into three categories; what the learner can do unaided, what the leader can do with guidance, what the learner cannot do. What the learner can do with guidance is called the zone of proximal development, because these are tasks they cannot yet perform independently, but are proximally close to mastering them.

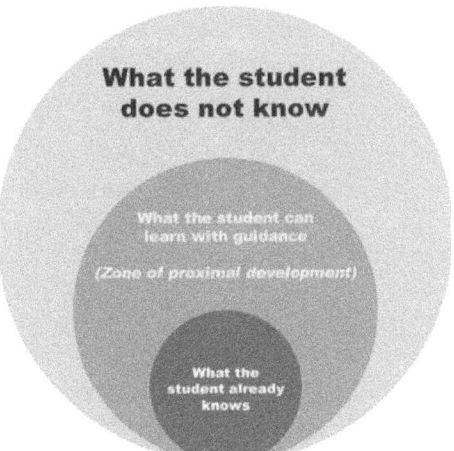

Vygotsky spent a lot of time studying how children learned new things, what enabled learning, and what blocked learning. What he found was groundbreaking. What he saw was that children who focused on tasks right outside of what they already knew (in the proximal zone), progressed towards the end goal (zone of what the student does not know) much faster. Children that tried to look at the end state first, bypassing tasks in the proximal zone, become discouraged and their learning pace suffered. Think of language development as an example. When children learn to speak, their vocabulary develops slowly and incrementally. If a child had to learn large words or their entire adult vocabulary immediately, the child's learning would be severely stunted. Children learn how to communicate most effectively when adults use language just *above* the child's current vocabulary (this is why many child development experts discourage using baby talk with children), otherwise known as vocabulary that is inside the child's zone of proximal development.

What ZPD shows us is that when it comes to goal acquisition, such as starting to learn a massive subject, focusing on what is just on the periphery of knowledge rather than the far distant abyss of the unknown, is when peak performance occurs. The child is in the zone. When an athlete is in the zone, she is operating at peak performance, which is normally a notch or two above her normal playing levels. She isn't a completely different player, she is just a tad faster or a tad more accurate, but it's extremely noticeable. ZPD has been applied to numerous other learning activities, such as mathematics, driving, teaching, and scaffolding.[21] When a child, student, or athlete is in the zone, they are performing tasks they have never been able (or rarely been able) to do unassisted before. They are psychologically energized and experiencing dopamine and adrenaline rushes because they have made a breakthrough. Think about the first time you rode your bike without training wheels as a child or first made it down the slope on your snowboard without falling. How ecstatic were you? You were still extremely far away from the lofty end goal of being a professional BMX rider or snowboard Olympian, but that didn't matter.

What's more important, notice how your inner critic disappeared? Many children who are on training wheels, time and time again, will tell themselves (and their parents) over and over that they cannot ride the bike on two wheels. It is too scary and difficult. They will fight you tooth and nail and proclaim that riding on two wheels is impossible. Then, when they make their first 2-wheel run without help, they are elated, and they boast about how great they are. In a matter of seconds, they went from being the most self-defeating child in the world to the best bike rider in the universe, in their minds. It's as if they don't remember ten seconds ago when they kept repeating that they couldn't do it. This is because the inner critic was extinguished. They completed a proximal task, without parental help, and life was good.

So, why not use the teachings from our first bike ride when we approach other goals? If our inner critic is loud and unruly when we think about long-term goals, forget about the long term and focus on the proximal. Instead of thinking about your graduate degree, plan your goals around just passing the current semester. Determine what is just outside your reach and shoot for that. Aim for your proximal zone. Chunk up your goals so that you can celebrate short-term wins, using the concept of proximal development, and get in the zone. Like when you took your first bike ride on two wheels, your inner critic will vanish.

Tame Your Inner Critic

Inner dialogue is powerful, when it is used to propel you forward rather than prevent you from reaching your destiny. No one understands your skills, your limitations, your fears, and your sources of power better than you do. This is a double-edged sword, though. Your inner critic plays on your deepest, darkest fears because it knows what they are. Fortunately, psychologists have discovered ways to tame that voice, so that it fades into the background and becomes inconsequential, or in the best case scenario, an inner advocate. During my research,[22][23] I have investigated things that mentally strong people do and don't do, compiling a list of eleven short ways to counter negative thoughts and live free from self-imposed limitations:

1. *Develop awareness of your thought patterns* – people often listen to their inner voice without even realizing it. Since Inner Aggression resides within the unconscious, it is sometimes difficult to understand when the consciously manifested inner critic arises from the depths. Evaluate your thinking to see if it is rooted in bias, a reflection of true events or the voice of something more sinister.
2. *Give some advice to your friend in the mirror* – when you find yourself listening to negative self-talk, give your friend some advice; only that friend, is you. Think about the type of advice you would give to a friend if they were in the exact situation as you. Chances are, you would be much more empathetic and compassionate to your friend when giving advice or feedback. Instead of saying things like "you are terrible," you would most likely say to your friend "better luck next time." Use the same approach when trying to tame your inner critic.
3. *Accept who you are, but don't stop improving* – the inner critic is powered by error detection and course correction. Not only in the psyche but literally in the same brain region! Your negative self-talk enflames when it thinks about all of the things you are not. If you accept who you are, there are no errors to detect, no courses to correct. The portion of your brain that exhumes your inner critic from the depths of your Inner Aggression is powerless if you accept who you are. That doesn't mean you should stop self-actualizing however. Always try to maximize your potential, while accepting who you are.
4. *Eliminate ruminating* – replaying events over and over in your head will always slant toward the negative because it activates the same portion of the brain that engages during self-defeating behaviors and

depressive thoughts. Study[24] after study[25] has shown that the longer you ruminate, the more negative your thoughts become. It's basically like gambling in Vegas where the house always has the advantage. You can win initially, but if you stay long enough, the house always wins. Rumination is the same way. A recent study[26] at Ohio University found that rumination increases inflammation in the body, meaning your negative thoughts can create actual physical, negative responses. You can't change the past, so consistently reflecting on how embarrassing something was or how poorly you performed will only feed the negative inner voice.

5. *Play "what would I do if these thoughts were true?"* – your inner critic loves to tell you lies. Why not call its bluff? If you are about to give a public speech and your inner voice is venturing toward the catastrophic, think about what would actually happen if you fell during your walk up to the podium or forgot your lines. When you think about them being true you realize that it isn't that bad – the audience would have a quick laugh and you would play it off, and the speech would go fine. Call your critic's bluff, play it out, and you'll see it isn't that bad if it did happen.

6. *Meditate* – one of the best things you can do is learn to meditate; learn to be mindful. There are millions of resources available on this subject, so I'll only mention the one that works for me – floating. A float tank is a sensory deprivation chamber that you would find at a spa, also called an isolation tank. It is soundproof, pitch black, and filled with skin temperature salt water, which gives the illusion that you are floating in space. It is a great way to sharpen your focus and let all your fears dissipate into the universe, which is helpful when trying to silence inner voices.

7. *Give your voice a funny name and write down your thoughts in the second person* – our inner critic tends to use first-person point of view a whole bunch. "I will fail," "it will embarrass me," "I can't do this," and so on. If you change the "I" to second-person point of view so it sounds more like "you will fail" or "you can't do this," you separate the inner critic from your identity, giving it less power and influence over your actions. Now that it is an external critic, give it a funny name just for the fun of it. This will help you keep it as an external critic.

8. *Challenge your inner critic head on* – much like calling your inner critic's bluff, you can talk back to your inner critic in your own defense. Many feel that the inner critic-to-psyche conversation is only one way, but it isn't. If your inner critic is challenging you, challenge it right back. Every negative statement that is proclaimed by the critic, offer up an equally positive one in rebuttal. For example, if your

critic says "you are going to embarrass yourself," simply respond with "no I won't, I will do great."

9. *Listen to your inner critic and change your behavior* – believe it or not, your inner critic may produce sound advice...sometimes. A broken watch is right twice a day, right? When your inner critic is sounding off, analyze the voice to see if there is any validity to its claims. For example, if your inner critic says "don't do that, you will hurt yourself," start to actually behave as if you aren't going to do it and see if your critic may have actually saved you from something.

10. *Treat it as an enemy* – this strategy means that your inner critic should be ignored, dismissed, fought against, and eventually overcome. Treating it as an enemy is the path to do so. This is a method recommended in the Diamond Approach[27] (a spiritual teaching that seeks dynamic enlightenment through transcendent truth) in Voice Therapy,[28] a common technique that taps into clients' core negative beliefs by identifying negative thought patterns that drive maladaptive behavior, and in Rick Carson's book, *Taming Your Gremlin*,[29] a guide on gaining freedom from self-defeating behaviors and beliefs. These methods all believe your inner critic is your nemesis and must be destroyed.

11. *Treat it as an ally* – other approaches recommend to treat your inner critic as an ally who should be transformed into a creative asset. Some view the inner critic as an entity that tries to help or protect us. It just lacks the "social skills" to communicate properly (most likely because psychoanalysts believe it resides within the malevolent id) so it only knows how to behave in a distorted, maladaptive way. Models such as Voice Dialogue,[30] a method that seeks to turn the critic into an inner asset, Internal Family Systems therapy,[31] an integrative approach to individual psychotherapy that combines systems thinking with the view that the mind is made up of relatively discrete subpersonalities, each with its own viewpoint and qualities, Inner Relationship Focusing,[32] a psychotherapeutic system for emotional healing and accessing positive energy, and Tibetan Buddhism,[33] all view the inner critic as a petulant child with unique insights that are extremely valuable. It is up to us to raise the child into an affable ally.

Focus on Building Your Self-Esteem

Self-esteem is one of the most formidable, provable, relatable, and understandable concepts in all of psychology. Everyone knows how they feel about themselves and how that feeling affects everything in their life. Focusing on self-esteem is a sure-fire way to eliminate self-defeating behaviors. Think of self-esteem as your defense against aggression – the more sure you are of yourself and your positions, the less power and influence your Inner Aggression will have on you. There are thousands of resources available on how to boost self-esteem, so I will highlight the specific tactics that I have discovered which are most effective in helping you specifically target your Inner Aggression and help keep self-defeating behaviors at bay.

Find natural ways to boost your oxytocin levels – In a study[34] performed at the University of California in 2011, scientists identified for the first time a particular gene's link to optimism, self-esteem, and Locus of Control, called the oxytocin receptor gene (OXTR). Oxytocin is a hormone that increases in response to stress and has often been referred to as the "love molecule." Considered one of the oldest known hormones, it has been traced back at least 400 million years to fish, meaning the human body has had a lot of time to develop natural ways to best utilize this neurochemical. Essentially, it is the chemical that produces feelings of trust and love toward others. Now, we know it is also related to self-esteem. The study highlights that some people have different combinations of OXTR variants[35] which predispose them to be able to love and trust more easily than others. But it is important to note that genetics only serves as a basis, not the entirety, of the love formula. Other studies have shown that regardless of how much oxytocin is currently in the brain and blood due to which variants you possess, *changes* in the levels relative to the absolute levels are what produce the feelings we desire. This means that regardless of our current levels, we can achieve those feelings of love by engaging in social activities that *change* our oxytocin levels in the blood and brain. Lab research has shown that there are natural ways to boost oxytocin via social interaction. Paul Zak, author of the *Morale Molecule: How Trust Works*, suggests these ten strategies:[36]

1. *Give and get lots of hugs* – touch raises oxytocin, reduces cardiovascular stress and improves the immune system. Just be sure you hug someone that wants to be hugged.
2. *Tell others you love them* – giving love also activates our natural oxytocin boosters. Chances are, you'll hear "I love you" back, giving you another dose, assuming the person you love does, in fact, love you back.
3. *Pet a dog* – animals are the best. Dog owners live longer, have less stress, and are much cooler than non-dog owners, according to me. Even if you aren't a dog person, give it a try.
4. *Ride a roller coaster or skydive* – oxytocin has been registered to spike up to 200% after moderately stressful events that are also exhilarating.
5. *Use social media, but not too much* – social media has been linked to higher levels of oxytocin because you can connect with others you

wouldn't normally be able to, but only in small doses, and as long as social media doesn't replace seeing your friends in real life.
6. *Soak in a hot tub* – other than being great family time, heat and water are two things that have been shown to produce oxytocin spikes.
7. *Meditate via "Metta"* – "Metta" refers to meditation where you focus on loving others (rather than clearing your own mind) and directing well-wishes their way. Lab studies have shown that this significantly boosts the hormone naturally.
8. *Share a meal* – nothing special about this one, just a time-tested way to bond with others and boost oxytocin.
9. *Give a gift* – lab studies have shown that people generally have higher spikes of the hormone when they give a gift, rather than receive one. Both are nice, but giving can certainly help give a boost.
10. *Listen with your eyes* – eye contact is always nice because it shows the person you are giving them your complete attention. This builds trust and strengthens social bonds.

This compendium of love-boosting strategies will also boost your self-esteem, ensuring that you do not fall victim to self-sabotage or engage in self-defeating behaviors.

Understand your "interpersonal vulnerability" dimension. Scientists have long known that our self-esteem is shaped by the appraisals we receive from others. More importantly, scientists have also discovered that low self-esteem is a major vulnerability factor for numerous psychiatric problems, such as eating disorders, anxiety disorders, and depression. But how exactly does self-esteem change when we receive feedback? Researchers at University College London devised a mathematical equation to specifically answer this question. The researchers used MRI scanners to measure brain activity within subjects who received feedback from strangers in the form of a thumbs up or a thumbs down after performing a task. They used computational models to understand the neural mechanisms at play when the subjects received positive and negative feedback from others. The original theory was a simple one – self-esteem would go up when positive feedback was received and go down when negative feedback was received. What the researchers discovered was something quite different. Self-esteem doesn't necessarily change solely based on the feedback being positive or negative. They instead found that *social prediction errors* had the greatest impact on the brain region and neural processes that most influence our self-esteem.[37]

Social prediction errors are miscalculations we make based on our expectations. When the participants of the study expected to be praised by the strangers but received a thumbs down, self-esteem took a hit. The researchers stated:

> We found that self-esteem changes were guided not only by whether other people like you, but were especially dependent on whether you *expected* to be liked...these social prediction errors -- the difference between expected and received feedback -- were key for determining self-esteem.[38]

Essentially, feedback received, whether good or bad, *that did not match what the subjects expected to receive,* caused the fluctuations in actual self-esteem. The researchers also found that the participants who had greater fluctuations in self-esteem during the experiment generally reported more symptoms of anxiety and depression. This correlated to increased brain activity detected by MRI scans in a part of the brain called the insula, a region of the brain that has a large role in body representation and subjective emotional experience. The researchers concluded by finding that greater fluctuations in self-esteem increased the risk for anxiety and depression symptoms, and those greater fluctuations were caused by increased social prediction error. Essentially, the more often you receive feedback that is contrary to your beliefs, the more prone to psychiatric disorders you are and the more your self-esteem will suffer.

John Lydgate, a monk and poet who lived around the 1400s, famously said "you can please some of the people all of the time, you can please all of the people some of the time, but you can't please all of the people all of the time." This phrase would also be adapted by Abraham Lincoln in a few political speeches as well. Essentially, there will always be those that don't like you, so a strategy that aims toward pleasing everyone all of the time with the hopes of always receiving positive feedback is futile. Even though an externalized attribution of our self-worth is a major component of social prediction error, the key is to focus inward on what we have control over. Luckily, there are two things that can be done to prevent social prediction errors and their effects:

1. *Keep your "sociometer" in check* – Our sociometer is a psychological gauge of the degree to which people perceive they are relationally valued and socially accepted by others.[39] In social settings, humans tend to constantly update their own sociometer based on every interaction with others, no matter how big or small. How often do we perceive the smallest slights against us – someone not returning a text message, someone didn't say "hello" to us emphatically enough, we didn't get a Christmas card, etc., - as "major" indications of how someone feels about us overall? Further exacerbated by social media, people overreact to trivial social stimuli, trying to constantly calculate a moving target of social acceptance. If you catch yourself constantly questioning whether someone likes you

and second-guessing every word you said or action you performed at the last social gathering, your sociometer is running amok. When our sociometer is constantly changing, our social prediction also changes along with it. Work to keep an accurate and honest representation of your self-view in social settings by paying no attention to inadvertent "slights" against you and by truly focusing on your sociometer. Use only objective feedback from others to gauge your current social acceptance. Don't try to guess other people's emotions, motives, preferences, or moods. This will ensure that your social prediction isn't always on the move, which will in turn minimize fluctuations in self-esteem.

2. *Learn how to accept feedback* – This is a big one. If I had to pick one overarching, omnipresent, area of development for all of humanity, it would be to develop the ability to receive feedback. People cringe at the thought of hearing what others think. Of the top leaders within Fortune 500 organizations that I have coached, learning how to receive feedback without being defensive is always at the top of their list of development goals. Failure of receiving feedback has a cognitive basis. Humans have a natural negativity bias and are hardwired to react to negative stimuli faster and more strongly. The fast twitch function of our reptilian brains enabled our survival in times of the hunter-gatherers, meaning that we are naturally wired to process negative threats much more quickly. Psychologists and neurologists have discovered that negative feedback is much more powerful than positive feedback due to a concept called "negativity bias." Ever notice how you can receive ten positive feedback statements and one negative feedback statement, and you will most likely focus on the negative? Two famous examples of the power of negativity bias were discussed in an article called "Negativity Bias, Negativity Dominance, and Contagion" in *Personality and Social Psychology Review*. Researchers found that marriages were only successful if positive acts outweighed negative acts 5 to 1. If the ratio was any less than that, divorce is considered imminent (husbands, remember this golden ratio when given your next honey-do list)! Another example that the researchers provide is fascinating. Guess how many lives a person would need to save to be "even" for committing a single murder. Five, ten, fifteen? The answer is twenty-five! A person convicted of one murder would have to save twenty-five separate people's lives for those surveyed to believe the score was even.[40] Negativity bias is powerful and affects our ability to receive feedback. Some easy ways to discover if you have experienced negativity bias is to examine if you've ever dwelled on: the one thing you forgot to say in a meeting versus all that you

remembered, the one bit of critical feedback versus the many positive ones, the one time someone let you down versus the many they didn't, the one bargain you missed over the many you got, or the one thing your partner did wrong or forgot over the many things they did right or remembered.[41] Overcoming the negativity bias that activates our defenses is the first step in learning how to accept feedback. By developing the ability to accept feedback, the social evaluations received from others will be much less jarring. In turn, this reduces the chances of social prediction error, helping to keep our self-esteem intact.

Inner Aggression is powerful because it can create inner voices that are deafening, debilitating, and incapacitating. Determining how aggressive we are, how that aggression affects our self-esteem and learning ways to quiet the tempestuous critics are all paths toward thinking on purpose. Next, we look at the domain which is related to Inner Passivity but is considered a conscious domain. Do you believe in luck, destiny, fate, or free will? Do you believe we create the events in our life or that life happens to us? This next domain is called our Locus of Control.

In Sum

- Much like our Inner Passivity, our Inner Aggression is an unconscious force within us that creates many self-defeating thoughts and behaviors on the conscious level. Common conscious manifestations of Inner Aggression include an inner critic, self-defeating personality disorder, negative self-talk, lack of self-esteem and self-acceptance, and a variety of other self-destructive behaviors.
- Our inner critic, or critical inner voice, or negative self-talk, refers to a subpersonality within humans that judges and demeans the person and is usually experienced as an inner voice that promotes feelings of shame, guilt, worthlessness, inadequacy, or failure.
- Self-defeating personality disorder is a pattern of self-defeating behavior that is rooted in our Inner Aggression as well as our psychic masochism. A person may avoid pleasurable experiences, may be drawn to relationships in which there is great suffering, or refuse help from others even when it is clearly needed.
- Self-esteem is normally the main target of our Inner Aggression. Self-esteem is defined as an individual's overall evaluation of their own self-worth.

- We can target our Inner Aggression by getting in the zone, taming our inner critic, and focusing on building our self-esteem.

CHAPTER 10 | LOCUS OF CONTROL

"You may not control all of the events that happen to you, but you can decide not to be reduced by them."

MAYA ANGELOU, American poet

"Only you can control your future."

DR. SEUSS

A term that is closely related to Inner Passivity is Locus of Control. "Locus of Control is the degree to which people believe that they have control over the outcome of events in their lives, as opposed to external forces beyond their control."[1] The full original name of the construct is Locus of Control of Reinforcement. The concept was developed by American psychologist Julian Rotter in 1954 and is a binary scale of internal vs. external.[2] One is said to have an internal Locus of Control if an individual believes that her behaviors are guided by her personal efforts and decisions. One is said to have an external Locus of Control if she believes that her behavior is guided by fate, God, luck, or other external circumstances. Quite simply, do you believe that your destiny is controlled by your own free will or predetermined by external forces? Widely used in education, health, clinical, and industrial-organizational psychology, the concept of Locus of Control is an important aspect of personality. The construct of Locus of Control is also prevalent in many prominent philosophical ideas. Determinism, the idea that all events are determined completely by previously existing causes, has a major external Locus of Control component.[3] Similarly, fatalism, the doctrine that posits that all actions and events are due to destiny and espouses an attitude that some future events are thought to be inevitable, was popularized in Friedrich Nietzsche's book *The Wanderer and His Shadow*.[4]

It is important to note that Locus of Control is a continuum, meaning that no one has 100 percent external or internal Locus of Control, though if you are 51% or more in one direction, that is said to be your Locus of Control. Generally, here are some characteristics of those with an internal or external Locus of Control.

Those with an internal Locus of Control:

- Take responsibility for their actions
- Are less influenced by other people's opinions
- Often do better at self-paced tasks
- Have a strong sense of self-efficacy
- Work harder to achieve the things they want
- Possess confidence in the face of challenges
- Are normally physically healthier, happier and independent
- Often achieve greater workplace success

Those with an external Locus of Control:

- Blame their circumstances on outside forces, such as luck or chance
- Don't believe their own efforts can change their situation
- Frequently feel hopeless or powerless in the face of difficult situations
- More often experience learned helplessness

Generally speaking, an internal Locus of Control is more desirable.[5] It is considered psychologically healthy for one to believe that he has control over the things that he is capable of influencing. People that believe their efforts drive success in situations tend to work harder and focus on more positive and healthy behaviors than people who believe that the outcome is not within their control. Many studies have been conducted on the relationship of Locus of Control and desired outcomes, such as health and overall well-being. Griffin wrote in "Locus of Control and Psychological Well-Being" that an external Locus of Control predicted variance in self-esteem, depression, and stress.[6] A strong internal Locus of Control has also been correlated to improved health in areas of obesity, alcoholism, smoking cessation, and diabetes, and to improved quality of life for those with HIV, migraines, kidney disease and epilepsy.[7]

However, there are certain situations where an internal Locus of Control can be detrimental. Much like we saw with excess virtue, too much can lead to instability if not equally balanced with competency or skill.

> Internals can be psychologically unhealthy and unstable. An internal orientation usually needs to be matched by competence, self-efficacy and opportunity so that the person is able to successfully experience the sense of

personal control and responsibility. Overly internal people who lack competence, efficacy and opportunity can become neurotic, anxious and depressed. In other words, internals need to have a realistic sense of their circle of influence in order to experience "success." Externals can lead easy-going, relaxed, happy lives.[8]

For example, someone with an internal locus who is terrible at a work task or sports might feel depressed or anxious if their efforts are solely responsible for the poor performance (as opposed to lack of natural talent). Generally speaking, an internal locus is preferred, but it is important to warn against the overly simplistic notion that internal is always better in all situations.

Locus of Control is found within many psychological constructs and measurements of psychological well-being and workplace performance. Rotter's Internal-External scale was one of the first scales to measure beliefs about control of reinforcement. Other notable assessments include the Stanford Preschool Internal-External Control Index, which measures control of reinforcement on children ages three to six, the Internal Control Index, which assesses variables pertinent to internal locus, such as cognitive processing, autonomy, resistance to social influence, self-confidence and delay of gratification, and the Core Self-Evaluations, which uses Locus of Control combined with measurement scales of neuroticism, self-efficacy, and self-esteem, to measure an individual's unconscious, fundamental evaluation of themselves.[9]

Locus of Control Versus Inner Passivity

Locus of Control is related to Inner Passivity and is a component of the purposeful cognition Index. The main difference is that Locus of Control is a product of your conscious thinking, where Inner Passivity is a product of your unconscious psyche. Think of Locus of Control as your own personal belief as to the genesis of your life's events and Inner Passivity as your unconscious lack of response or awareness to how you feel about those events. If you have a high degree of Inner Passivity, coupled with a high external Locus of Control, you are most likely to believe that you have bad luck, a bad relationship with God, or are repenting for sins you committed in a former life (if you believe in Jung's theories of the collective unconscious), combined with an overly docile approach to addressing those feelings. In this case, you will develop feelings of angst and acrimony that produce a multitude of negative external behaviors. If you have an internal Locus of Control combined with a high degree of Inner Passivity, you will be able to introspect on those feelings of passivity and convince your mind of a better path forward. Conscious thoughts about your Inner Passivity, or utilizing purposeful cognition, will help you battle this unconscious construct that is at the root of much of human suffering. Much like how Inner Passivity can be assessed and targeted, your Locus of Control can also be assessed and changed.

Positive Outcomes

Locus of Control has been researched for many decades and is linked to many positive, desired outcomes in a variety of situations. A longitudinal study at the University of Bristol and Emory University found that teenagers are less likely to be overweight if their parents had a positive attitude during pregnancy, meaning parental Locus of Control affects child obesity.[10] A study in the *Journal of Behavior & Information Technology* found that Locus of Control is positively correlated to technostress, or more simply put, those with an external locus are more easily stressed out by their smartphones, social media, and work emails.[11] Other studies found an internal locus helped with relieving severe migraines,[12] dealing with co-worker rudeness,[13] developing environmental awareness in children,[14] and many other fascinating studies. One that is of significant importance when investigating the relationship between Locus of Control and purposeful cognition is a study done by researchers at Boston Children's Hospital, published in the *Journal of Molecular Psychiatry* in 2016. The study states:

> Clinical anxiety affects up to 30 percent of Americans who are in great need of better treatments with fewer side effects. A study from Boston Children's Hospital, published September 6 by the *Journal of Molecular Psychiatry*, finds that certain neurons in the hypothalamus play a central, previously unknown role in triggering anxiety. Targeting them, rather than the whole brain, could potentially provide a more effective treatment for anxiety and perhaps other psychiatric disorders.[15]

The experimenters showed that blocking a stress hormone called corticotropin-release hormone, or CRH, within a specific group of neurons within mice erased all of the animals' natural fears. CRH is the hormone that was discovered over 40 years ago that coordinates our fight or flight responses. This response is obviously vital to our survival against physical threats, but when activated in response to symbolic threats, activated at the wrong time, or too intensely, it creates anxiety and depression. CRH blocking drugs are currently being researched as possible alternatives to SSRI inhibitors, such as Prozac, Paxil, and Zoloft, and benzodiazepines, such as

Valium, Ativan, or Xanax, with mixed results. What scientists discovered was that it was not feasible to block CRH throughout the brain, but by targeting specific nerve cells in the paraventricular nucleus, an area of the hypothalamus which releases stress hormones such as cortisol, they were able to dramatically reduce anxiety behaviors within rodents. The researchers go on to state:

> We already knew that CRH controlled the hormonal response, but the big surprise was that the behavioral response was completely blunted...it was a very robust finding: Every parameter we looked at indicated that this animal was much less inhibited... it was a total surprise to us that the *Locus of Control* is in a tiny part of the hypothalamus.[16]

The researchers found that by targeting neurons that directly affected fight or flight responses and anxiety, dramatic behavioral changes occurred. This was evident when the mice with the deletion "walked elevated gangplanks, explored brightly lit areas and approached novel objects" when the other mice did not. The mice no longer had fear and their outlook on the world, and subsequent behavior changed. This aligns to other research on fight or flight responses, which conclude that fear and behavior are closely linked.[17] When our fight or flight response is activated, we are perceiving that an external threat that is out of our control is coming our way and our response is a fast-twitch defense mechanism that ultimately decides our mindset and behavior. Fear of that external threat also brings anxiety, so over thousands of years, humans have been conditioned to associate anxiety with externalized fear, meaning that anxiety is a natural pair with having an external Locus of Control. What the researchers at Boston Children's Hospital discovered was that by targeting the anxiety neurons of mice, the Locus of Control within those mice changed.

This is an amazing finding! No psychologist, scientist or researcher to date has been able to pin down exactly where our Locus of Control resides within our psyche. The Boston Children's Hospital research, along with other studies, suggest that Locus of Control rests within certain neurons in our hypothalamus that are associated with our anxiety and stress responses. An internal Locus of Control is rooted in feelings that we are in control, we are empowered, and we are resilient, which are opposite feelings of fight, flight, fear, and anxiety. Remember, nobody is in control of what events happen to them. Locus of Control is adjusting how we think about and respond to those events, which ultimately guide our destiny. As Epictetus, the famous Greek philosopher, famously said all those years ago, "it's not what happens to you, but how you react to it that matters." According to this research, the key to developing an internal Locus of Control could reside within the hypothalamus and our neurons. Obviously, not many people have access to CRH blockers, so how can we use mental strategies to develop an internal locus? The answer lies within neuroplasticity and mirror neurons.

Develop an Internal Locus of Control

The hypothalamus is a small region of the brain, located at the base of the brain near the pituitary gland, and it is the endocrine system's link to the nervous system. It is responsible for maintaining homeostasis within the body, producing and inhibiting hormones, and stimulating key processes such as heart rate, blood pressure, body temperature, electrolyte balance, thirst, appetite, weight, and sleep cycles. The hypothalamus is also responsible for the secretion of many pituitary hormones. Some of the primary ones include:[18]

- Corticotropin-releasing hormone (CRH), which helps regulate stress, metabolism and immune response.
- Gonadotropin-releasing hormone (GnRH), which ensures normal function of ovaries and testes.
- Growth hormone-releasing hormone (GHRH), more commonly known as Human Growth Hormone, which affects bone and muscle mass.
- Oxytocin, which is the chemical that produces feelings of trust and helps us sleep.
- Prolactin-releasing hormone (PRH) or prolactin-inhibiting hormone (PIH), also known as dopamine, which gives us feelings of happiness and euphoria.

So in summary, the hypothalamus is responsible for our stress response, overall health, our sexual function, how much muscle we have, how well we sleep, if we can trust others, and our feelings of happiness. Sounds important! Wouldn't it be great if we could influence our hypothalamus, without using drugs like human growth hormone or CRH blockers? The good news is, we can. We can do this by a process called neuroplasticity and understanding how certain neurons, specifically mirror neurons, operate.

According to research in *Human Molecular Genetics*, there are an estimated 20,000 human protein-coding genes within our bodies that we are born with.[19] These carry all of the genetic material of our ancestors, which biologically determine many of our traits. These genes align with "nature" in the old nature versus nurture debate. However, at birth, a baby's brain contains over 100 billion neurons, which are the cells responsible for transmitting information via electrical and chemical signals all throughout the central nervous system, through a system of axons, dendrites, synapses, and a whole lot of other complicated stuff. Neurons form neural pathways over a person's entire life, meaning that our existential experience shapes what pathways are formed, how information is carried throughout our brains, and which sections of our brains activate during certain stressors or experiences. So while our genes give us our nature, neurons are influenced by nurture. The way that we can purposely target how those neural pathways are influenced is through neuroplasticity.

Neuroplasticity was discovered by a Polish neuroscientist named Jerzy Konorski in 1948 when he observed how neural structures in a brain could change. In the 1960s, it was discovered that these neural structures could reorganize themselves in response to a traumatic event, which led to the discovery that stress alone could not only change neural function but also how the brain itself was organized. Researchers learned that the brain reorganizes itself through a mechanism called "axonal sprouting" where undamaged axons can grow new nerve endings to connect (or reconnect) to other nerve endings to create a new pathway. Think of it like a new road in your neighborhood that connects two other, previously unconnected roads. These were amazing findings because historical research claimed that the brain was a non-renewable organ, meaning that brain cells were finite, fixed, and unable to be regenerated.[20] Now we understand that our brains can form new connections and pathways. Specifically, our brains can form stronger connections (structural neuroplasticity) and new connections (functional neuroplasticity). Neuroplasticity has been shown to help in recovery from strokes and traumatic brain injuries, enhance memory, create more effective learning, and enhance certain senses. Essentially, neuroplasticity refers to the brain's ability to adapt and to the physiological changes that happen as a result of how we interact with our environment and think about events. Our brain adapts and reorganizes in response to our changing needs. While there are hundreds of strategies to engage in neuroplasticity boosting behaviors, they all sum to one common idea[21] – the notion that one can improve cognitive function and neuron growth through targeted exercises and purposely thinking about new ways of doing things. Our thoughts can reshape our brains and the neural networks within us. As an example, if we learn a musical instrument, the brain will form new neural pathways so we can more quickly access the brain function needed to make music. Even activities such as dancing, learning new vocabulary, and reading, creates new neural networks. We construct new neural pathways by purposely doing new activities because we have to think about how to complete those activities. Think of it as muscle hypertrophy for your brain.

In the 1980s, neurophysiologists discovered a specific type of neuron called a mirror neuron. These neurons fire both when an animal (or human) commits a particular act or observes that same act performed by another.

These mirror neurons are thought to be the primary driver of learning a new behavior simply through observation and mimicking. Primates learn through a complex system of imitation and replication, and thanks to YouTube, humans increasingly learn in this fashion as well. I am sure you know some people that can simply learn a new trick, dance, or behavior simply by watching someone else do it first. This is because the mirror neurons fire and encode the observer with the knowledge, or more specifically how to fire certain neurons, to also perform the task. This means that we can watch others perform a task, neuroplasticity encodes our neurons, and we now know how to perform the task. How amazing is that? Mirror neurons help us create new neural pathways through simple observation. Since mirror neurons engage when we *perceive* another person doing a task, this can also be turned inward as well, since perception can refer to both external and internal observation. Humans have a reflective ability to introspect and look at certain actions we solely commit as if two different people committed them. For example, we can buy a new sports car, and our emotional brain is ecstatic but our rational brain is anxious. We can step back and view both systems as a whole, seeing the dichotomy of experience from a higher mental perch. One person committed the act, but we have the ability to see two (or sometimes more) processes at work within our brains. This means our mirror neurons can fire when we cogitate about our different brain functions. This is our path to developing an internal Locus of Control, by using neuroplasticity, mirror neurons, and a concept referred to as the common coding theory.

Common coding theory describes how our perceptions and physical movements are linked, or essentially, how our thoughts affect our behaviors. The common coding theory claims that there is a shared representation, or a common code, for both how we perceive a particular event and our actions/behaviors in response to that event. Roger Sperry, a neurologist who won the Nobel Prize in Physiology or Medicine in 1981, argued that humans have what is called a perception-action cycle that is the primary driver of nervous system function, meaning that perception is a means to action and action is a means to perception.[22] This infers that our perceptions shape our actions. If we can change our perceptions, we can change our behaviors, and vice versa. Within the brain, perception is located in the occipital lobe in the primary visual cortex near the back of the brain, where behaviors are generated from a mix of midbrain amygdala function and prefrontal cortex function. We can extrapolate then that perception and action are distinct entities within our brains that have an ability to "look at each other" and affect each other's functions.

Now, let's combine all three of the concepts of neuroplasticity, mirror neurons, and common coding theory and we come up with an amazing formula! We know that neuroplasticity means that we can form new neural pathways. We know that mirror neurons engage in neuroplasticity simply by observing others' behaviors, giving us new knowledge and abilities. We know that common coding theory suggests that our perceptions and actions affect each other and come from different brain regions, meaning that we can engage our mirror neurons internally because these regions can view each other. This all concludes that we can shape our neural networks by changing our perceptions about events, or that by purposely (and positively) thinking about events, we can positively change our neuron networks, which can affect domains such as Locus of Control.

In summary, *positive thinking* about all events that happen is the key to developing an internal Locus of Control. Positive thinking is the most powerful tool you have in shifting your Locus of Control, because it creates new neural pathways, reduces anxiety, and ultimately drives positive behaviors. It's that simple. Through my experience working with many who have shifted from an external to an internal Locus of Control, here are some techniques you can engage:

- Positively think about all events and outcomes, even if they are negative. This will minimize your anxiety and fight or flight response. Remember that Locus of Control is conscious (where Inner Passivity is unconscious) so we can change it by positively thinking about things.
- Look for instant feedback. Try to only engage in tasks that have a quick outcome post-action. If you shorten the feedback loop between actions and results, you will spend less time ruminating about what went wrong, what you could have done better, etc. Perform the act, obtain the result, learn the lesson, and move on.
- Take responsibility for everything that happens in your life, whether it is good or bad. This will shift your mindset from a victim of fate to a driver of destiny. As long as you believe you can influence the outcome and you are responsible for that outcome, when the situation arises again you will get a more favorable result.
- Develop emotional intelligence, specifically problem solving, reality testing, decision making, and optimism skills. Emotional intelligence is discussed in detail in chapter 11.
- Engage your mirror neurons and find someone who has a strong internal Locus of Control and shadow them. Watch how they behave, when they get upset, and their responses to given situations.
- Limit negative self-talk and weak language. Negative talk, such as "I have no choice" and "I can't" should be replaced with "I choose not to" or "I won't."

- Have the mindset that people make their own luck. There is such thing as random chance, but that is different than luck, good or bad. You cannot control what happens, but you can control how you respond.

But what happens if we cannot think positively? The mind can sometimes seethe with malevolence, prohibiting our ability to think clearly and positively. Next, we look at the domain which can block our path towards positive thinking. The fourth domain is called our Cognitive Distortions.

In Sum

- One is said to have an internal Locus of Control if an individual believes that her behaviors are guided by her personal efforts and decisions. One is said to have an external Locus of Control if she believes that her behavior is guided by fate, God, luck, or other external circumstances.
- Those with an internal Locus of Control:
    - Take responsibility for their actions
    - Are less influenced by other people's opinions
    - Often do better at self-paced tasks
    - Have a strong sense of self-efficacy
    - Work harder to achieve the things they want
    - Possess confidence in the face of challenges
    - Are normally physically healthier, happier and independent
    - Often achieve greater workplace success
- Those with an external Locus of Control:
    - Blame their circumstances on outside forces, such as luck or chance
    - Don't believe their own efforts can change their situation
    - Frequently feel hopeless or powerless in the face of difficult situations
    - More often experience learned helplessness
- An internal locus needs to be coupled with skill and competency or it can lead to undesirable outcomes.
- Locus of Control and Inner Passivity are related – Locus of Control is conscious while Inner Passivity is unconscious.
- Research suggests that Locus of Control is located within specific neurons in the hypothalamus, meaning that we can use neuroplasticity, mirror neurons, and common coding theory to specifically target the changing of our Locus of Control through the power of positive thinking.

CHAPTER 11 | COGNITIVE DISTORTION

"Superstition is foolish, childish, primitive and irrational – but how much does it cost you to knock on wood?"

JUDITH VIORST, American writer

"I became insane, with long intervals of horrible sanity."

EDGAR ALLAN POE

We tend to trust what goes on in our brains. We trust that our appraisals of ourselves and others are accurate, that our memories are precise and that our evaluations of social situations correctly produce maximized outcomes. We believe what our eyes see and how those events are interpreted in our brains. While this can certainly be the case some of the time, research has consistently proven that our brains can lie to us. Aaron Beck, a psychiatrist and professor who is often referred to as the father of cognitive therapy, found that while working with depressed patients that they experienced negative streams of thought that seemingly arose spontaneously. Referring to them as "automatic thoughts," he classified them into three categories: negative ideas about themselves, the world, and the future.[1] These three areas would soon become known as Beck's Cognitive Triad.

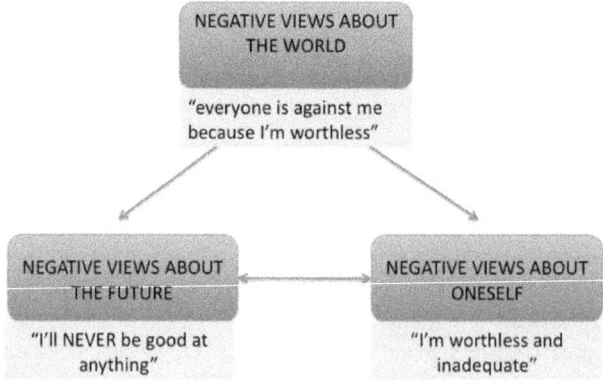

Beck discovered that these three key elements often made up the belief system among patients that led to systematic depression. The triad involves automatic, spontaneous and seemingly uncontrollable negative thoughts in these three areas. Beck used the triad as a way to help patients identify and evaluate thoughts that they had about particular subjects, leading them to think more realistically about them, which led to emotional healing. Beck and his colleagues would use this form of talk therapy to treat disorders including depression, bipolar disorder, eating disorders, drug abuse, anxiety disorders, personality disorders, and many others, by creating a system of treatment called Cognitive Behavioral Therapy, or CBT.

Cognitive Behavioral Therapy

CBT is a powerful approach to therapy because it addresses depression that is rooted in false assumptions and distorted thinking. Beck was able to connect distorted thinking patterns to patients' symptoms and developed a framework that allowed patients to change their thinking, which in turn, eliminated various symptoms of depression and anxiety. Remember that within the cognitive perspective of psychology, our thoughts drive our experiences. So if these thoughts are distorted, it can drastically affect our ability to have positive life experiences and outcomes.

David Burns, a student of Beck and another pioneer into depression and treatment research, wrote in his 1989 book *Feeling Good: The New Mood Therapy* about eleven Cognitive Distortions. Research after his book has added a few more, for a total of sixteen. They are:[2][3][4]

1. *All-or-Nothing Thinking / Polarized Thinking* - also known as "Black-and-White Thinking," this distortion manifests as an inability or unwillingness to see shades of gray. Those who suffer from this distortion only see things in terms of extremes. For example, something is either amazing or terrible, you are either perfect or a total failure, or it is only hot or cold.
2. *Overgeneralization* - within this distortion, a person comes to a conclusion based on one piece of evidence or a single incident. For example, a student may receive a C on one test and conclude that she is stupid and a failure. A single event represents a never-ending pattern of defeat.
3. *Mental Filter* - similar to overgeneralization, the mental filter distortion engages a person's negativity bias full bore by focusing on a single negative event while excluding all the positive events. For example, a husband might dwell on a single negative comment made by his wife and view the relationship as hopelessly lost, because he is ignoring the years of positive comments and experiences.

4. *Disqualifying the Positive* - within this distortion, the person acknowledges positive experiences but rejects them instead of embraces them. For example, a skater that scores a goal in hockey may believe it was due to random luck instead of her skills, facilitating the continuance of negative thought patterns even in spite of evidence to the contrary.
5. *Mind Reading* - this distortion is one of two that fall under "Jumping to Conclusions." This distortion manifests as the inaccurate belief that we know what another person is thinking. For example, we may see a person frowning and assume that they are upset, without possessing any other confirming evidence to their state of mind.
6. *Fortune Telling* - this distortion is the second of two that fall under "Jumping to Conclusions." This refers to the tendency to make conclusions and predictions based on little to no evidence and holding them as absolute fact. This is common in people who are single and profess that they will never find love because they haven't found it yet. There is no way to know what the future holds, even if past and current experience align with that thinking.
7. *Catastrophizing* - also known as Magnification or Minimization, a person believes that disaster will strike no matter what. Also known as the "Binocular Trick" because of how it skews perspective, this distortion involves exaggerating the importance or meaning of things or minimizing the importance or meaning of things. A person may exaggerate the importance of significant events, such as a mistake or an achievement, and apply that significance to all life events.
8. *Emotional Reasoning* - Emotional reasoning refers to the acceptance of one's emotions as fact. An example of this can be described as "I feel it, therefore it must be true."
9. *Should Statements* - Should statements are statements that you make to yourself about what you "should" do, what you "ought" to do, or what you "must" do. When applied to others, they impose a set of expectations that will likely not be met, because we are inferring that the other person is not currently living up to a standard with their actions.
10. *Labeling and Mislabeling* - These distortions are when we assign judgments of value to ourselves or others based on one instance or experience. Similar to overgeneralization, an example of this would be labeling yourself as a complete failure in life for getting a D on one exam.
11. *Personalization* - this distortion involves taking everything personally or assigning blame to yourself for no logical reason to believe you are to blame. This distortion leads a person to believe everything is

his fault when things go wrong, often leading to a sense of psychological martyrdom.
12. *Control Fallacies* - this distortion is double-sided, meaning that a person can believe they are helpless victims that have no control over anything or that they are in complete control of everything. Both beliefs can be equally as damaging as they are delusional.
13. *Fallacy of Fairness* - this distortion leads a person to judge every experience by its perceived fairness. He will likely feel anger, resentment, and hopelessness when he inevitably encounters a situation that is not fair.
14. *Fallacy of Change* - this distortion involves expecting others to change if provided enough peer pressure (can be positive or negative). This distortion is normally accompanied by a belief that our happiness and success rests on other people. This leads us to believe that forcing those around us to change is the only way to achieve what we want. For example, those who think "if I can get my spouse to simply stop doing [insert behavior] then my life will be amazing," are engaged in this distortion.
15. *Always Being Right* - in other word, these are perfectionists. Those engaged in this distortion often struggle with Imposter Syndrome, a psychological pattern in which an individual doubts their accomplishments and has a persistent internalized fear of being exposed as a "fraud." It is the belief that we must always be right at all costs. With this distortion, the idea of being wrong is absolutely not possible or acceptable.
16. *Heaven's Reward Fallacy* - considered one of the most popular distortions since it is often a theme of movies, this distortion manifests as a belief that one's struggles, suffering, or hard work will result in an eventual reward. Sometimes, our hard work and sacrifices do not directly lead to desired results. This often results in disappointment, frustration, anger, and even depression when the awaited reward does not materialize.

One of the core concepts of CBT is understanding that facts are not opinions and that emotions are not facts. Emotions do a great deal for us in providing wonderful life experiences, giving us intuitions in social interactions, producing feelings of love, trust, admiration, and protecting us when fears arise. While there are many resources available to you on CBT, I have found in my doctoral research that one aspect of emotionality is at the core of distorted thinking. That dimension is referred to as our emotional intelligence.

Fight or Flight

Before diving into emotional intelligence, it is important to understand where our "fight or flight" impulses come from. Thanks to research performed under the biological perspective, we now understand that there is a neural basis for the human fight or flight response. According to evolutionary psychologists, the brain evolved from the "bottom up," developing an original core responsibility for our survival before any higher levels of cognition could be developed within the brain. Once mammals evolved, the brain was responsible for processing emotions. This core function is located in the midbrain in a section called the amygdala. This portion of our brain acts as the body's sentinel, constantly scanning the environment for threats that can harm or kill us, triggering the HPA axis that was mentioned in chapter 8. The amygdala has an ability to highjack other portions of our brain and change the hierarchy of mental processes when it senses fear, preoccupying attention and diverting all neural resources, conscious and unconscious. The amygdala is also responsible for sending energy to our limbs, muscles, and throughout our neurotransmitters instantaneously, giving us an ability to fight or flight in a nanosecond when responding to threats. While this gives us an ability to react to threats immediately, we often do not have time to cognitively think about our response or behaviors.

We now live in a world where there are very few physical threats. Predators aren't trying to eat us, many have shelter and readily available food, and most of the industrialized world doesn't live among warring tribes where we have to fear new people we encounter. We do however live in a world with symbolic threats, due to personal issues with others, social media bullying, or competing for romantic relationships, to name a few. However, the amygdala still functions today the same way it always has. That is why it is often referred to as our primitive or reptilian brain – it has yet to evolve past its originally intended function. When we perceive modern threats, the amygdala highjacks our nervous system the same way it has for thousands of years, narrowing attention, shuttering mental processes to the background, and ultimately affecting our behavior. Emotional intelligence is the process of cognitively and consciously identifying all of the emotions that process in our amygdala so that we can behave accordingly.

So why does the amygdala have so much power and influence in our lives? This is all due to the physical pathway of the electrical signals that interpret our life experience. In the 17th century, philosophers like John Locke advocated empiricism, which is the theory that states that all knowledge comes from our primary sensory experience, as opposed to rationalism, which is the theory that claims all ideas, reason and deduction are innate. The biological perspective has provided evidence that empiricism can account for much of our mental processes and subsequent behavior, due to those somatic pathways. Think for a moment, how the chair feels that you are sitting in. How your clothes feel on your skin and how the temperature feels on your body. All of these senses are converted into electrical signals that aggregate in your nervous system, travel along your spinal cord, and enter the back of your head near the base of your brain. Those electrical signals have to travel all the way to the prefrontal cortex *before* you can have a rational thought about what those signals mean. The main issue is that those electrical signals must *first* pass through the limbic system (which is where the amygdala resides) before it reaches the prefrontal cortex.

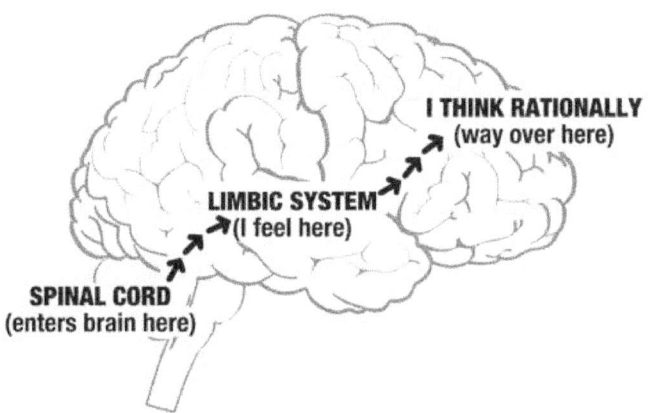

Graphic from Emotional Intelligence 2.0

The amygdala processes these emotions at lightning speed, often well before the prefrontal cortex receives those signals and produces rational thoughts about them. The amygdala takes these signals and creates a response instantaneously, which is normally a primal response geared toward the fight or flight instinct. *This means that we feel every impulse before we can generate a thought about that impulse.* By the time the prefrontal cortex gets the signal, the amygdala has already decided what it wants to do. It is up to the prefrontal cortex to quickly scan all available information in the brain to determine if the amygdala's desired response is in our true best interests or not. For example, let's say a person is agitating you, creating feelings of anxiety. The amygdala receives those signals and instantly engages the fight instinct. You are ready for battle. Now, by the time your prefrontal cortex receives the signal, your muscles are tense and you are ready to punch this person. Your prefrontal cortex puts the brakes on and says "wait! this person is your manager!" So, instead of slugging that person, you simply smile and nod and go about your day. Your prefrontal cortex, or rational thoughts, altered your amygdala's desired behavior because in the long run, being employed (and out of jail) is better than satisfying the amygdala's fight instinct. Jonathan Haidt wrote in the *Happiness Hypothesis* that:

When some regions of the hypothalamus are stimulated directly with a small electric current, rats, cats, and other mammals can be made gluttonous, ferocious, or hypersexual, suggesting that the limbic system underlies many of our basic animal instincts. Conversely, when people suffer damage to the frontal cortex, they sometimes show an increase in sexual and aggressive behavior because the frontal cortex plays an important role in suppressing or inhibiting behavioral impulses.[5]

This is where emotional intelligence comes in. Emotional intelligence seeks to shorten that communication loop between the amygdala and the prefrontal cortex by giving us an ability to identify and label emotions as they happen, ensuring we do not act in primal fashion when responding to fight or flight scenarios, but rather behave with respect to rectitude, societal norms, and morality.

Emotional Intelligence

Often, our prefrontal cortex gets it wrong. We incorrectly label our emotions and subsequently misunderstand what those emotions are trying to tell us. According to research, only 36% of people were able to accurately identify emotions as they happen.[6] That means that 64% of the time, we misinterpret what our primitive brain is trying to tell us! Developing emotional intelligence is crucial in battling Cognitive Distortion and obtaining overall success in life. Emotional intelligence is defined by Reuven Bar-On, a leading pioneer and researcher into emotional intelligence, as "a set of emotional and social skills that influence the way we perceive and express ourselves, develop and maintain social relationships, cope with challenges, and use emotional information in an effective and meaningful way." Emotional intelligence is the concept of drawing upon the wisdom of our emotions as a way to avoid Cognitive Distortions and think clearly about what the emotions are trying to convey to us. But why is it so difficult to decipher our emotions? The answer lies in the basal ganglia, a group of brain structures found deep within the cerebral hemisphere.

According to Daniel Goleman, a leading researcher and scholar in emotional intelligence, the basal ganglia is the part of the brain that observes everything we do in life, analyzing our performance in a variety of situations and our subsequent feelings about them. Essentially, our unique life wisdom, which is a result of all of our life experiences, is stored in the basal ganglia. Think of it as your own personal library and archive. The basal ganglia tries to communicate with us in a multitude of situations, offering wisdom to us during times when we need it the most. The main issue is that the basal ganglia is so primitive, that it has *no connection to the verbal cortex* of our brain. It cannot communicate to us in words; it can only communicate to us in feelings. When the basal ganglia is trying to warn us, it cannot create vocabulary or memory to engage with the prefrontal cortex; it can only create emotion. This is why our thoughts are often distorted – we are trying to interpret the ancient language of the basal ganglia through modern words and phrases. Its two main areas of connectivity to us are to the emotional centers of the brain, such as the amygdala, and the gut. This is the scientific rationale behind gut feeling and intuition – our basal ganglia is scanning our library of life wisdom, ethics, morality, and values, and communicates to us whether it believes that a situation is right or wrong. Because of this lack of direct connectivity to our verbal cortexes, emotions either go unnoticed, miscategorized, or misinterpreted, leading to Cognitive Distortion, and in some cases, a deterioration of physical health.

An interesting side note that is related to thinking on purpose is the subject of the gut microbiome. There is research that demonstrates a link between gut health and mental health. A procedure, dating all the way back to 4th-century China that is now referred to as fecal microbiota transplant, or FMT, involves treating neurotoxicity and other adverse gut microbiome conditions by taking fecal matter from a healthy donor and implanting it into the colon of an ailing patient. Apart from the undesirable visualization that describing the procedure brings, it has been proven to improve the health of the gut microbiome with resounding success.[7] But researchers have recently discovered something else - that FMT recipients had *positive mental effects after* the implants.[8] In a paper published in 2005 in *Medical Hypotheses*, researchers claimed that probiotics have a role in the treatment of depression. They wrote:[9]

> We have shown that people who are clinically depressed have less diversity in the bacteria in their gut than people who are not depressed. The question now is how can we improve the diversity of our bacteria.

This finding led them to the claim that changing the composition of microbiota in the gut affected emotional behavior. Essentially, physical gut health affects emotional and mental health. The researchers performed studies on mice, and eventually humans, to learn of a communication superhighway that contains over 100 million neurons known as the gut-brain axis, or GBA. This research finally established the direct connection between the basal ganglia and the gut. Research in the *Annals of Gastroenterology* claims the following:[10]

> The gut-brain axis (GBA) consists of bidirectional communication between the central and the enteric nervous

system, linking emotional and cognitive centers of the brain with peripheral intestinal functions. Recent advances in research have described the importance of gut microbiota in influencing these interactions. This interaction between microbiota and GBA appears to be bidirectional, namely through signaling from gut-microbiota to brain and from brain to gut-microbiota by means of neural, endocrine, immune, and humoral links...In clinical practice, evidence of microbiota-GBA interactions comes from the association of dysbiosis with central nervous disorders (i.e. autism, anxiety-depressive behaviors) and functional gastrointestinal disorders. In particular, irritable bowel syndrome can be considered an example of the disruption of these complex relationships, and a better understanding of these alterations might provide new targeted therapies.

This is an amazing finding! Researchers have concluded that bacteria in your gut affects mental states, emotionality, and even brain chemistry. This is because the basal ganglia is one of the main users of that GBA axis superhighway. The gut brain is connected to the head brain via the vagus nerve, known as the longest nerve in the human body, weaving a complex path from your cranium, through your face, and down into your abdomen. Also known as the wandering nerve due to its vast connection system throughout the body, we know now that the vagus nerve is part of a feedback loop where *positive emotions can drive physical health and vice versa.*[11] Understanding our emotions (through emotional intelligence) leads to better physical well-being just as much as being in top physical condition leads to better mental well-being. The establishment of the GBA axis and vagus nerve function proves this.

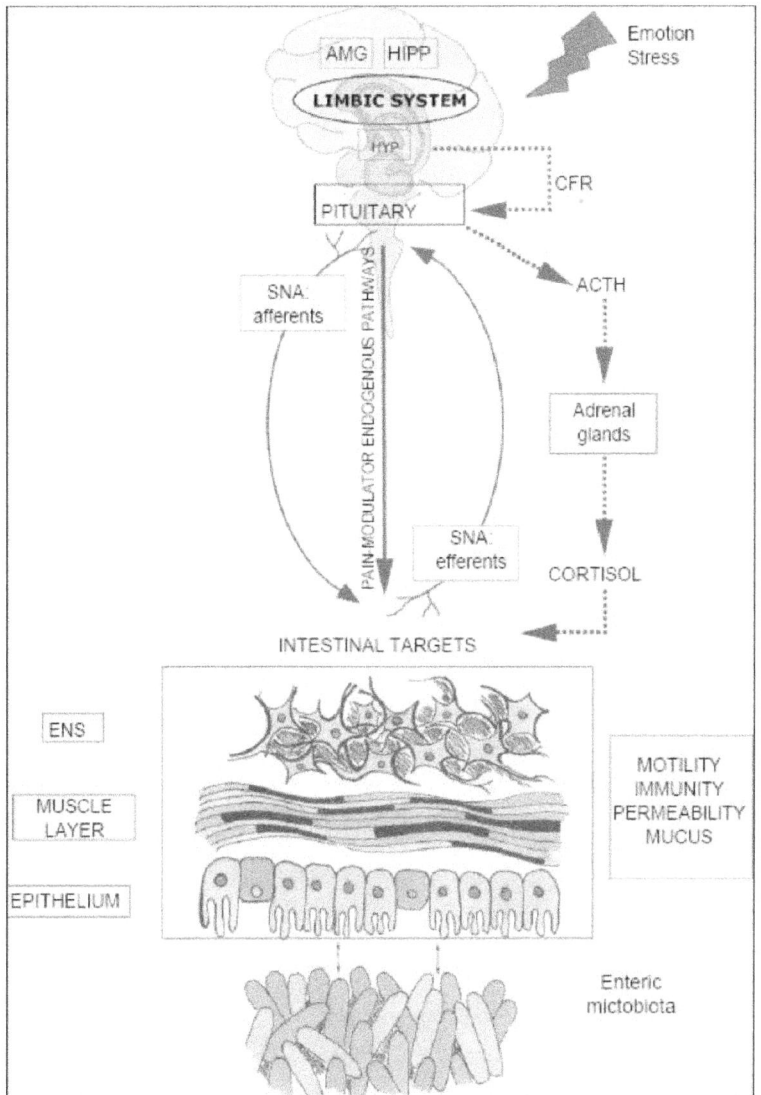

Microbiome Gut-Brain Axis Structure[12]

It is a difficult concept to grasp at first – this notion that your gut has such influence over your mental state. But continuing research in the area of gut biome health finds more evidence of its importance to mental health. For example, 95% of the body's serotonin, the brain chemical responsible for mood regulation, is found in the gut. Researchers discovered[13] that a majority of children with ASD (autism spectrum disorder) display gastrointestinal symptoms.[14] In experimental trials, mice that experienced memory problems, dementia, and other cognitive difficulties, reversed some of these symptoms with probiotic therapy. Other research[15] has shown that "dysbiosis and alterations of the gut microbiome composition have been shown to contribute to the development of several diseases in humans, such as inflammatory bowel disease, type 2 diabetes, metabolic syndrome, obesity, allergies, colorectal cancer, and Alzheimer disease."

This research has linked gut microbiome health to mental health, since we now know one of the ways that the basal ganglia communicates to us is through the GBA axis (the other way is through the amygdala). When the basal ganglia is in distress or feels that it is not being listened to, physical health can deteriorate, starting with the gut. Maybe developing an ability to think on purpose is simply a function of keeping a healthy gut! At the very least, if you maintain a healthy gut microbiome, you won't need an FMT transplant any time soon.

Focusing on gut health is certainly one way to appease the basal ganglia. Developing your emotional intelligence is the other. Developing emotional intelligence enhances the ability for our prefrontal cortex to be aware of what our basal ganglia is trying to convey to us through emotionality. This is why *Emotional Self-Awareness* is a core skill within emotional intelligence, prevalent across all major models of emotional intelligence within the *Encyclopedia of Applied Psychology*. Being able to pay attention to these subtle cues that arise from emotionality is to have access to the oldest, most powerful parts of our brain. Think of emotional intelligence as the Rosetta stone, finally bridging the gap between an ancient language (the basal ganglia and emotions) to a modern language (the prefrontal cortex and rationality).

Other skills within the realm of emotional intelligence include assessments of our own inner strength and confidence, our propensity to remain self-directed and openly expressive of our thoughts and feelings, our ability to develop relationships based on trust, our ability to understand how emotions impact our ability to make decisions (remember the Damasio study highlighted in chapter 6), and how we use the emotions associated with our ability to cope with change and unfamiliarity.

Emotional intelligence skills have been correlated to a variety of desired life outcomes and are often considered one of the best predictors of success. IQ is often thought to be a major predictor of life success, but research has shown that this is not true. Thomas Stanley, the author of *The Millionaire Mind*, wrote about research he performed on 733 self-made millionaires in the US. These were millionaires that were not born with money but instead made their fortunes on their own. He asked them to rate the top thirty factors most responsible for their success. Of the thirty, the top five factors were:

1. Being honest with all people
2. Being well disciplined
3. Getting along with people

4. Having a supportive spouse
5. Working harder than most

All five of these factors are rooted in emotional intelligence. IQ only ranked 21 out of 30 (when doctors and lawyers were removed from the sample, IQ ranked 30 out of 30). Other research[16] highlights that EI is responsible for 58% of job performance, 90% of top performers have high EI, and people with high EI make $29,000 more than their low EI counterparts. Below is a graph[17] that shows a correlation of IQ to Income (net worth). As you can see, there is essentially zero correlation.

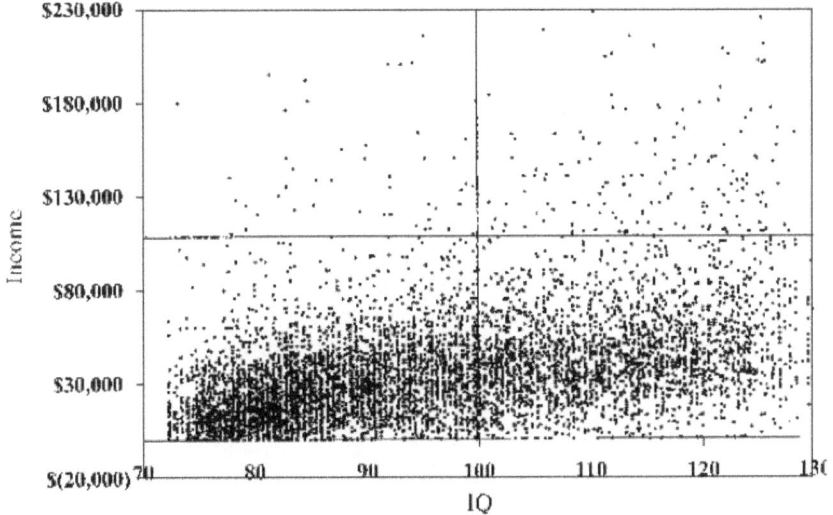

Let's try an example. Think about the best manager you ever had. Think about why he or she was a great manager and write it down, say it out loud or just think to yourself about the reasons he or she was a great manager. For example, they could have been a great listener, generous, etc.

...

Ok, time is up. Now when thinking about the best manager you ever had, and why that person was the best you ever had, did you say it was because they were "smart"? If you did, that is pretty rare. I have performed this exercise with thousands of teams and I've never heard it. No one has ever proclaimed, "they were the best manager I had because they were so smart!" Normally, it's because of attributes like honesty, patience, great listening, or empathy. All are aspects of emotional intelligence. A Gallup poll of more than 1 million U.S. workers found that the number 1 reason people quit their jobs was due to a bad boss or immediate supervisor. This is why you may have heard the adage "people don't leave bad companies; they leave bad managers." This extends the power of emotional intelligence to the workplace as well, since you now know that focusing on building emotional intelligence skill creates the best bosses.

While emotional intelligence is considered a powerful set of skills that ultimately determines success in life, it is important to note that balance is the key. As mentioned in chapter 8 under the Inner Passivity skill of "Aim for Your Average," too much of any particular skill can be detrimental. Emotional intelligence skills can be "overused." Emotional intelligence skills such as self-regard, self-actualization and emotional self-awareness are important skills to develop, but in excess, they can create feelings of overconfidence or goal achievement blindness (where you only focus on achieving your goals and nothing else). Other skills, such as empathy, assertiveness, and reality testing are important to develop, but too much empathy can lead to someone never being able to deliver bad news, being too assertive can lead to a lack of communication ability or strong leadership, and being too grounded in reality can affect creative thought processes. It is important to understand the role that emotions play – they connect our rational brains to our primitive brains. Our primitive brains are much more skilled in assessing risk and danger, but our rational brains put those fears into context. If we rely too much on our emotions, we won't be able to navigate complex social situations delicately or perform the cognitive functions that make us human, such as math, rationality, and higher-level reason. If we rely on logic too much, we miss the cues from our mental sentinel that wishes to protect us from harm and we miss out on feelings of love, trust and social bonding from others. The key is to not overuse either but to strive for an even balance between rationality and emotionality.

Bias, Decision Paradoxes, and Heuristics

Another aspect of our thinking that adds to Cognitive Distortions are mental processes referred to as cognitive bias, decision paradoxes, and mental heuristics. There are a few decision-making theories used in finance, economics, and psychology but the most prevalent one that is related to Cognitive Distortion is the "Expected Utility Theory." The expected utility theory deals with the analysis of situations where people must make a decision without knowing which outcomes may result from that decision, or put simply, they must make a decision under *uncertainty*. The theory claims that people will choose the act that will result in the highest expected *utility*, which is defined as the sum of the products of probability and utility over all possible outcomes. In other words, as long as the numbers support a particular decision, under this hypothesis, leaders should always choose the highest utility, or *best possible mathematical outcome*. After all, this makes sense. As rational, mathematical, intelligent creatures, we should be able to look at multiple scenarios and choose which one has the best mathematical outcome.

The issue is that these mathematical calculations (our rationality) are overridden by the mental elements of cognitive bias, mental heuristics, decision paradoxes, and irrationality, which all drastically alter decision-making processes, even in the best of us.

Heuristics are essentially mental shortcuts that lead to problem-solving conclusions which ease the cognitive load of the decision making. These shortcuts are a summation of our knowledge, experiences, and overall life story. Often, heuristics are a good thing. Otherwise, we would sit around all day and critically analyze every situation or scenario, and do a cost/benefit analysis on the food we eat and the TV shows we watch. Nothing would ever get done! However, these heuristics sacrifice *accuracy for speed*, which leads to incorrect conclusions. These are referred to as cognitive biases. Cognitive biases are tendencies to think in certain ways that can lead to systematic deviations from a standard of rationality or good judgment. The key thing to understand is that mental biases lead to breakdowns in rational thinking. Biases normally fall into four main categories, which are:

1. what should we remember
2. too much information
3. need to act fast
4. not enough meaning

The Cognitive Bias Codex shows the top 200 biases, all of which have different ways to distort our thinking (the graphic can only be read in full if blown up to four feet tall or higher since it contains so much detail. Do an internet search for the codex if this interests you).

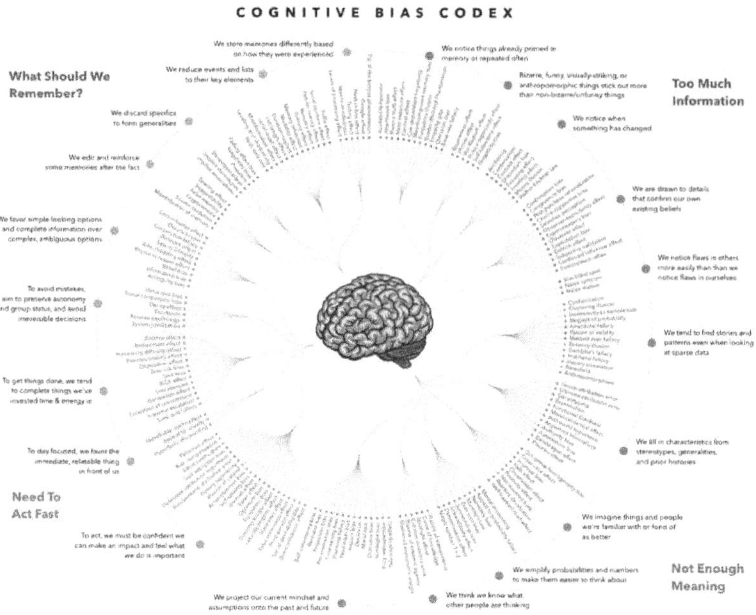

Let's review one paradox that I run into often in my coaching work, which is referred to as the Allais paradox. The Allais paradox was developed by Maurice Allais in a 1953 journal paper titled "Le Comportement de l'Homme Rationnel devant le Risque: Critique des Postulats et Axiomes de l'Ecole Americaine" [translated as The Rational Man's Behavior in the Face of Risk: Criticism of Postulates and Axioms of the American School] and it describes the empirically demonstrated fact that individuals' decisions can be *inconsistent with expected utility theory*. This paradox is usually explained with the Allais experiment which is shown here:[18]

An individual is asked to choose one between the following gambles:
Gamble A: 100% chance of receiving 100 million
Gamble B: 10% chance of receiving 500 million
            89% chance of receiving 100 million
            1% chance of receiving nothing

And another amongst the following:
Gamble C: 11% chance of receiving 100 million
            89% chance of receiving nothing
Gamble D: 10% chance of receiving 500 million
            90% chance of receiving nothing

Let's first look at gamble A and B, which would you prefer?

...

Did you choose A or B?

Most choose A, even though B has a higher expected utility if you do the math (Gamble A has an expected utility of 100 vs. Gamble B has an expected utility of 139). Most give added weight to a result that has *absolutely no risk*. This is what famous psychologists Daniel Kahneman and Amos Tversky dubbed the *Certainty Effect*, a powerful cognitive bias that alters rational decision making.

Now let's look at gamble C and D, which would you prefer?

...

Did you choose C or D?

If you followed expected utility theory and applied the learning from the first experiment, you would think most would choose C, but most choose D (Gamble C has an expected utility of 11 vs. Gamble D has an expected utility of 50). In the first gamble (A vs. B), the *less risky choice is preferred over a higher expected utility*, while in the second gamble (C vs. D) a *higher expected utility is preferred over a less risky choice*. This is what Kahneman and Tversky dubbed the *Pseudo-Certainty Effect* (another one of the cognitive biases) where although people normally prefer certainty over uncertainty, if the scenario is described or approached differently, individuals will prefer or ignore the uncertainty that was previously rejected in a preceding scenario. Essentially, the Allais paradox proved that humans do not always act in the best interest of maximizing utility or minimizing risk, and that decision-making processes can align with certainty or uncertainty, depending on perceived risk and how the question is framed.

So why is this important? It means that humans are irrational and decision making rarely follows logic! Gelengül Koçaslan decided to test this and wrote in the *Journal of Neuroquantology* in a paper called "Quantum Interpretation of Decision Making Under Risk"[19] that those who experience irrationality, or behave in a "different reality," often make different decisions under risk than others. This means that IQ, personality, and decision-making theories such as the expected utility hypothesis, *do little to predict how one will make important decisions while under risk,* because decisions are often made in the irrational epicenters of our brain (more specifically the amygdala within the limbic system) *before* risk is assessed in our rational prefrontal cortex. Think back to the brain graphic of how electrical signals travel up the spine and toward the prefrontal cortex where rational thought can occur.

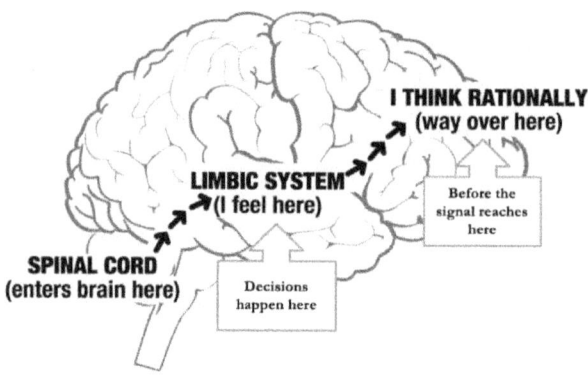

This means that due to the way our bodies are wired, our emotional centers make decisions before our rational centers even know the impulse exists. Decisions on how we behave are solidified before our IQ, personality, and rationality even show up to the party. Like Damasio discovered in *Descartes Error*, our decision making ability is heavily impacted, if not solely influenced by our emotions, which leads to cognitive biases and distortions. This led Damasio to the groundbreaking discovery that humans make decisions based on emotions, then apply facts later on to substantiate the decision. I will repeat that because it is one of the most important facts about emotionality and rationality that you can understand. Humans make decisions based on emotions, then apply facts later on to substantiate the decision. This means that our rational thoughts are essentially enslaved to the decision that is already made by our emotional systems, which can lead to Cognitive Distortion, irrationality, and cognitive dissonance.[20]

How to Overcome Your Cognitive Distortions

You may be thinking, if we are dominated by our reptilian brains and enslaved by our emotions, why even bother? It is because emotional intelligence is considered a dynamic skill set that can be developed if specifically targeted. Our primitive brain had a million-year head start on our prefrontal cortex, which means that we need to spend extra time ensuring that our thoughts are clear and our emotions are well defined, to ensure we can think on purpose. What separates humans from other species is that we have the power to use rationality as a system of checks and balances for our primitive, emotional brain. Even though the prefrontal cortex was the last part of our brain to evolve and is the last section of our brain to receive the electrical signals that frame our perception, it is still vital to our human experience that we seek to maximize its relationship with our reptilian brain. Increasing our emotional intelligence by developing our verbal construct, which helps interpret what our emotions are trying to tell us, is the key. There are hundreds of resources available on Cognitive Behavioral Therapy and eliminating Cognitive Distortions. I will offer the three key strategies that I have discovered in my research which will specifically target actions that hinder our ability to think on purpose.

Avoid Zahavian Signals

In 1975, Israeli biologist Amotz Zahavi developed a hypothesis to explain how evolution led to what he referred to as "honest" or "reliable" signals between animals that actually were not honest; they were meant to deceive one another. Often referred to as the handicap principle, a Zahavian signal is a way for an animal to demonstrate its fitness, strength, or prowess to other animals, either in an attempt to mate or dissuade the other animal from attacking. For example, when in the wild, certain animals exhibit strange behavior in the face of imminent threats. An impala, which is a medium size antelope found in eastern and southern Africa, will exhibit a peculiar behavior called "stotting"[21] when it spots a predator.

A young impala "stotting"

Rather than run away, giving the predator a chase that it is expecting and immediately revealing to the predator its escape capabilities (or lack thereof), the impala "demonstrates" that a pursuit by the predator would be wasted effort, because the impala possesses such "strong" abilities and can waste energy dancing around, despite the threat of imminent danger. According to researchers, if the impala simply invests a little bit of energy in this signal to show the cougar that a chase would be futile, it may not have to evade the cougar because she would choose another animal for its meal. This way, the impala saves vital energy by stotting rather than sprinting, and if the cougar is actually capable of catching the impala, the stotting is a bluff that ultimately leads to the impala's survival as well. Similar behavior is found across many animals, such as larks that sing while being chased, peacocks that fly to attract mates and many others. The Zahavian signal conveys that the signaler possesses the prowess, energy, or capability to demonstrate the signal, which in turn conveys a sense of status that either makes the signaler a preferred mate or a difficult meal. It is an honest signal that has a hidden motive.

Humans exhibit Zahavian signals as well. We are always finding ways to demonstrate our fitness, status and power to other humans, either in an attempt to attract mates or dominate peers. You see this clearly in purchases, such as cars, houses, and other luxury items. Humans will often buy expensive items to signal to others that they can "waste" money on such an item, conveying that they have so many resources available to them, that they can spare those resources and energy on frivolous items such as luxury cars. Now, the key distinction here is the *intended deception in the signal*. Essentially, it's all about the bluff. I am all for nice things, big houses, and fast cars. I believe people should celebrate success and give their loved ones the best things in life they can. But only if they can truly afford it and it isn't a Zahavian signal to others.

A more common description of this behavior is called "keeping up with the Joneses," an English idiom that refers to the comparison to one's neighbor as the benchmark for social status through the accumulation of material goods. When you signal to others that you are fit, wealthy, or powerful through conspicuous consumption, it leads to Cognitive Distortion because you will initially feel real benefits from it. People will praise your new car, cherish your new house, and your social status will rise, albeit for a short while, because your status is built on a foundation of sand. This distorts social perception, which feeds back into your self-esteem, creating a toxic cycle that will eventually harm you. As an example, obesity used to be the Zahavian signal of choice before the Industrial Revolution. Obesity would signal that you had an ability to procure and eat plenty of food – more than you actually needed. But this would come at the expense of your health, agility and muscle strength. Signaling your status to others via obesity weakened you in the long run. Nowadays, most Zahavian signals are demonstrated by purchasing things that we cannot afford.

The reason that keeping up with the Joneses creates a vicious, unsustainable cycle, is that it creates real effects on our happiness that are based off incorrect or distorted facts. A recent study at the University of Colorado Boulder found that when it came to sexual intercourse, people were not happy with it based on the frequency alone, but only became happy if that frequency was higher than others. "Having more sex makes us happy, but thinking that we are having more sex than other people makes us even happier."[22] The researchers concluded that the biggest driver of happiness was the *relative frequency compared to others*, as long as it was just a tad bit higher. This meant that the participants who had sex twice a week and thought their neighbors only had it once, were happier than those who had it ten times a week but thought that their neighbors had it thirteen. The fake construct of keeping up appearances, and being slightly better, drove happiness more than the actual facts.

Social status has always been an important aspect of society, which has its obvious rewards. If you were sinking on the Titanic in 1912 and you were of high status, then it was more likely that you had a lifeboat available to you. But now in an age of credit cards, easy money and loans, humans can easily fake social status through Zahavian signals. We can deceive others by conspicuous consumption, keeping appearances with our neighbors and peers. This leads to Cognitive Distortion because we are putting forth a false reality while putting our own financial and mental health at risk.

Another form of Zahavian signaling that does not involve purchases is how we post on social media. Status updates on social media are often Zahavian signals. People will post the best things in their life, the most flattering picture taken, their "healthy" meal that they "always" eat, or pretend that they just woke up and look perfect. Many studies have been done to show the dangers of social media and its negative effect on self-esteem, self-control, and other factors. For example, a recent study done at the Columbia Business School showed a link between posters who desperately sought after "likes" on social media and rising body-mass indexes and credit card debt.[23] Essentially, trying to signal to people in an artificial online world created real detrimental consequences in the physical world. Seeking positive feedback, even if that feedback was rooted in deception, was considered more important than financial and physical health to the participants. Engaging in Zahavian signaling created a distorted reality where a superficial thumbs-up in an artificial world had actual negative effects.

The key is to not engage in Zahavian signaling. Again, if you truly can afford the fancy car, if you do look like that when you wake up, and you aren't purchasing or posting to keep up with the Joneses, then go for it! Another study at Cornell University found one group was immune to the dopamine rush that most get when a "like" is received on a social media post. That group is those with a sense of purpose.[24] The researchers defined a sense of purpose as "ongoing motivation that is self-directed, oriented toward the future and beneficial to others." The researchers found that purposeful people can see where they want to be in the future and can act by attaining those goals. This subset of people did not chase artificial positive reinforcement at the expense of their long term future. Purposeful people were immune to positive reinforcement from an artificial online world, not allowing it to distort their actual world. Imagine that, "purposeful" people were better off. Ensure that you do not engage in Zahavian signaling, don't keep up with the Joneses, and have your social media posts mimic your real life. This will keep Cognitive Distortion at bay, enhancing your ability to think on purpose.

Separate Facts and Opinions

One of the first activities you would perform if you participated in CBT would be an exercise called "Fact or Opinion." Many of our Cognitive Distortions come from misinterpreting our feelings, then turning those misinterpreted feelings into "facts." As noted earlier, only 36% of people can accurately identify emotions as they happen. We cannot control our basal ganglia or amygdala. We cannot limit the flow of electrical signals in our brain. The emotions keep coming, regardless if we want them to or not. That is why our rational brains often disregard feelings, filing them away into the depths of our psyche if we determine them to not be relevant at the moment. It is because we have so many of them! But when we label our emotions, are we labeling them correctly? Here is an exercise to see.

Take the fifteen statements below and decide whether that statement is a fact or an opinion. Don't over think it, just try to label each one of these, writing down in this book or on a separate piece of paper if the statement should be considered a fact or an opinion:

1. I'm an evil person.
2. Jo told me that she didn't like my comment about her.
3. No one will ever love me.
4. Nothing ever goes right.
5. This will be a catastrophe.
6. I'm self-centered.
7. There's something wrong with me.
8. I'm not as attractive as she is.
9. I failed the exam.
10. I am overweight.
11. He screamed at me.
12. I'm a lazy person.
13. I didn't give my brother money when he asked.
14. My legs are too big.
15. Everyone thinks I'm ugly.

Being able to make the distinction between fact and opinion is the key to eliminating many Cognitive Distortions. Being able to quickly distinguish between fact and opinion has been linked to high levels of mental stability and is a core component of our ability to think on purpose. Now, let's see how you did.

1. I'm an evil person. *Opinion*
2. Jo told me that she didn't like my comment about her. *Fact*
3. No one will ever love me. *Opinion*
4. Nothing ever goes right. *Opinion*
5. This will be a catastrophe. *Opinion*
6. I'm self-centered. *Opinion*
7. There's something wrong with me. *Opinion*
8. I'm not as attractive as she is. *Opinion*
9. I failed the exam. *Fact*
10. I am overweight. *Fact*
11. He screamed at me. *Fact*
12. I'm a lazy person. *Opinion*
13. I didn't give my brother money when he asked. *Fact*
14. My legs are too big. *Opinion*
15. Everyone thinks I'm ugly. *Opinion*

How many did you get right? If you didn't get at least 12 of the 15 correct, then you have some work to do. People are estimated[25] to have around 70,000 thoughts a day. If you take your 80% pass rate from the above example and apply that to your daily thought counter, that means that 14,000 of your thoughts *each day* might be distorted. 14,000! Now, for those in relationships, you double that to account for your partner. That means between the two of you, in a single day, there could be over 28,000 distorted thoughts. Thoughts that aren't true, are mislabeled, are incorrect, or irrational. Do you see where this is going? We can compound this even further if we try to classify those thoughts as positive or negative. In 2005, the National Science Foundation published a finding that 80% of human thoughts each day are negative. Thousands of negative thoughts each day that are distorted can drive one mad! Now you see the importance of eliminating distortion. This begins with understanding the difference between fact and opinion.

One common exercise that will help you examine your irrational thoughts is called "putting your thoughts on trial." In this exercise, you are judge, jury, and executioner. On second thought, since you are the only one on trial, let's get rid of the executioner. You are the defense attorney, prosecutor, and judge. There, that's better. In this exercise, you are trying to determine the accuracy of your thoughts. Let's do an example if you have an irrational thought. Here are the roles:

Defense: Gather evidence in support of your thought. Evidence can only be used if it's a verifiable fact, meaning no guesses or opinions.

Prosecution: Gather evidence against your thought. Evidence can only be used if it's a verifiable fact, meaning no guesses or opinions.

Judge: Come to a verdict regarding the thought after hearing evidence from both sides. Is the thought accurate and rational? What is your verdict?

By doing this exercise, you lay out both sides of a thought, trying to gather evidence for both sides. What you will often find is that there is little to no evidence for the defense attorney of irrational thoughts; her case will crumble before the judge. This provides you objective evidence in the courtroom of your mind that the irrational thoughts do not stand up to cross-examination.

Summon the Challenger, Bring an Anchor

Anxiety is an extremely dominant force in the human psyche. Many psychologists believe that anxiety and depression are the two "foundation" elements of most, if not all, negative emotional disorders that exist today, meaning that most mental disorders can be traced back to a feeling of at least one of the two. Anxiety is one of the oldest studied disorders as well, with vague references dating all the way back to Hippocrates in 460 BCE. Ancient Epicurean and Stoic philosophers sought techniques to achieve "anxiety-free" states. In the 17th century, Robert Burton described anxiety in *The Anatomy of Melancholy*, a famous medical textbook that uses melancholy as the lens through which all human emotion is scrutinized. Anxiety has long been the champion of all emotional disorders.

A key distinction between depression and anxiety that is useful to know with respect to Cognitive Distortion is that depression is a symptom of focusing on the past while anxiety is a symptom of focusing on the future. Many, if not all, Cognitive Distortions are irrational thoughts about the future, since the future hasn't happened yet. According to research:[26]

> In the *DSM-5,* anxiety is defined as the anticipation of future threat; it is distinguished from *fear*, the emotional response to real or perceived imminent threat. Further, the term *worry* in *DSM-5* adds an additional nuance by referring to the cognitive aspects of apprehensive expectation.

It is important to note that anxiety is a normal emotion. From an evolutionary viewpoint, it promotes survival by encouraging people to steer clear of dangerous places. It is when anxiety and worry are *excessive* that generalized anxiety disorders start to emerge. According to the *DSM-5*, generalized anxiety disorder includes the following:[27]

> A. Excessive anxiety and worry (apprehensive expectation), occurring more days than not for at least 6 months, about a number of events or activities (such as work or school performance).
>
> B. The individual finds it difficult to control the worry.
>
> C. The anxiety and worry are associated with three (or more) of the following six symptoms (with at least some symptoms having been present for more days than not for the past 6 months):
>
> Note: Only one item required in children.
>
> 1. Restlessness, feeling keyed up or on edge.
>
> 2. Being easily fatigued.
>
> 3. Difficulty concentrating or mind going blank.
>
> 4. Irritability.
>
> 5. Muscle tension.
>
> 6. Sleep disturbance.
>
> D. The anxiety, worry, or physical symptoms cause clinically significant distress or impairment in social, occupational, or other important areas of functioning.
>
> E. The disturbance is not attributable to the physiological effects of a substance (e.g., abuse of a drug, a medication) or another medical condition (e.g., hyperthyroidism).
>
> F. The disturbance is not better explained by another medical disorder (e.g., anxiety or worry about having panic attacks in panic disorder, negative evaluation in social anxiety disorder [social phobia], contamination or other obsessions in obsessive-compulsive disorder,

separation from attachment figures in separation anxiety disorder, reminders of traumatic events in post-traumatic stress disorder, gaining weight in anorexia nervosa, physical complaints in somatic symptom disorder, perceived appearance flaws in body dysmorphic disorder, having a serious illness in illness anxiety disorder, or the content of delusional beliefs in schizophrenia or delusional disorder).

So how do we eliminate anxious thoughts? We *challenge* them. A champion can only be defeated when a worthy challenger comes forth. Within CBT, there is a process to identify irrational thoughts and replace them with rational ones, which will ultimately help you manage anxiety. With practice, this process becomes easier to complete over time. The challenge process is listed here:

1. *Think of what triggers your anxiety.* Think of common situations in your daily life that create anxiety spikes in your thoughts, such as sitting in traffic, talking to your Mom, or getting ready to prepare dinner.

2. *Think about the likelihood that something will actually go wrong.* Remember, anxiety is the unhealthy emotion we experience when we overestimate the likelihood that something in the future will go wrong. We get into a frenzy thinking about all of the possible outcomes, creating irrational thoughts about the event itself.

3. *Fast forward to the event.* Think about three outcomes if this event was to occur: the worst possible outcome, the best possible outcome, and the most probable outcome.

4. *Determine if it still matters.* Now that you have identified the three outcomes take a look at the worst possible outcome. Write down the following - if that outcome did occur, would it still matter tomorrow, next month, or next year?

With this exercise, you are challenging your irrational thoughts while jotting down the rational outcomes. This forces you to notate what is most likely to occur and question whether or not the extreme outcomes would make any difference in your life, in the unlikely event that the worst outcome did come to fruition. This process is reinforced with a cognitive bias that we can use for good, referred to as the anchoring bias.

Anchoring bias is the tendency for humans to put more weight on the first piece of information offered than on everything else that follows. That information serves as an anchor for the subsequent thoughts you are about to have. You see this tactic in sales all of the time. You can walk into a store and see something on sale for $9.99, but if you also see that price right after seeing a sign that says "originally $19.99," you will believe much more strongly that the $9.99 price is a deal. Original price vs. the discount price, monthly vs. annual plans – all anchoring techniques to produce a feeling within you to get you to buy something. Anchoring can also be used to establish a range if we think about two pieces of information together, such as an upper and lower bound, or in this case, the best and worst possible outcomes. If we identify the best and worst possible outcomes, we establish a "range" of outcomes, where our thinking becomes bound to only ponder events *between* those extremes. The natural tendency will be to use these anchoring points to ensure that our thinking is pointed inward toward the middle, reinforcing the most likely outcome. By challenging our irrational thoughts, we can document the possible outcomes and use anchoring to push us towards the middle, which will be much more closely aligned with rationality.

In Sum

- Aaron Beck, a psychiatrist and professor who is often referred to as the father of cognitive therapy, found that while working with depressed patients that they experienced negative streams of thought that seemingly arose spontaneously. Referring to them as "automatic thoughts," he classified them into three categories: negative ideas about themselves, the world, and the future. These three areas would soon become known as Beck's Cognitive Triad.
- CBT is a powerful approach to therapy because it addresses depression that is rooted in false assumptions and distorted thinking. Beck was able to connect distorted thinking patterns to patients' symptoms and developed a framework that allowed patients to change their thinking, which in turn, eliminated various symptoms of depression and anxiety.
- The sixteen most common Cognitive Distortions are: All-or-Nothing Thinking, Polarized Thinking, Overgeneralization, Mental Filter, Disqualifying the Positive, Mind Reading, Fortune Telling, Catastrophizing, Emotional Reasoning, Should

- Statements, Labeling and Mislabeling, Personalization, Control Fallacies, Fallacy of Fairness, Fallacy of Change, Always Being Right, and Heaven's Reward Fallacy.
- The amygdala has an ability to highjack other portions of our brain and change the hierarchy of mental processes when it senses fear, preoccupying attention and diverting all neural resources, conscious and unconscious.
- The amygdala takes these signals and creates a response instantaneously, which is normally a primal response geared toward the fight or flight instinct. *This means that we feel every impulse before we can generate a thought about that impulse.* By the time the prefrontal cortex gets the signal, the amygdala has already decided what it wants to do.
- Emotional intelligence is defined by Reuven Bar-On, a leading pioneer and researcher into emotional intelligence, as "a set of emotional and social skills that influence the way we perceive and express ourselves, develop and maintain social relationships, cope with challenges, and use emotional information in an effective and meaningful way."
- Another aspect of our thinking that adds to Cognitive Distortions are mental processes referred to as cognitive bias, decision paradoxes, and mental heuristics.
- The three key strategies that I have discovered in my research which will specifically target actions that hinder our ability to think on purpose are to Avoid Zahavian Signals, Separate Facts from Opinion, and Summon the Challenger.
- Take care of your gut. Eat some yogurt.

CHAPTER 12 | EMOTIONAL DISTORTION

"Leadership's First Commandment: Know Thyself."

Leadership Proverb

"The only way to change someone's mind is to connect with them from the heart."

RASHEED OGUNLARU, British author

Emotional intelligence, casually short-handed to EI or EQ (for Emotional Quotient), refers to an "array of interrelated emotional and social competencies, skills and behaviors that determine how well we understand and express ourselves, get along with others, cope with challenges, and use emotional information in an effective way."[1] According to the *Encyclopedia of Applied Psychology,* there are three major models of emotional intelligence:

1. the Mayer-Salovey model which defines this construct as the ability to perceive, understand, manage and use emotions to facilitate thinking;

2. the Goleman model which views it as an assortment of emotional and social competencies that contribute to managerial performance and leadership; and

3. the Bar-On model which describes EI as an array of interrelated emotional and social competencies, skills and behaviors that impact intelligent behavior.[2]

Essentially, EI is considered a set of dynamic skills, completely separate from personality or IQ, that has been shown to predict many facets of human behavior and workplace performance.[3] The concept of a social intelligence has been studied for over a hundred years, ever since Edward Thorndike noticed in the 1920s that the best factory worker didn't necessarily make the best foreman. He noticed that leadership required a different social skill set that was distinct and separate from the technical proficiency that normally denoted high-level performance in a particular role. Hundreds of research studies within the last decade have shown that enhancing your EI is extremely important because possessing high EI shortens the communication process between the prefrontal cortex and the amygdala, as described in the previous chapter. This leads to quicker reactions, better decisions and more favorable life outcomes.

EI covers a wide range of emotional skills that can be organized into four pillars: Self-Awareness, Self-Expression, Interpersonal and Social Interaction, and Stress Management.[4] Self-awareness is often considered the most vital of the emotional pillars because it indicates the strength of the mental relationship between the prefrontal cortex and the emotional regions of the brain. When you lack emotional self-awareness, an onslaught of negative outcomes is right around the corner. From misinterpretation of social cues to the creation of false memories, a lack of emotional self-awareness can have a profound negative impact on your overall well-being. A lack of emotional self-awareness leads to the fifth domain of the Purposeful Cognition Index. That domain is called Emotional Distortion.

How Memories Are Made

In psychiatry, confabulation is a memory error defined as the production of fabricated, distorted, or misinterpreted memories about oneself or the world, without the conscious intention to deceive.[5] Those who confabulate often develop incorrect memories, ranging from small deviations to extreme fabrications, and are generally steadfast about their recollections even in the face of overwhelming contradictory evidence. As you can imagine, this can drastically affect your overall well-being. So, what causes us to confabulate?

Back in chapter 5 you learned about the weapon focus effect, one of the many studies that show how eyewitness testimony is unreliable. This effect was due to certain memory focusing activities during enhanced levels of stress. Another reason eyewitness testimony, especially that which requires long-term memory recall, is unreliable is because of how memories are created in the brain. More specifically, how memories are labeled as they are being stored and filed away.

The hippocampus is a major component of the brain that belongs to the limbic system. Its main function is to consolidate all pertinent information it has recently acquired and to process that information from short-term memory into long-term memory. MRI scans have shown that in Alzheimer's disease and other forms of dementia that the hippocampus is one of the first brain regions to sustain damage. It is the region of the brain that forms new memories about episodic events that we experience and encodes those memories, storing them away until they are ready for retrieval. It also happens to be neighbors with the amygdala and basal ganglia, since they are all located in the limbic system together.

Think for a moment about the last concert you went to. Do you remember how you felt? Do you remember how excited you were to go or how pumped you were when you heard your favorite song? Were you sad when it ended? Chances are, you remember these feelings very clearly. Now, can you remember what color shirt the lead singer was wearing or the third song that was played? Chances are, you can't. This isn't due to the adult beverages you were most likely consuming either. This is because your emotional regions of the brain (amygdala and basal ganglia) are next-door neighbors to your memory conversion region (hippocampus), while your prefrontal cortex lives in a completely different neighborhood with no direct road to it. This is why you will rarely remember what someone said to you, but you will always remember how they made you feel. Anita Roddick, best known as the founder of The Body Shop, a UK-based cosmetic company, famously said, "whenever we wanted to persuade our staff to support a particular project we always tried to break their hearts." She understood that getting people motivated was simply a function of stoking emotion, not promoting facts or statistics.

A recent study in *Cerebral Cortex* cites that the hippocampus actually does much more than form memories. It also plays an important role in imagining *future* events. When humans construct future scenes in the mind, it occurs in the hippocampus.[6] Other studies have shown that the hippocampus drives brain-wide functions of connectivity in the cerebral cortex, which is the largest region of the mammalian brain. The study cites that:

> The cerebral cortex plays a key role in memory, attention, perception, cognition, awareness, thought, language, and consciousness. In other words, low-frequency activities of the hippocampus can drive the functional integration between different regions of the cerebral cortex and enhance the responsiveness of vision, hearing and touch. These results indicated that the hippocampus can be considered as the heart of the brain, a breakthrough in our knowledge of how the brain works.[7]

Other studies[8] have found that the processes which produce human bravery are also found to occur within the hippocampus. Bravery is oftentimes in response to ambivalence within the mind, where anxiety is telling you to do one thing, but social norms or extenuating circumstances dictate that you should do the opposite. Anxiety is essential for survival because it protects us from harm, but in cases where anxiety runs amok, bravery is when humans act in defiance to that anxiety.

With the hippocampus being the "heart of the brain," it is easy to see how important it is to our overall cognitive functioning. The confluence of many mental processes occurs in this vital region. However, this vital region has a weakness; a kryptonite that drastically reduces its ability to operate correctly, often leading to sharp vicissitudes of fortune. That weakness is Emotional Distortion.

The Source of Emotional Distortion

Emotional Distortion is the fifth domain of the Purposeful Cognition Index and it refers to the *absence of key EI characteristics* which ensure that our hippocampus is operating at an optimal level. Emotional Distortion is the privation of purposeful thinking because it affects our memories about events, spatial awareness, navigation abilities, and reality testing. Put more simply, it is a lack of emotional self-awareness, which drives errors in memory creation and social perception.

Emotional self-awareness is defined as the ability to understand one's own emotions, where they come from, and how they impact our thoughts and actions. It is considered a cornerstone EI skill because it is one of the only skills that is present within all of the major models of EI. When you have high levels of emotional self-awareness, you have an ability to view both positive and negative emotions as vital feedback and you have an ability to differentiate between similar emotions (such as anger and sadness or excitement and anxiety). Those with high levels of emotional self-awareness tend to their feelings, are aware of how their mood impacts others, recognize when they are upset, and understand how emotions impact relationships, social interactions, and overall performance. As mentioned in the previous chapter, almost 64% percent of people have low levels of emotional self-awareness, meaning that they cannot accurately identify emotions as they occur. This leads to Emotional Distortion, and ultimately, dysfunctional hippocampus operation. The hippocampus is besotted with emotionality because the emotions felt during an event often label how the event is stored within long-term memory. Emotional self-awareness ultimately determines how you remember your life's events, since emotions are tied to memory creation. If you are unable to differentiate between slight nuances in emotion due to Emotional Distortion, then your memories could be tainted, false, or flat out untrue (which is the case in confabulation). When you reflect on past events that elicited powerful emotionality, yet cannot distinguish between apoplectic rage or extreme sorrow, or differentiate between cautious optimism or subtle trepidation, how can you be sure that your memories are true? The answer is, you can't. Think of Emotional Distortion as the labeling mechanism for your memories. When it is time to recall an event, the label is the first thing you pull out of the mental drawer, which in turn affects how you recall that event. Your emotions at the time of memory creation label the memory, which are then recalled at a later date. If your emotions are distorted, your recall will be distorted as well.

How to Overcome Your Emotional Distortions

The epigraphs at the beginning of this chapter describe a powerful idea. The idea that we must first seek to know ourselves and the notion that we must protect ourselves against those that use emotions in Machiavellian ways to guide our behavior. Emotional Distortion is the lack of emotional self-awareness, which ultimately drives errors in cognition and incorrect memory labeling. It opens the door for others to easily persuade us and affect our perception of events. Emotional Distortion blocks our ability to think on purpose. When you are unable to discern what your basal ganglia is trying to tell you or you let your fight or flight impulses drive your behavior, you miss the ability to maximize emotional and social competencies that ultimately drive desired business and personal outcomes. Overcoming Emotional Distortion is a function of developing emotional self-awareness. You can eliminate Emotional Distortion by understanding what is causing your emotions and correctly identifying those feelings, so that when your short-term memory is converted to long-term memory, you will have a correct label of the event. Based on my post-doctoral research in emotional intelligence and working with leaders in various industries, I have found three main ways to eliminate Emotional Distortion.

Understand Your Body Map

Remember, you can never eliminate emotions nor would you really want to. What kind of life would that be? Your emotional centers of the brain do not value parsimony; they create an abundance of emotions every minute of every day and are never parsimonious in their constant churn of new feelings. This profusion of emotions is generated long before you first consciously recognize that you are feeling them. The key is to understand how your body feels the emotion *before* your prefrontal cortex thinks about that emotion. Researchers have found that humans can feel emotions in the physical body long before we can actively think about the emotion. Somatosensory feedback is associated with emotional experiences and researchers have discovered a map of bodily sensations that are associated with different emotions, enabling earlier detection of certain feelings.

In a 2014 study published in *Proceedings of the National Academy of Sciences*,[9] scientists discovered that emotional bodily sensations reflect culturally universal sensation patterns. Much like how a smile has universal meaning across cultures, emotional sensation in the body also seems to be universal. The researchers evaluated bodily sensations associated with six basic emotions (anger, fear, disgust, happiness, sadness, and surprise) and seven non-basic emotions (anxiety, love, depression, contempt, pride, shame, and envy) as well as a neutral state. They concluded that "discernible sensation patterns associated with each emotion correspond well with the major changes in physiological functions associated with different emotions." This means that humans have an ability to identify emotions by paying attention to somatosensory feedback and physiological responses to situations. Basically, emotions create somatic sensations in the body that can be used to identify emotional patterns and responses. See the graphic from the study below:

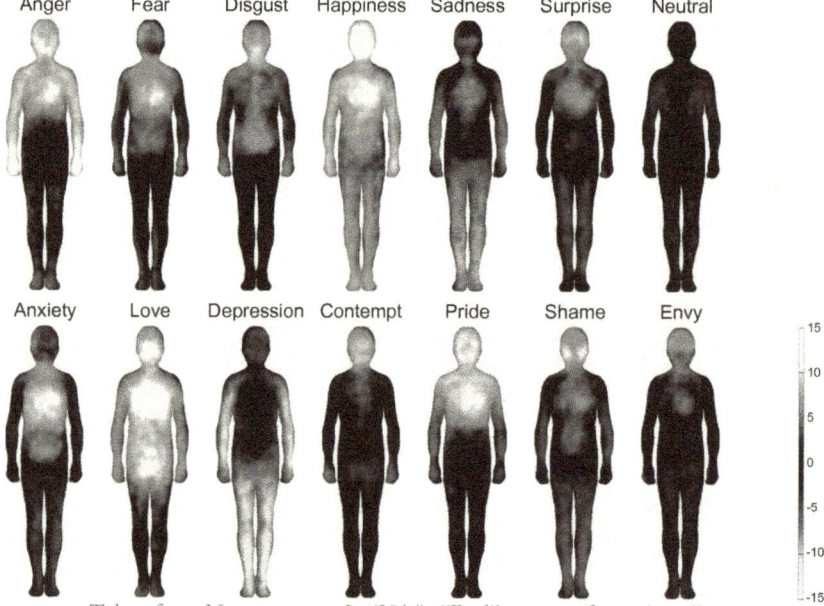

Taken from Nummenmaa, L. (2014). "Bodily maps of emotions."

Since emotionality creates universal physiological responses within humans, this means that we can use these bodily responses to map our own emotions within certain social situations. By paying attention to physiological responses, you can start to create your own body map which identifies emotions before your prefrontal cortex eventually decides to get around to thinking about that emotion. Common physiological responses are:

- Shaking
- Sweating or sweaty palms
- Nausea

- Dry mouth
- Faster breathing
- Heart palpitations
- Panic attacks
- Dizziness
- Butterflies in stomach

When you feel these bodily responses, actively work to identify the emotion that the situation is generating. This will help you create your own body map, which will be essential in developing your own emotional self-awareness. Think of it as a poker tell. In poker, a tell is considered an unconscious event by the individual that signals what behavior is next. The more you play against an opponent, the more you are able to recognize certain patterns (tells) that predict their upcoming deception. The key is to pay attention and link unconscious events (tells) to behaviors (hands played). The same works in mapping your own bodily responses. If you work to create your own body map, you will eventually be able to have actionable insight into raw emotions that you are experiencing well before your prefrontal cortex has a logical thought about that feeling. You are giving your logical brain a preemptive advantage in identifying and categorizing the emotion.

By creating your own body map you will be able to have an "additional" label when you convert the memories of the event to long-term storage, since you will have a physiological response that coincides with your cognitive label. Emotional feelings are associated with discrete, yet partially overlapping maps of bodily sensations, which ultimately frame your emotional experience.[10] For example, decreased limb sensation has been associated with sadness, increased sensation in the upper limbs has been associated with anger, sensations around the throat and stomach have been associated with disgust, sensations in the chest have been associated with fear and surprise, while total body sensations have been associated with happiness. Understanding your physiological responses will ultimately lead to better emotional processing and emotional self-awareness. Both of which lead to the elimination of Emotional Distortion because you are correctly labeling memories as they are encoded.

Label Your Emotions

Robert Plutchik, an American psychologist who authored more than 260 articles on the study of emotions, created a psychoevolutionary theory of basic emotions. In his book, *Emotion – A Psychoevolutionary Synthesis*, he describes ten postulates upon which he posited emotions are based:[11]

1. The concept of emotion is applicable to all evolutionary levels and applies to all animals including humans.
2. Emotions have an evolutionary history and have evolved various forms of expression in different species.
3. Emotions served an adaptive role in helping organisms deal with key survival issues posed by the environment.
4. Despite different forms of expression of emotions in different species, there are certain common elements, or prototype patterns, that can be identified.
5. There is a small number of basic, primary, or prototype emotions.
6. All other emotions are mixed or derivative states; that is, they occur as combinations, mixtures, or compounds of the primary emotions.
7. Primary emotions are hypothetical constructs or idealized states whose properties and characteristics can only be inferred from various kinds of evidence.
8. Primary emotions can be conceptualized in terms of pairs of polar opposites.
9. All emotions vary in their degree of similarity to one another.
10. Each emotion can exist in varying degrees of intensity or levels of arousal.

From these ten postulates, Plutchik's research claims that there are approximately 34,000 distinguishable emotions that humans can experience. 34,000 emotions would be impossible to categorize individually so he distilled them into eight primary emotions – anger, fear, sadness, disgust, surprise, anticipation, trust, and joy.[12] From this, he created a wheel of emotions that illustrates bipolar emotions: surprise vs. anticipation, trust vs. disgust, anger vs. fear, and joy vs. sadness. His graphic illustrates these eight primary emotions and also provides labels for various intensities of these emotions.[13]

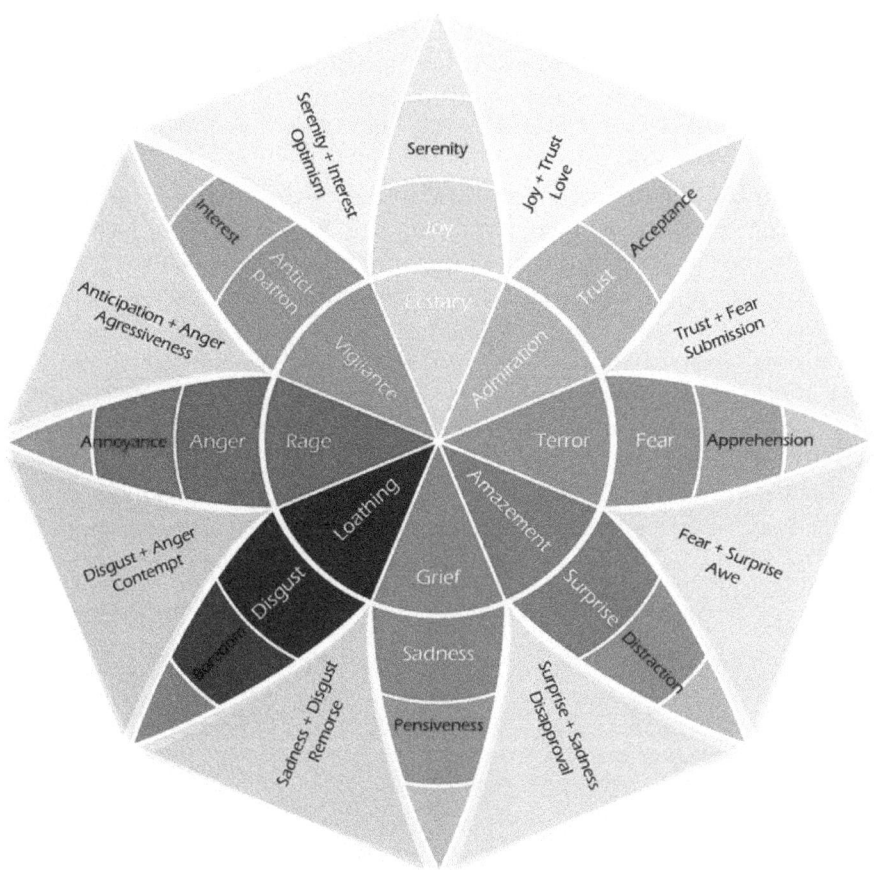

Building upon this wheel, Tiffany Watt Smith, author of *The Book of Human Emotions*, expanded upon the model to create a list of emotions that totals 154.[14] No wonder why humans have a hard time differentiating between the slight nuances of emotions. With so many emotions available to us, how can we know exactly what it is that we are feeling at any given time? The key is that we have to actively work to label these emotions at the moment they occur.

Researchers at UCLA published a 2012 study which claims that naming or labeling your emotions *as they occur* reduces the impact that they have on you.[15] Psychologists asked 88 people who were afraid of spiders to voluntarily hold a giant tarantula. The subjects were divided into four groups. The first group was asked to describe the emotions they felt as they approached the sizable arachnid, for example, saying "I am *anxious* or *terrified* of this spider." The second group was asked to speak in more neutral terms that did not convey their fear but were designed to minimize the experience itself, such as "I am not afraid of this tiny spider; it can't hurt me." The third group was asked to say something completely irrelevant and the fourth group was asked to not say anything at all. The researchers found that the first group was able to get the closest to the spider and exhibited the least amount of emotional arousal when doing so. The participants that labeled their fear and anxiety were able to reduce the effects of the powerful emotionality that the situation generated. The researchers concluded that labeling emotions as they occurred was a powerful mechanism which reduced the overall potency of the emotion, allowing for increased performance in the given task.[16]

The scientists concluded that the group that was able to get the closest to the spider exhibited "affect labeling." The participants who used a larger number of negative words to describe their emotions did better in terms of how close they were willing to get to the spider and in their physiological skin-sweat response. But why does this happen? Why does labeling emotions, which is essentially the practice of pairing verbal tags with emotional senses, reduce the effects of those negative emotions? The answer lies in the portion of the brain known as the right ventrolateral prefrontal cortex, a region that is involved in labeling our feelings and reactions but is also associated with regulating our emotional responses.

A 2007 study published in *Psychological Science* found that affect labeling disrupts amygdala activity in response to affective stimuli.[17] The researchers state the following:

> Putting feelings into words (affect labeling) has long been thought to help manage negative emotional experiences; however, the mechanisms by which affect labeling produces this benefit remain largely unknown. Recent neuroimaging studies suggest a possible neurocognitive pathway for this process, but methodological limitations of previous studies have prevented strong inferences from being drawn. A functional magnetic resonance imaging study of affect labeling was conducted to remedy these limitations. The results indicated that affect labeling, relative to other forms of encoding, diminished the response of the amygdala and other limbic regions to negative emotional images. Additionally, affect labeling produced increased activity in a single brain region, right ventrolateral prefrontal cortex (RVLPFC). Finally, RVLPFC and amygdala activity during affect labeling were inversely correlated, a relationship that was mediated by activity in medial prefrontal cortex (MPFC). These results suggest that affect labeling may diminish emotional reactivity along a pathway from RVLPFC to MPFC to the amygdala.[18]

Essentially, the researchers discovered that affect labeling created a neurological response within the amygdala that reduced the effects of the emotions being produced. The inverse was also true. If there was no affect labeling as emotions were being produced, the negative emotions exhibited maximum potency.

Labeling your emotions has a dual benefit. By labeling your feelings (instead of trying to minimize the situation like the second group did in the tarantula study) you get into the habit of properly identifying emotions as they occur, which boosts your emotional self-awareness. You also reduce the powerful effects of negative emotionality by using affect labeling to keep the formidable amygdala at bay. This will reduce physiological responses that indicate anxiety or fear and allow you to perform better on tasks.

Recognize That There Are No Bad Emotions

The leitmotif throughout this book has been the concept of psychological dualism. Most of the research in psychology throughout all of human history has promulgated this dichotomy, with notions of the conscious vs. the unconscious or the bright side vs. the dark side. However, when dealing with Emotional Distortion, a proven technique that helps foster emotional self-awareness is to eliminate the idea that emotions are good and bad. If you want to eliminate Emotional Distortion, *all* emotions should be viewed as good.

Think for a moment about the emotions that we normally consider bad: sadness, grief, disgust, loathing, anger, rage, terror, or fear, to name a few. We develop an antagonistic relationship with these emotions, which is certainly understandable because they are difficult to experience. Even within those that willingly engage in psychic masochism, negative emotions can still be arduous. This leads us to suppress the emotions, which you now know is extremely detrimental to overall mental and physical health. Instead, you should view bad emotions as data. They are providing you valuable information. What is that fear telling you? What is that anger telling you? Remember, the amygdala and the fight or flight responses it produces are some of the oldest evolutionary processes within the human brain that are designed to protect us from harm. Why would we ignore warning signs that are designed to help us, simply because we don't like how the warning signs make us feel? That is similar to not heeding a verbal warning to get out of the ocean because a shark is coming, simply because you don't like the sound of the lifeguard's voice.

Emotions are neurohormones that are secreted as we perceive the world around us.[19] They are used to label our perceptions and to motivate us to take a specific action, such as fight or flight. For example, fear tells us that imminent danger is near and that all of our available focus should shift toward avoiding that danger. Sadness gives us insight into what we care about, what we love, and how it feels when we lose it. When you are emotionally self-aware, you are tuned into these emotions and also tuned into what they are trying to tell you. If you believe that emotions are bad and you actively suppress them, you might miss the shrill-voiced lifeguard telling you about the shark in the water.

The key is to think of the emotion as trying to communicate a *need*. What is it that your body needs at the exact moment that you are feeling the powerful negative emotion? If you view the emotion as bad and ignore it, you are essentially ignoring a need. Remember back to Maslow's Hierarchy of Needs – the path to self-actualization comes from consistently meeting base-level needs and then subsequently meeting higher-level needs. Joshua, Freeman, CEO of Six Seconds – The Emotional Intelligence Network, suggests following these three core principles to ensure that you view all emotions as good, or at least, view all emotions as serving a vital purpose:[20]

> 1. Emotions are signals that serve a function. They should not be "blindly obeyed," but nor should they be ignored.
>
> 2. There is an innate connection between needs and emotions. In trying to make sense of your own or another's feelings, consider that they might be signals about a core need.
>
> 3. Although feelings can be uncomfortable and overwhelming, resist the urge to judge them – and to judge yourself and others for having them. Instead, consider that each feeling is part of a larger story, a story of what's truly most important.

Eliminating the duality which views emotions as good or bad will ensure that you don't inadvertently, or purposely, avoid bad emotions because they are unpleasant. Remember, just because you ignore the emotions, doesn't mean they go away. The emotional energy is built up over time and manifests itself into undesirable behaviors and outcomes. Viewing all emotions as good will enhance your emotional self-awareness because you will pay attention to what each emotion is trying to communicate to you, which will ultimately lead to an elimination of Emotional Distortion. As the Roman philosopher Seneca once said, "let tears flow of their own accord: their flowing is not inconsistent with inward peace and harmony."

In Sum

- Emotional Distortion is the fifth domain of the Purposeful Cognition Index and it refers to the *absence of key EI characteristics* which ensure that our hippocampus is operating at an optimal level. Emotional Distortion is the privation of purposeful thinking because it affects our memories about events, spatial awareness, navigation abilities, and reality testing. Put more simply, it is a lack of emotional self-awareness, which drives errors in memory creation and social perception.
- There are three major models of EI: the Mayer-Salovey model, the Goleman model and the Bar-On model. All three view emotional self-awareness as the cornerstone of emotional and social intelligence.
- Confabulation is a memory error defined as the production of fabricated, distorted, or misinterpreted memories about oneself or the world, without the conscious intention to deceive. Those who confabulate often develop incorrect memories, ranging from small deviations to extreme fabrications, and are generally steadfast about their recollections even in the face of overwhelming contradictory evidence.
- The hippocampus is a major component of the brain that belongs to the limbic system. Its main function is to consolidate all pertinent information it has recently acquired and to process that information from short-term memory into long-term memory. It is often referred to as "the heart of the brain."
- Emotional self-awareness is defined as the ability to understand one's own emotions, where they come from, and how they impact our thoughts and actions. It is considered a cornerstone EI skill because it is one of the only skills that is present within all of the major models of EI.
- Overcoming Emotional Distortion is a function of developing emotional self-awareness. You can eliminate Emotional Distortion by understanding what is causing your emotions and correctly identifying those feelings, so that when your short-term memory is converted to long-term memory, you will have a correct label of the event.
- Understanding your physiological responses will ultimately lead to better emotional processing and emotional self-awareness. Both of which lead to the elimination of Emotional Distortion because you are correctly labeling memories as they are encoded.
- Labeling your emotions has a dual benefit. By labeling your feelings (instead of trying to minimize the situation like the

second group did in the tarantula study) you get into the habit of properly identifying emotions as they occur, which boosts your emotional self-awareness. You also reduce the powerful effects of negative emotionality by using affect labeling to keep the formidable amygdala at bay.

- Viewing all emotions as good will enhance your emotional self-awareness because you will pay attention to what each emotion is trying to communicate to you, which will ultimately lead to an elimination of Emotional Distortion.

CHAPTER 13 | PART II SUMMARY

"The beginning is the most important part of the work."

PLATO

"All achievements, all earned riches, have their beginning in an idea."

NAPOLEON HILL, American author

Part II centered around one core idea – the notion that humans can develop an ability to think on purpose. Owning our own thoughts, or thinking on purpose, is the key to reducing our Inner Passivity, blunting our Inner Aggression, establishing an internal Locus of Control, and eliminating Cognitive and Emotional Distortions.

Our Inner Passivity creates a wide range of reactions to situations where we let life pass us by and take things for granted. Inner Passivity creates overwhelming feelings of apathy, drawing us into states of self-doubt and indifference, often disguised as a seductive languor.

Our Inner Aggression does quite the opposite, constantly chastising, berating, and admonishing us, playing on our deepest and darkest insecurities and using those to block our ability to achieve life's goals. These two unconscious states manifest into conscious behaviors, creating a bevy of symptoms that create undesired outcomes in our lives.

Locus of Control is the psychological construct that refers to how strongly we believe that we have control over the events and experiences of our lives. The ancient Egyptians believed in a God of fate and destiny. Shai (pronounced as Shay) was believed to be born with each person and was responsible for the protection or misfortune of each individual. They believed that Shai, along with other Gods, completely controlled all the events of their lives. Other more modern religions like Judaism and Christianity believe that free will is a product of the intrinsic human soul and that God created human beings specifically with free will in mind. In modern psychology, an internal Locus of Control, or belief in free will, has been linked to greater happiness and fulfillment in life.

Cognitive Distortions, which are faulty beliefs about ourselves, our friends, the present, or our past or future, cloud our thinking and alter our ability to think clearly, or think on purpose. They produce anxiety, one of the most powerful human emotions and also one of the most destructive. Finding ways to eliminate Cognitive Distortions are at the root of Cognitive Behavioral Therapy, a powerful set of proven techniques that have helped millions of people strive for mental health without the use of medications or drugs.

Emotional Distortions result from a lack of emotional self-awareness. Emotional Distortion is the antithesis of purposeful thinking because it affects our memories about events, spatial awareness, navigation abilities, and reality testing. When our emotions are heavily distorted they can drive errors in memory creation and color how we perceive reality. Our emotions are warning signals from our unconscious psyche to our conscious selves. If we ignore these emotions or these feelings become distorted, we are not able to heed warnings that can help us navigate social situations effectively, protect us from psychological harm, or even physically save our lives.

These five domains all have one thing in common that has been alluded to many times thus far in this book. They all possess a duality to them, a bimodal attribute which contains two maxima. We are either passive or active, aggressive or calm, external or internal, distorted or clear. Remember back at the beginning of the book, I highlighted that a common theme was present within all the research pertaining to the psyche – the notion that the mind seeks truth, accuracy, and fidelity on the one hand, yet has a deliberate desire to behave in unreasonable ways on the other. The mind has a proclivity for this duality. The mind seems to have an isomorphic ambivalence about its preferred default state. This means that it is up to us to purposely drive the desired state that we want. We must think on purpose.

Remember back to René Descartes, who posited the notion of "I think, therefore, I am." He claimed that thoughts make us real. Solipsism, the philosophical idea that only one's mind is sure to exist, postulates that everything outside of one's mind is unsure. According to Descartes, everything that we gain from sensory experience could be erroneous and could very well be a hallucination (or a simulation). Jonathan Haidt said it best in his book, the *Happiness Hypothesis*. He wrote:

> In philosophy class, I often came across the idea that the world is an illusion. I never really knew what it meant, although it sounded deep. But after two decades studying moral psychology, I think I finally get it. The anthropologist Clifford Geertz wrote that "man is an animal suspended in webs of significance that he himself has spun." That is, the world we live in is not really one made of rocks, trees, and

physical objects; it is a world of insults, opportunities, status symbols, betrayals, saints, and sinners. All of these are human creations which, though real in their own way, are not real in the way that rocks and trees are real. These human creations are like fairies in J.M. Barrie's Peter Pan: they exist only if you believe in them. They are the Matrix (from the movie of that name); they are a consensual hallucination.[1]

Descartes expanded upon this position by looking at the world through incertitude. Referred to as Cartesian doubt, he advocated the philosophical position of methodological skepticism, theorizing that humans can only be completely sure of their own, singular existence, by first doubting all beliefs and then determining which beliefs could be *certain* were true. Via this method, the only belief that is certain to be true is that we exist, because we have thoughts. Nothing else is certain. Thinking makes us real. From this, Descartes proposed two arguments, the dream and the demon.[2]

The dream argument is the notion that the act of dreaming provides preliminary evidence that the senses of perception that we use to distinguish between reality and dreams cannot be trusted, leading to the conclusion that we should be skeptical of any state that is dependent on our senses. Essentially, there is no way to differentiate between dreaming or being awake. He surmised that while one dreams, one does not normally realize they are dreaming, so wouldn't the opposite also be true? Sometimes referred to as the "Zhuangzi paradox," this is a concept found in many philosophies such as Daoism, Buddhism, and simulation hypothesis.[3]

The evil demon, or malicious demon, argument suggests that an omnipotent demon is responsible for our entire existence. This would be similar to the machines in *The Matrix*, who run the simulation that humans do not know they are in. Under this argument, Descartes wrote in *Meditation On First Philosophy* that because of this, we could not trust our senses, because an all-powerful demon shaped our experience by deceiving our perceptions.

Within both of these arguments, we again see a duality of states. Within various philosophies throughout time, ones that are either rooted in doubt or true knowledge, the mind's dyad dominates the notion of human existentialism. This leads us to a modern concept which encapsulates the notion of duality that is ubiquitous within psychological concepts and philosophical teachings throughout history.

The Bright Side and the Dark Side

The bright side and the dark side are what modern psychologists refer to when they speak of the conscious and the unconscious. Dr. Robert Hogan, an American psychologist who is known for his innovations in personality testing, leadership development and organizational effectiveness, has authored more than 300 journal articles and countless books on personality psychology about conscious and unconscious states of mind. In 1990, he published a paper titled "The Dark Side of Charisma," where he discussed the difference between good and bad leaders with respect to their bright and dark sides:

> They have charisma...these are flawed managers, whose glittering image masks a dark destructive side...dark-side traits are conceptualized as extreme extensions of the "bright-side" traits of the Five-Factor Model that often have counterproductive effects. We predict which dark-side traits will be related to ratings of "too little" and "too much" of four leader behaviors and how low levels of Emotional Stability may accentuate the relationship between dark-side traits and excessive leader behavior.[4]

Essentially, he claimed that the dark side creates an imbalance (too little or too much) of the traits normally exhibited by the bright side. In a later article where he reflects on his 1990 article, he writes:

> The bright side of personality describes people's performance when they are paying attention to the normal rules of self-presentation, when they are controlling the way others perceive them and, therefore, trying to create a good impression. The dark side describes people's behavior when they are *not paying attention* and/or don't care about creating a good impression; this happens when they are emotionally upset, when they are stressed or ill, when they are under the influence of chemical substances, or when they are simply being themselves. The dark side often emerges when individuals are dealing with someone whom they perceive as having a lesser status than they do – such as subordinate employees. The bright side represents maximal performance whereas the dark side represents typical performance. *People move continuously and unconsciously back and forth between the two sides of personality*. In essence, the bright side reflects faking and the dark side represents the real person. As Freud would say, however, the real person is usually something to be avoided. Please note two additional points about the dark side. First, it doesn't refer to hidden psychic desires that suddenly emerge under potentiating circumstances (like a full moon). Rather, the dark side refers

to *how people behave when they are not paying attention*. Second, most people are unaware of how they behave when they are just being themselves. In this sense, *therefore, the dark side really is unconscious* – because it is outside conscious awareness. But the secrets of the dark side are readily accessible because they are captured by a person's reputation – other people can tell you about your dark side. What you do with that information is up to you.[5]

Psychologist Daniel Kahneman wrote a best-selling book on the subject in 2011 called *Thinking: Fast and Slow*. In collaboration with Amos Tversky, he summarized decades of research on his central thesis of the dichotomy between two systems of thought. He posits that System 1 is a fast, instinctive and emotional system, where System 2 is a slow, effortful, logical, calculating system. System 1 is responsible for intuition and based on simple mental rules (heuristics). System 2 is the rational center that is based in logic. Essentially, Kahneman was describing the relationship highlighted earlier between the amygdala and prefrontal cortex. Examples he provides to highlight this dichotomy between systems are shown here:

Things System 1 can do:

- localize the source of a specific sound
- complete the phrase "war and ..."
- display disgust when seeing a gruesome image
- solve 2+2=?

Things System 2 can do:

- give someone your phone number
- park into a tight parking space
- determine the price/quality ratio of two washing machines
- determine the validity of a complex logical reasoning
- solve 17 × 24
- brace yourself before the start of a sprint
- point your attention towards the clowns at the circus[6]

The whole premise of his book is that there is a fast system and a slow system, and that understanding the differences and relationship between the fast and the slow, the conscious and the unconscious, were vital to purposeful thinking.

Jonathan Haidt developed another prominent body of knowledge on the subject of mind duality in two of his books, *The Happiness Hypothesis* and *The Righteous Mind*. In these texts, he elaborates on a metaphor that corresponds to Kahneman's Systems 1 and 2 thinking, providing us the notion of an emotional side and rational side of the brain. The analogy he uses is of an elephant and a rider. The elephant represents the emotional side of the brain while the rider represents the rational side. His analogy is simple; the rider is a more intelligent being and attempts to control the elephant but the elephant does what it wants to. The elephant (emotion) goes where it wants to go, regardless of how much the rider (rationality) commands, directs or punishes the animal. It times of disagreement, the elephant always wins. It is only when the two work in tandem does maximum efficiency and harmony occur. The rider has the ability to motivate the elephant toward the intended path, through rewards such as carrots, but in the end, the bigger, dumber, stronger elephant determines their ultimate direction. The rider is infinitely smarter and aware of his existence, while the elephant may not even be aware of his own existence. Even so, the elephant always wins in disputes, because the rider has no access to the *real* causes of the elephant's behavior.[7]

Predating Haidt, Hogan, and Kahneman, Carl Jung built upon Freud's theory of the id and created the shadow archetype. Jung believed that the shadow, or dark side, included everything outside the light of human consciousness. He viewed the shadow as the unknown dark side of the personality that was instinctive, irrational, and the source of decision paralysis and ultimate confusion within the conscious human psyche. He claimed that the life-long struggle of the individual was to *develop and retain awareness of the shadow while not identifying with it*. A delicate balance that drove some mad if they failed to keep distance and descended into darkness.[8]

This leads us to Part III. You have learned all of the psychological principles to date that have led the treatment of mental health to its current state. You have learned about the five domains that block our ability to think on purpose, the power of the unconscious mind, and the supremacy of our emotional brain over our rational brain. A theme that is prevalent in all of the different perspectives and theories is the notion that we must somehow unveil the darkness that resides within us while ensuring that it does not seduce us. We must shine a light on the sinister forces within our mind, but not identify with them.

Part III will review three core areas that need to be maximized in order to achieve success in life: being a leader, developing relationships, and living in the present. The next section will highlight how each of the five domains negatively affects these core areas, provide you strategies to eliminate these domains and reveal how you can take the Purposeful Cognition Index assessment.

Part III

CHAPTER 14 | LEADING ON PURPOSE

"A leader is a dealer in hope."

NAPOLEON BONAPARTE, French Emperor

"Leadership is a choice, not a position."

STEPHEN COVEY, American author

Are leaders born or are leaders made? Again, the duality of nature vs. nurture presents itself! While there are certain innate qualities that need to be present for a leader to thrive, leadership is considered a skill set that can be developed and maximized over time. For those of you who may not agree, I'll ask it another way. Are there any naturally born pilots? Of course not! You certainly need to be born with two eyes and a certain attitude to be successful, but you also need to be taught specific skills to operate a machine at Mach 6. Leadership is the same way.

There are many different paths one can take to learn the skills of leadership as there is not a single, stand-alone way to lead others. Everyone possesses a different leadership style, which is a product of how you were taught to lead combined with what your natural tendencies are. Leadership style is defined as the *way a person uses power* to lead other individuals, groups, or organizations toward a common objective. According to research within leadership theory, there are a few main styles that are omnipresent within academic research and practical business application.

Autocratic (also known as authoritarian) leadership is a style where all of the power resides with a single individual. The leader holds all authority and responsibility, and all decision-making goes through the autocratic leader. It is considered an outdated leadership style due to its uncollaborative nature. One of the more famous examples of autocratic leadership that led to one's demise is the Roman emperor Caligula. He was a ruler that was considered insane, egomaniacal, capricious, and sadistic, and was the first Roman emperor that was assassinated. Many historians attribute his death to a disdain for his autocratic leadership style. Most of the literature[1] describes his quest for avarice and total control as the two central causes of his ultimate downfall.

Democratic leadership is the obverse of autocratic leadership, where subordinates are heavily involved in decision making. The democratic leader has final say but chooses to delegate authority, communicate upward, downward and sideways throughout the organization, and encourage fairness, creativity, and honesty. Indra Nooyi, the former CEO of PepsiCo, is considered a leader who consistently showcased this style of leadership during her time leading the company, often getting heavily involved at a personal level with employees to solicit as many ideas and opinions as possible.

Charismatic leadership is a style where leaders create powerful self-images that draw others close to them. These leaders influence others by projecting strengths of their personality, exuding passion and boosting motivation among the followers. Charismatic leaders manifest their power through their persona, which sometimes leads to an inflated sense of ego. Often mercurial in nature, charismatic leaders tend to operate "off the cuff" and tend to focus on the specific tasks that will bolster their self-image, even if it isn't what is best for the organization. There are many examples of charismatic leaders throughout history, with some notable examples such as Winston Churchill, Adolph Hitler, Fidel Castro, Vladimir Lenin, and Napoleon Bonaparte.

Laissez-Faire leadership is a style that is based on trust. This type of leader delegates responsibility to others to make decisions, allows team members to work at their own pace and provides maximum flexibility for workers to thrive. The Laissez-Faire leader believes in the self-actualization of others as a mechanism that should be fostered by allowing them room and space to operate. Mahatma Gandhi is considered one of the most famous within this leadership style because he believed that people should lead by example and be the change they wish to see in the world around them.

Transformational leadership is a style that promotes engagement, inspiration and striving for an ultimate vision. The transformational leader is known to be a visionary and is confident in his view of the future, which is often very different from the known present. He is resolute in his idea of how things should be and enables those around him to help achieve that purpose. Steve Jobs, the former CEO of Apple, was known for challenging employees to always think bigger and inspired them to be extraordinary.

Servant leadership is a style where the leader's primary purpose is to enable others to perform their best. Often operating in the shadows, those who are servant leaders believe in removing roadblocks for employees and finding ways to maximize the talent around them. The servant leader will often deflect praise and recognition to her team. Martin Luther King, Jr. is often considered one of the greatest servant leaders because he did not want to be the leader of the Civil Rights Movement in the US, but he knew that there was a need for equality so he put other people's needs ahead of his own.

All of these leadership styles are vastly different from each other in terms of their focus and application.[2] They are different in their approaches to people management, focus, environment, delegation, responsibility, and accountability. However, there is a single element that is universally transitive across all the styles. They each require the leader to *act with purpose* to showcase their *authentic* selves. Followers will not follow unless a leader is authentic.

Authenticity is the cardinal attribute that bolsters leadership power and promotes followership across all forms of leadership. If you want to persuade someone to follow you into battle, they have to know that you are being authentic and believe in the cause yourself. We often judge a person's authenticity by the level of passion and commitment they have for what they are saying and doing. Stephen Joseph, author of *Authentic: How to be yourself and why it matters*, writes that authentic people possess a certain number of common characteristics that communicate psychological maturity and optimal cognitive functioning. They:[3]

1. Have realistic perceptions of reality.

2. Are accepting of themselves and other people.

3. Are thoughtful.

4. Have a non-hostile sense of humor.

5. Can express their emotions freely and clearly.

6. Are open to learning from their mistakes.

7. Understand their motivations.

Joseph suggests that these characteristics are universal across all cultures and leadership styles. All seven of these can be obtained by thinking on purpose. By eliminating Emotional Distortion, you will have realistic perceptions of reality and develop an ability to express emotions freely. Eliminating Cognitive Distortion will allow you to be thoughtful and accepting of yourself and others. Minimizing Inner Aggression will help you develop a non-hostile sense of humor and develop an ability to learn from your mistakes. Reducing Inner Passivity will help you understand where your motivations truly come from.

If one is not true to oneself, they are considered to be unauthentic. No matter what leadership style you subscribe to, none of them will be effective without authenticity, even if you display high levels of passion and commitment. Unauthentic people show unhealthy defensive functioning and psychological immaturity in times of mounting stress. According to Joseph, inauthentic people:

1. Are self-deceptive and unrealistic in their perceptions of reality.

2. Look to others for approval and to feel valued.

3. Are judgmental of other people.

4. Do not think things through clearly.

5. Have a hostile sense of humor.

6. Are unable to express their emotions freely and clearly.

7. Are not open to learning from their mistakes.

8. Do not understand their motivations.

You can easily see how Inner Passivity, Inner Aggression, Locus of Control, Cognitive Distortion, and Emotional Distortion can all create these characteristics if they are left unchecked. Developing an ability to think on purpose ensures that you are working toward the characteristics that bolster authenticity.

What Leaders Do

Jack Welch, the former CEO of General Electric and one of the most influential leaders of all time, wrote in his 2009 book *Winning* about eight rules of effective leadership. These rules are listed as simple tasks, but are in and of themselves paradoxes, because they can be contradictory, ambiguous, or differing when you read them all together. As an example, one of his rules says that you should show energy and passion while showing a constant can-do attitude, while another rule says to constantly question your people. One rule says to act with authority while another says to admit to mistakes. The key is knowing which of these rules to implement at the right time.

The list in its entirety is not meant to be applied all at once to every situation, but to be strategically applied individually, yet also simultaneously. Hence the paradox. Knowing how and when to apply these rules is easier when you have developed an ability to think on purpose and can lead with authenticity. Thinking on purpose will give you the cognitive agility to correctly apply the proper combination of these rules while being genuine and sincere. That is where true power comes from. Below are the eight rules of leadership with additional steps of how thinking on purpose can help you master each rule:[4]

1. Leaders relentlessly upgrade their team, using every encounter as an opportunity to evaluate, coach, and build self-confidence. You should never be static and believe that your team is the best it can be. Even professional sports teams that win championships have extremely busy off-seasons, upgrading the coaching staff and tweaking line-ups. After the Washington Capitals finally ended their Stanley Cup drought and won in 2018, they changed their head coach and shuffled their roster in the off-season. Jack says that you have to do these three things:

1. Consistently evaluate talent to make sure people are in the right jobs. Provide support to those who are and move out the ones who aren't.

2. Coach, guide, and help people improve their performance in every way possible.

3. Build self-confidence of everyone on your team through encouragement, authenticity, and recognition.

Each of these can be achieved by developing an ability to think on purpose. Evaluating talent is a tough task, and those who suffer from Cognitive or Emotional Distortions will have a difficult time assessing the talent of those around them. Being able to remain objective and do what is best for the company is difficult with distorted thinking. Inner Passivity and Inner Aggression crush your ability to coach others and build your own self-confidence, so if these domains are running amok within your psyche, how can you coach and build self-confidence in others? Self-confidence is emotional energy that snowballs throughout an organization as it builds. Much like how the flight attendant tells you to first secure your oxygen mask before you help others, leadership is the same way. If you don't take care of yourself first, you won't be able to help or lead others. Leading on purpose ensures that your talent assessments are objective and socially responsible, increases your ability to coach and help others self-actualize, and gives you the tools to radiate the type of authenticity that will create infectious self-confidence within the organization.

Purposeful Cognition domains which affect this leadership rule –
Inner Passivity, Inner Aggression, Cognitive Distortion, and Emotional Distortion.

2. Leaders make sure people not only see their vision, but they also live and breathe it. A vision, by itself, is not real. A vision is something that you want to achieve in the future that you do not currently have now. By definition, it is distinct and dissimilar from the present. The present is real; the future is unknown. It is important to set a vision because it is a collection of goals that are organized into one achievable outcome that will move your organization from the current state toward a desired future state. A powerful vision can create instant psychological inertia that propels an organization toward a better future. But as with most future-thinking, communicating a vision can often promote feelings of anxiety within the organization. Leaders who establish a powerful vision also need to be equipped with the tools to ensure that future-thinking doesn't also create organizational anxiety.

Leaders who wish to master this rule should first ensure that their own anxiety isn't baked into the organizational vision. Remember that anxiety is defined as the anticipation of future threat; it is distinguished from fear, which is the emotional response to a real or perceived imminent threat. Your vision for the future of those you lead should be grounded in optimism and positivity, not a defensible position for a future perceived threat. If you ensure that your vision is geared toward achieving the desired business outcome rather than geared toward avoiding future peril or danger, anxiety won't have an ability to weave itself into your divination. Developing an ability to lead on purpose will allow you to become a visionary leader, one who does not operate in the present due to a future fear, but due to a potential opportunity.

> *Purposeful Cognition domains which affect this leadership rule –*
> Inner Passivity, Inner Aggression, Locus of Control, Cognitive Distortion, and Emotional Distortion.

3. Leaders get into everyone's skin, exuding positive energy and optimism. A powerful contagion permeates from the leadership of an organization. "The leader's mood, is for lack of a better term, catching."[5] A leader's mood spreads throughout the organization and affects the motivation and attitudes of workers throughout the entire company. A study done by the California Institute of Technology claims:

> Our belief as to whether we will likely succeed or fail at a given task -- and the consequences of winning or losing -- directly affects the levels of neural effort put forth in movement-planning circuits in the human cortex, according to a new brain-imaging study by neuroscientists.[6]

The researchers used fMRI images to conclude that positive neural activity preceding goal-directed behaviors led to increased output over negative neural activity. Essentially, if you think you can, it creates a self-fulfilling prophecy via increased mental activity and output that enables the desired outcome vs. if you think you can't. Being positive and optimistic enhances brain function which allows you to achieve your goals easier. This optimism is infectious within organizations, and it all begins with the leader. Understanding that you can affect the neural activity and output of others simply by being positive and optimistic is an essential quality of leadership. Leaders with an internal Locus of Control and minimal levels of Emotional Distortion are able to perform this flawlessly.

> *Purposeful Cognition domains which affect this leadership rule –* Locus of Control, Cognitive Distortion, and Emotional Distortion.

4. Leaders establish trust with candor, transparency, and credit.

Throughout this book, you have read about the various mental and emotional processes that produce feelings of trust and how this feeling is accelerated when you feel safe and believe that your voice is being heard. You learned how oxytocin in the brain produces feelings of trust. As a leader, if you can replicate those feelings within others via candor, transparency, and credit, you will develop a lifelong following of loyal supporters that will follow you into any battle.

Trust is important because people do their best work within environments that *do not punish failure*. Think about any innovation that has occurred within the last 100 years. They all started as a "crazy" statement that someone *had to feel safe enough to proclaim* within a room full of their peers.

> "Hey, imagine if these buggies could run on their own, without horses?"

> "Listen, what if people could talk to each other across town with a device that they hold in their hand?"

> "This might sound crazy, but what if all of the libraries in the world were accessible on one device in your living room?"

> "I have this crazy notion that the Earth rotates around the Sun, not vice versa... thoughts?"

Inventors of world-changing technology and ideas had to feel safe enough to mentally develop the idea and then publicly propose it to their peers. If the innovator felt that he could not trust his peers, felt that he would be ridiculed, or believed that leadership would take credit for the idea, they simply would never have proposed the idea in the first place. I have consulted with many organizations where workers were scared to suggest new ideas, due to a lack of trust in leadership. This led to ideas never being socialized. A true leader will create an environment where sincerity is valued, credit is recognized publicly, and the culture is oozing with such optimistic transparency that workers will have no reservations about proposing wild ideas. Developing an ability to lead on purpose, specifically eliminating Inner Passivity and Inner Aggression, will ensure that your leadership style avoids the combative and focuses on the collaborative, which will permeate throughout the organization.

Purposeful Cognition domains which affect this leadership rule – Inner Passivity and Inner Aggression.

5. Leaders have the courage to make unpopular decisions and gut calls. Jack was onto something when he created this rule. Leaders are great at building consensus and collaborating with others to reach organizational decisions, but leaders should also be equipped with an ability to go against the grain, follow their gut, and make a decision that goes against consensus. Jack writes:

> Much has been written about the mystery of the gut, but it's really just pattern recognition, isn't it? You've seen something so many times that you *just know* what's going on this time...leaders are faced with gut calls all the time...you've got no proof, but you've got a real uh-oh feeling in your stomach. Listen to your gut. It's telling you something.[7]

Luckily, you now know that a gut feeling is actually the basal ganglia trying to communicate life wisdom to you. Ensuring that your thoughts are not distorted and that your emotional intelligence is highly developed will enable you to listen to your gut and make the difficult calls that leaders must make. Possessing a high emotional intelligence also helps you develop the courage needed to make those calls.

A 2018 study by Stanford Medicine investigated what neural activities occurred before displays of fear and acts of courage within mice. The mice were subjected to threatening stimuli that resembled a looming predator while certain cells in their brains were being stimulated. The researchers found that there is a mechanism referred to as the "brain switch." The brain switch comes from two brain pathways which are critical in determining how the brain responds to visual threats. At the fork in the road of these two pathways, the ventral midline thalamus (vMT) acts as a relay station (or traffic cop) and takes all of the sensory information that was just seen or heard and sorts out where in the brain to send that information. When the researchers specifically targeted stimulating the medial prefrontal cortex in the mice (where we think about the emotions we feel), the mice responded with courage to the spurious predator, often standing their ground, rattling their tails, or acting with aggression.[8] When the researchers diverted signals away from the prefrontal cortex (much like how the vMT would naturally do), the mice froze in place and cowered with fear. The mice that used their prefrontal cortexes were able to act courageously while the mice who didn't engage their thinking centers were paralyzed with distress. Thinking on purpose, which heavily engages your prefrontal cortex, will activate the same regions of the brain responsible for courageous mice behavior within the study. Leading on purpose enables bold behavior, which allows you to go against the grain in times where a tough leadership decision is needed.

> *Purposeful Cognition domains which affect this leadership rule* – Locus of Control, Cognitive Distortion, and Emotional Distortion.

6. Leaders probe and push with a curiosity that borders on skepticism, making sure their questions are answered with action. One of Jack's most famous postulates is "an individual contributor's job is to have all of the answers; a leader's job is to have all of the questions." Leaders need to question everything – from the accuracy of reports to the company status quo. Leaders need to be skeptical, but not cynical; insistent, but not aggressive. The leader needs to know exactly how much of each behavior to dial up without going overboard.

The emotional intelligence skills of *optimism* and *assertiveness* are heavily involved in this leadership rule. These skills are also extremely delicate, meaning that using them a tiny bit too much or too little comes across as a completely different behavior. For example, the skill of assertiveness, which is the ability to communicate feelings in a non-offensive way, exists within the tiny space between being passive or aggressive. Only those that toe the line perfectly can exhibit behaviors of assertiveness which allow you to get your point across without being offensive or off-putting. Optimism is a bit different because it doesn't exist in-between two other powerful emotions, but because the smallest amounts of pessimism can destroy massive amounts of optimism. A metaphor that highlights the prodigious power that pessimism has over optimism is the relationship between oil and water. According to research findings,[9] a single drop of oil can contaminate a million drops of drinking water. Pessimism is the same way. The dyspeptic among us often drown out the Pollyannaish. Remember how profound of an impact that the negativity bias has on our brain. Negativity heavily outweighs positivity in terms of the psychic power of each lone act. Emotional Distortion further compounds this. Those who have high levels of Emotional Distortion will not be able to elegantly toe this emotional line and properly engage these powerful EI skills when needed.

In *Winning*, Jack describes how many of his middle managers would always respond to his questions with "we'll look into it," whenever they were probed with a direct inquiry. Early in his leadership career he took that answer as sufficient and moved onto the next topic, only to eventually discover that many of his middle managers never looked into anything. They were putting him off. Whether the middle managers realized it or not, they essentially delayed organizational decision-making on key issues, which led to losses of market share, reduction in profits, and an exodus of talent. Jack realized that he needed to force his subordinates for answers. Even if the answers were "I don't know," that would still trigger an action by leadership to align resources to the problem to figure it out. By leading on purpose, you can be optimistic and assertive, which will allow you to probe for answers to questions that are not easy to come by.

> *Purposeful Cognition domains which affect this leadership rule –* Locus of Control, Cognitive Distortion, and Emotional Distortion.

7. Leaders inspire risk taking and learning by setting the example.

Leaders don't know everything. As with the previous rule, it is the leader's job to have all of the questions. If the leader already knew all the answers, there would be no questions to ask! Leaders can use their ability to question to promote two other important traits within employees – risk-taking and learning.

Researchers at the University of Turku in Finland made an important discovery when analyzing the brains of risk-takers:[10]

> We expected to find that young men who spend time considering what they are going to do in a given risk situation would have more highly developed neural networks in their brains than those who make quick decisions and take chances...this has been well documented in a series of studies, but our project revealed the complete opposite.

The researchers found that men who were risk-seekers had larger sections of brain white matter. White matter comprises of the brain's total neural network, accounting for over 160,000 kilometers in length. White matter transmits signals via nerve impulses and acts as the brain's superhighway of communication. High risk-takers showed less hesitation, higher optimism, and a more internalized Locus of Control over the low risk-takers within the study. Brain scans revealed that the high risk-takers had higher activation of white matter, which ultimately contributed toward higher learning, developing stronger coping strategies, and activation of the caudate nucleus, the portion of the brain responsible for enhanced reward processing under peer influence.[11] Essentially, risk-takers are smarter, and their brains reward them for it.

This can be applied to leadership as well. One of the best things a leader can do is to create a "learning organization." A learning organization is "an organization that is skilled at creating, acquiring, and transferring knowledge, and at modifying its behavior to reflect new knowledge and insights."[12] A learning organization has a systematic approach to problem-solving, encourages experimentation, doesn't punish failure, learns from past experiences and others, and understands how to weaponize knowledge to continue market dominance. Some of the most valuable companies in the world are masters of organizational learning, and it all begins with the behaviors of its leaders. By inspiring risk-taking, leaders can also inspire organizational learning to grow organically within the workforce. Leading on purpose allows for calculated risk-taking, which can make the organization smarter. Think of it as activating the white matter of the organization's brain.

Purposeful Cognition domains which affect this leadership rule –
Inner Passivity, Inner Aggression, and Locus of Control.

8. Leaders celebrate. Momentum is a hard thing to come by in leadership. Momentum helps propel work efforts toward success when your projects hit inevitable organizational roadblocks. Roadblocks are plentiful, and leaders will face thousands of them in their careers, but momentum is fleeting and ephemeral. When momentum emerges, even if for a moment, a great leader must capitalize.

John Kotter, most famously known for his 8-step process for leading change, examined research that spanned over four decades to determine the best process for leading organizational change. These steps include:

1. Create a sense of urgency
2. Build a guiding coalition
3. Form a strategic vision
4. Enlist a volunteer army
5. Remove barriers
6. Generate short-term wins
7. Sustain acceleration
8. Institute change

All of these steps are designed to maximize change success, regardless of the context of the change effort itself. This is because the process isn't designed to maximize technology adoption or amplify customer satisfaction (though these are wonderful side effects of the process). The process is designed to *create and sustain* organizational momentum.

Think of momentum like a rolling snowball. A snowball is fragile and has diminutive power as it begins its descent down the hill. As it tumbles down the slope, various boulders in its path could easily dismantle the snowball in its early stages. Only when the snowball has become a juggernaut, in both size and speed, can it stand a chance against an immovable object.

Organizational change is the same way. There are many boulders in your path and your change effort will start as a tiny snowball that you can hold in your hand. The only way to blow through resistance is to gain momentum. Kotter's 6th change management step (generate short-term wins), which matches Welch's 8th leadership step (leaders celebrate), are both designed to create this momentum.

Short-term wins are "proof of progress." Whether the win is big or small, the win *motivates*. Motivation equals momentum. The win proves that you are on the right track. Many successful teams celebrate daily! I have even seen teams celebrate "the best idea that failed." Celebrating often is important.

Holding off celebrations for only major milestones or until the end of the project will minimize your chances of success because employee motivation will decline as time passes. Celebrating is one of the only ways to reactivate the motivation-machine that sustains organizational change. Celebrating creates a culture where people are excited to show up and talk about how great things are, all of which continues building momentum. According to research,[13] the more you celebrate, the greater the chances that you will win.

Researchers at the University of Groningen found that cheering convincingly increased overall chances of success. The researchers describe the effect that cheering had on the outcome of penalty kicks in a soccer match; a concept that they referred to as "emotional contagion." The authors of the study wrote the following:[14]

> We examined the association between celebratory responses after successful soccer penalty kicks and the outcome of a penalty shootout. Individually displayed post-shot behaviors in penalty shootouts held in World Cups and European Championships (N = 151) were rated on the presence of universally distinct and recognizable behaviors associated with positive emotions. Using chi-square analyses we investigated which behaviors were associated with winning the shootout, when the relative standing between the teams was equal. *Players who engaged in certain celebratory post-shot behaviors were more likely to be in the team that ultimately won the penalty shootout.* In particular, celebrations including both arms were associated with winning the shootout. *It was more likely that the next kick taken by an opponent was missed after a player displayed these behaviors after a goal than*

when he did not. The findings are interpreted in terms of emotional contagion – that is, the transference of emotions from individuals onto teammates and opponents. It is suggested that the individual expression of post-performance emotions serves a direct purpose in enhancing future team performance and that emotional contagion is an important process in the context of elite sport performance.

Essentially, the team that cheered harder scored more and the opposing team scored less. The emotion from celebrating the goal fed into the motivation of the next shooter and also demotivated shooters from the other team. Emotional contagion created psychological momentum. Leaders within organizations can achieve a similar result, simply by celebrating. Leading on purpose allows for leaders to take a step back, commemorate achievement and recognize efforts of others. This not only helps generate momentum but also makes work fun. So celebrate your wins with both hands in the air!

> *Purposeful Cognition domains which affect this leadership rule –* Inner Aggression, Locus of Control, and Emotional Distortion.

Anyone can be a leader. Leadership is not a title, a position, or a birthright. You can be a leader to your children by setting the right example, to your peers by doing the right thing in times of ethical ambiguity, and to your society by being socially and morally responsible. Leading on purpose first starts with your ability to think on purpose and by understanding that anyone can be a leader at any time. You just need to step up to the plate once your number is called.

In Sum

- Leaders are not born, they are made.
- Leadership style is defined as the *way a person uses power* to lead other individuals, groups, or organizations toward a common objective.
- There is a single element that is universally transitive across all the styles. They each require the leader to *act with purpose* in order to showcase their *authentic* selves. Followers will not follow unless a leader is authentic.
- Thinking on purpose will give you the cognitive agility to correctly apply the proper combination of Jack's rules while being genuine and sincere. That is where true power comes from.

- Self-confidence is emotional energy that snowballs throughout an organization as it builds. Much like how the flight attendant tells you to first secure your oxygen mask before you help others, leadership is the same way. If you don't take care of yourself first, you won't be able to help others.
- A powerful vision can create instant psychological inertia that propels an organization toward a better future. But as with most future-thinking, communicating a vision can often promote feelings of anxiety within the organization. Leaders who establish a powerful vision also need to be equipped with the tools to ensure that future-thinking doesn't also create organizational anxiety.
- Trust is important because people do their best work within environments that *do not punish failure*. Think about any innovation that has occurred within the last 100 years. They all started out as a "crazy" statement that someone *had to feel safe enough to proclaim* within a room full of their peers.
- Leaders need to be skeptical, but not cynical; insistent, but not aggressive. The leader needs to know exactly how much of each behavior to dial up without going overboard.
- Short-term wins are "proof of progress." Whether the win is big or small, the win *motivates*. Motivation equals momentum. The win proves that you are on the right track.

CHAPTER 15 | RELATING ON PURPOSE

"The most important thing in life is to learn how to give out love, and to let it come in."

MORRIE SCHWARTZ, American author and professor

"Love looks not with the eyes, but with the mind, and therefore is winged Cupid painted blind."

WILLIAM SHAKESPEARE

One of the most influential books ever written was *How to Win Friends and Influence People,* by Dale Carnegie. Published in 1936, the book highlights basic, yet profound, techniques to handle people, get others to like you, and win people to your way of thinking. The book is credited with influencing major icons of our popular culture – positive icons such as Warren Buffet, who took Dale Carnegie's course when he was 20-years-old and still hangs the diploma in his office to this day, and negative icons such as Charles Manson, who used what he learned in the book to manipulate women to kill on his behalf.[1] The book continues to have a significant influence to this day because it captures a single notion – the idea that to achieve what we want in life (whether noble or nefarious), we need help from those around us. You may have heard the saying, "what other people think of you is none of your business." This is bad advice. What other people think of you matters and you should make it your business to know what others think so that you can positively influence those thoughts.

Consider the you that you know. This is called your *identity*. Freud would posit that your identity is hardly worth knowing at all, because you are the only person in the world that knows your identity, and it is something that you made up.[2] By this point in the book, you should realize how proficient the mind is at creating fantasy worlds that are disconnected from reality. Your identity is a fantasy; it is only in your head, and no one else will ever be privy to it. Another old saying, "you should only care what you think about yourself," is not only outdated, it is dangerous. People hire us, talk to us, befriend us, love us, engage with us, and experience life with us, *based on their view of who we are*, not based on our view of who we are.

Robert Hogan describes the external view as our *reputation*.[3] Our reputation is what the rest of the world sees when they look at us. As a psychological construct, over 100 years of research suggests that our identity is almost impossible to study objectively while our reputation is fairly easy to assess. Hogan (and many other psychologists throughout time) posit that the best predictor of future behavior is past behavior, a construct that is easily measured by asking other people to objectively assess that behavior. There is a widely accepted taxonomy of reputations that can be used to objectively assess someone's behavior from an external rater's point of view. This is what a 360-degree assessment, or "360" for short, accomplishes.

Let's imagine for a moment that you and I are having a conversation, sharing a nice bourbon. In our conversation, there are actually six separate people present. They are:

1. Who I think I am (my identity)
2. Who you think I am (my reputation)
3. Who I really am (which is some mix of the previous two)
4. Who you think you are (your identity)
5. Who I think you are (your reputation)
6. Who you really are (which is some mix of the previous two)

Which one is the real me? Which one is the real you? A 360 assessment helps you quantify this. There are many versions of 360 assessments available that align to personality, emotional intelligence, or some other leadership dimension, but they all have the same structure. You will take the assessment about yourself and you will identify others, known as raters, to take the same assessment about you. Normally, your raters are organized into groups, such as your manager, peers, direct reports, friends, family, or others. When you get the results back from your 360, you will be able to compare your identity results (your "self" scores) with your various reputation results (your rater scores). Are you really the affable fellow that you think you are? Does your feedback to your peers, which you believe comes across as constructive, instead come across as derisive or scoffing? A 360 assessment will be able to tell you this because it compares how you view yourself to how others view you, helping you consolidate those viewpoints.

How we relate to others is an essential factor of the human experience. Additionally, our own internal view of how our behaviors come across, or more specifically, how accurately our identity matches our reputation, is also one of the most important facets of the human condition. When our identity varies wildly from our reputation, that is referred to as a gap. All 360 assessments are designed to help identify those gaps and provide rudimentary strategies to help you close those gaps, *often focusing solely on external behaviors*. Many assessments do not focus on the *internal cognitive processes* that prohibit our identity from aligning with our reputation. The Purposeful Cognition Index is the first assessment targeted at identifying and developing these internal cognitive processes to help you develop an ability to think on purpose. Thinking on purpose provides you an ability to use the strategies in this book to shrink your identity-reputation gaps, to win friends and influence people, and to maximize your relations for your benefit. From this, you will develop the ability to relate on purpose.

Mutually Satisfying Relationships

You hear the axioms all the time; "it isn't what you know, it's who you know" or " it isn't about your net worth, it's about your network." These all highlight the importance of interpersonal relationships over other factors, such as IQ, experience, or access to resources. For the moment, let's exclude romantic relationships from this section and only discuss peer relationships, both inside and outside of work.

"Interpersonal Relationships" is a core EI skill of the Bar-On model of emotional intelligence and is defined as the ability to develop and maintain mutually satisfying relationships. *Mutually satisfying* is the key term. In order for a relationship to be considered mutually satisfying, both parties need to feel that they each get something better out of being in the relationship that they would not otherwise have on their own. Similar to the notion that $1 + 1 = 3$, meaning that one person's attributes combined with another person's attributes create a 3rd shared set of characteristics that each can draw from for their own greater benefit. This mutual benefit is derived from a system of both being able to "give" and "take," where trust and compassion drive higher levels of satisfaction and benefit for all parties. How we relate to people is based on our ability to develop trust and portray compassion, by promoting the behaviors that communicate acts of "give" and "take." Psychologist Edward Thorndike noticed in the 1920s that the best factory foreman wasn't necessarily the best factory worker. Technical expertise did very little to translate to successfully leading teams and getting along with other people. He discovered that a social intelligence (which has since become emotional intelligence) was responsible for success at higher levels of leadership that required interacting with other people. Relating to others was the best predictor of overall success once workers vacated roles that required technical expertise alone. It's too bad that over 100 years later, organizations still promote the technically proficient and overlook the socially skilled when it comes to job advancement and succession planning.

Those who portray high levels of the Interpersonal Relationships skill come across as authentic, are known by many at a deeply personal level, are at ease in social situations, and look forward to engaging with others. Having an ability to relate on purpose gives you the ability to show your authentic self and have confidence in social situations that require multiple levels of human interaction. Many might assume that these skills are only useful in professions that require a large amount of human interaction, such as a teacher, social worker, retail manager or other "people professions." But research has shown that even in professions where there is not a lot of interaction with others, having an ability to relate on purpose still yields immense benefit. The reason is because of what psychologists Samuel Turner and Deborah Beidel refer to as "social effectiveness."[4]

Turner and Beidel studied how people performed in social situations and discovered that social anxiety is a major inhibitor of performance. Many company leaders erroneously believe that social anxiety is due to a lack of skill that is required in a given situation. Essentially, the belief is that you are nervous because you cannot physically perform the task ahead of you. This bolsters the false notion that higher technical proficiency leads to less anxiety, which in turn leads to better performance in the social arena. You wouldn't be anxious if you had the skills, right? If that were the case, professional actors and singers would no longer get nervous. But some of the best performers of our time, such as Adele, Rihanna, and Garth Brooks, to name a few, still get extremely anxious before performing.

By now, you know anxiety is *not caused* because of a lack of physical skill. It generates from our proclivity to ruminate about the future. You also know by now that thinking on purpose reduces anxiety in a variety of ways. If anxiety in social situations blocks an ability to develop and maintain mutually satisfying relationships, then using the same skills to think on purpose will also help you develop an ability to relate on purpose. Since Carnegie's book has stood the test of time, let's use his examples and show how thinking on purpose can help you master each of his principles, giving you an ability to relate on purpose and develop mutually satisfying relationships:[5]

Fundamental Techniques in Handling People

Don't criticize, condemn, or complain. Complaining activates our inner critic and promotes defensiveness within others, which activates their inner critic. Activating Inner Aggression within ourselves and those around us certainly doesn't help develop mutually satisfying relationships, because it triggers an "us" vs. "them" mentality. Instead, engage in the common humanity approach.

Give honest and sincere appreciation. Appreciation creates positive emotions in both the giver and receiver - positive emotions limit both Cognitive and Emotional Distortion.

Arouse in the other person an eager want. Motivation is a powerful thing. Inner Passivity is a powerful force that diminishes action. If you find what produces the feelings of want and desire in another, you will help lessen Inner Passivity.

Six Ways to Make People Like You

Become genuinely interested in other people. "Genuine" is the key word here. By becoming interested in other people, you display your authentic self. Authenticity comes from understanding your emotions and how your emotions affect your behavior.

Smile. This is the best way to activate the mirror neurons of others in a positive way. A smile is universal and is the first step toward positive outcomes in any situation.

Remember that a person's name is, to that person, the sweetest and most important sound in any language. Remember that our senses create emotions before they create cognitive thoughts. This means that we can stack the deck toward positive cognition if we know what first creates positive emotions. Use a person's name to achieve this.

Be a good listener. Encourage others to talk about themselves. By encouraging others to talk about themselves, you get insight into their desires and fears. If you listen closely, you can hear their inner critic, and respond accordingly with positive counsel.

Talk in terms of the other person's interest. When someone hears another person talk in terms of their own interest, that helps validate their own thinking. This helps you reduce any Cognitive Distortion that they may have about a given topic, producing feelings of safety and community.

Make the other person feel important – and do it sincerely. Similar to being genuine and authentic, if you make the other person feel important, you will lessen their distorted thinking by making them feel safe and providing validity to their interests.

Twelve Ways to Win People to Your Way of Thinking

The only way to get the best of an argument is to avoid it. Arguments activate Inner Aggression. If you can avoid them, you don't feed your aggressive psyche.

Show respect for the other person's opinions. Never say "You're wrong." Telling someone that they are wrong doesn't convince them that they are actually wrong, it makes them defensive and feeds into Cognitive Distortion.

If you're wrong, admit it quickly and emphatically. Taking ownership when you are wrong helps maintain your internal Locus of Control.

Begin in a friendly way. This one is pretty straight forward!

Start with questions to which the other person will answer yes. This is a salesman's trick because saying yes activates the portions of the brain which produce feelings of trust and connection. Saying yes creates agreement, which produces oxytocin and other trust hormones.

Let the other person do a great deal of the talking. Similar to being a good listener, this helps silence another person's inner critic.

Let the other person feel the idea is his or hers. When someone feels that the idea was theirs, it bolsters an internal Locus of Control. When an idea isn't theirs, it promotes feelings of an external locus.

Try honestly to see things from the other person's point of view. Similar to talking in another's terms of interest, if you can see how another person sees a particular topic, it will help lessen Cognitive and Emotional Distortion that a contentious situation may bring on.

Be sympathetic with the other person's ideas and desires. Similar to the notions of authenticity and being a good listener mentioned previously. Sympathy creates connection.

Appeal to the nobler motives. This helps people identify their real reasons for doing things. If you appeal to the nobler motives, you break down levels of distortion within others to identify true intentions.

Dramatize your ideas. Drama produces feelings. Remember that people will always remember how you made them feel, not what you said. This helps get people's emotions on your side.

Throw down a challenge. A challenge is essentially a test of Locus of Control. By challenging others, you give them the chance to display their inner locus.

Be a Leader: How to Change People Without Giving Offense or Arousing Resentment

Begin with praise and honest appreciation. Praise creates positive emotion. Positive emotion creates positive cognition.

Call attention to people's mistakes indirectly. This method ensures that you don't create defensiveness, which also activates someone's inner critic.

Talk about your own mistakes before criticizing the other person. This method also reduces feelings of defensiveness and ensures that others can hear your feedback clearly without Emotional Distortion getting in the way.

Ask questions instead of giving direct orders. Asking questions to others promotes feelings of competence within them. This helps them bolster their internal locus.

Let the other person save face. When a person can't save face, their inner critic and Inner Aggression will run rampant.

Praise every improvement. This tactic helps reduce the inner critic.

Give the other person a fine reputation to live up to. This helps others self-actualize, promoting emotional intelligence and reducing various distortions.

Use encouragement. Make the fault seem easy to correct. This uses positivity to reduce Inner Aggression.

Make the other person happy about doing what you suggest. This also uses positivity to reduce various distortions.

These are a few small ways that thinking on purpose can help you use these time-tested methods to win friends, influence people, and develop mutually satisfying relationships, showing you the psychological effects which are created from each of these strategies. Using these positive strategies will help you avoid a miasma of social negativity that can cloud your interactions and block your ability to relate on purpose to those around you.

The Social Interaction

Humans are highly social creatures. Even the most recluse of us need social interaction of some sort to be psychologically healthy (that is why solitary confinement in prison is considered the most severe punishment available). Haidt writes, "Having strong social relationships strengthens the immune system, extends life (more than does quitting smoking), speeds recovery from surgery, and reduces the risks of depression and anxiety disorders."[6] Scientists have discovered proof that the evolution of human intelligence and larger brain sizes are due to social interaction.[7] Essentially, what separates modern humans from our primitive ancestors is the ability to be social. Evolutionary benefits come from our capability to interact with others. This is true in the animal kingdom as well, where larger brains are found within animal species that are more social. Humans spend most of our time with others in groups. These groups are what distinguish us from other mammals because humans are not the fastest, biggest or strongest mammals on earth, yet we are the most dominant species on the planet. We have learned to use group and social interaction to our benefit, providing protection, community, and purpose, but also because social interaction improves our cognitive performance. Researchers have discovered that social interaction itself has a direct correlation to enhanced mental functioning and that by associating with groups we each help bolster the intelligence of others.[8]

Because of these cognitive boosting factors, social interaction is extremely addicting, even to the most introverted among us. Take addiction to mobile devices for example. (Isn't it interesting that the only types of people that call their customer base "users" are drug dealers and technologists?) Early theory on mobile-device habits and smartphone addiction centered on a notion that the new technology provided introverted people a way to become even more anti-social, allowing them to avoid face-to-face interaction with others because they could interact with the world through a device. But researchers who recently investigated dysfunctional use of smart technology discovered that mobile-device habits are not anti-social, they are hyper-social. Cognitive anthropologists (those that study the evolution of cognition and culture) published a study in *Frontiers in Psychology* that the most addictive smartphone features all tap into the human desire to connect with other people. So it isn't the device itself that is addicting or the cloak of anonymity that it provides so alluring, it is the ability to connect with those that we would otherwise not be able to connect with that is so addicting. The researchers write:[9]

> There is ample evidence to support the claim that smartphone use is inherently prosocial, and by extension, that this prosociality is a core locus of smartphone addiction. First, the majority of smartphone use is spent on social activities such as social networking, text messaging, and phone calls. Even less interactive smartphone use, like information seeking or surfing the web, has now become implicitly social: 'likes,' views, and comments are social indices of prestige and collective attention. Second, individuals who use their devices for primarily social purposes are quicker to develop habitual smartphone use. These findings suggest that it is not just the smartphone itself that is addictive but rather the—direct or indirect—social interaction it enables.

The researchers also highlight how humans have a desire to monitor and be monitored by others. We like to watch people and we like it when others watch us. Anyone who has ever raised a toddler knows this from the years of "watch me, watch me!" screams during any activity. Humans require constant input from other humans to provide a sense of identity and a guide to culturally appropriate behavior. What other people think of us provides validation of our behavior. What other people think of us matters. Social interaction is what separates us as a species and humans crave it on all levels.

In sociology, social interaction is a dynamic, changing sequence of actions and events between individuals or groups. When people interact, they design rules, roles, symbols and language to communicate. Microsociology, one of the main focuses of sociology, is centered on everyday social interactions, mainly face-to-face interaction. Microsociology is unique in that it is based on interpretative analysis, not an empirical observation, meaning that it aims to offer insights into how a given person, within a given context, interprets a phenomenon. This implies that two people can interpret the same event differently. Social status and social roles within microsociology fulfill broader societal and cultural contexts with sociology, meaning that daily face-to-face interactions between humans and groups eventually bubble up to form the overall culture. Face-to-face interaction is one of the basic elements of a social system[10] and there are a few distinct philosophies that attempt to provide a model for this microsocial construct.

Intersubjectivity is the psychological relationship between people and is often considered the obverse of solipsistic thinking (remember that solipsism is the philosophical idea that only one's mind is sure to exist). Intersubjectivity refers to shared meanings constructed by people during their interactions with each other. When people interact, their interactions create mutual understanding, which eventually turns into community, law, and beliefs. Intersubjectivity posits that communities form due to shared social experiences and interactions, which are different from other communities that form different values and beliefs from different social interactions. This is why you see different values and beliefs among different communities, tribes, or countries. The collective thoughts and interactions make up the social system. A German philosopher named Edmund Husserl recognized the importance of intersubjectivity and developed an approach called phenomenology, which he described as the study of the structures of experience and consciousness. Phenomenology, derived from Greek for "that which appears," looks at how judgments, perceptions, and emotions create conscious experiences for humans. According to Husserl, what people think creates the human experience. How humans interpret phenomena shapes a greater understanding of human nature than anything else. Within this discipline, the only ways to study consciousness are to look at human behavior, subjective experience, and systematic reflection. Phenomenologists reject the concept of objective research and traditional data.[11] Let's take empathy as an example. Empathy is defined by Bar-On as the ability to recognize, understand, and appreciate how other people feel. Those who have high empathy can articulate their understanding of another person's perspective and show respect for those feelings. But feelings are subjective. In phenomenology, empathy refers to the experience of one's body as another.[12] You focus on the subjectivity of another's feelings and create those feelings within yourself, giving you an appreciation of them and an ability to recognize and appreciate how the other is feeling. Your interaction is based on the subjective experience, not any objective data. What the other person thinks matters because it is affecting how you think, in turn shaping your human experience and how you feel. Your experience of the phenomenon structured your experience. Whether the phenomenon itself was "real" or not, is irrelevant. Your mental and physiological functions that derived from the phenomena were real. Since Husserl, seven different types of phenomenology have emerged:[13]

1. Transcendental constitutive phenomenology studies how objects are constituted in transcendental consciousness, setting aside questions of any relation to the natural world.
2. Naturalistic constitutive phenomenology studies how consciousness constitutes things in the world of nature, assuming that consciousness is part of nature.
3. Existential phenomenology studies concrete human existence, including our experience of free choice and action in concrete situations.

4. Generative historicist phenomenology studies how meaning—as found in our experience—is generated in historical processes of collective experience over time.
5. Genetic phenomenology studies the emergence/genesis of meanings of things within one's own stream of experience.
6. Hermeneutical phenomenology studies interpretive structures of experience.
7. Realistic phenomenology studies the structure of consciousness and intentionality as "it occurs in a real world that is largely external to consciousness and not somehow brought into being by consciousness."

While one could certainly write a series of books just on this subject alone, the main takeaway here is that the human experience is as much subjective as it is objective. Scientists can use data, neurological study, and objective analysis to construct existential models of consciousness, but subjective interpretation of phenomena in microsocial interactions are just as important, if not more so. But how does developing an ability to think on purpose affect our subjective interpretation of face-to-face interactions and social phenomena? Because purposeful cognition dramatically affects our social interpretations through a theory called symbolic interactionism.

Symbolic Interactionism

Remember back at the beginning of the book where I mentioned that some believe we live in an artificial simulation? Guess what; I am one of them! (I fess up to this in the Part II summary endnotes section.) But not in the type of simulation you are thinking about, as portrayed in *The Matrix*, where artificially intelligent machines are keeping humans in a digital coma by producing an alternate reality where our brains reside, to harness BTUs produced from our bodies. But rather a type of simulation that is deliberately emblematic and purposely created to reside above the core, physical layer of our reality. As humans, we live in a symbolic world composed of shared understanding and social context that is often different from what is "real."

Symbolic interactionists believe in our physical reality, meaning that the world we are experiencing does indeed exist, but also believe that humans cannot respond to this reality directly. According to symbolic interactionists, we can only respond to *the social understanding of reality*. According to the theory, there are three assumptions that frame symbolic interactionism:[14]

1. Individuals construct meaning via the communication process.
2. Self-concept is a motivation for behavior.
3. A unique relationship exists between the individual and society.

These assumptions quantify the notion that the individual derives the meaning of reality from the interaction with others, uses the concept of the self as a guide for actions and behaviors, and has a relationship with "reality" that no one else has. Think of it like this, your relationship with your parents is unique, even if you have nine siblings that grew up in the same household. This is because of small differences in communication and experiences growing up that your other siblings did not have. It is the same between the individual and society. Each one of us has a unique relationship with reality, due to our social understanding of reality.

Herbert Blumer, an American sociologist who further expanded upon the symbolic interactionism theory that was originally conceived by George Mead in the early 1900s, developed three premises from these three original assumptions.

Premise 1: Humans act toward things on the basis of the meanings they ascribe to those things.[15] Blumer posits that individuals behave toward objects in their world based on the personal meanings that the individual has already given those items. Think of an item that has sentimental value to you, but no value to another. You both will behave drastically different toward that object. It exists in the same physical reality for both of you, but your unique meaning creates unique behaviors.

Premise 2: The meaning of such things is derived from, or arises out of, the social interaction that one has with others and the society.[16] This premise explains the social interaction that one has with other humans and how the meanings that result from those interactions drive behavior. According to Blumer, people do not simply interpret or define the actions of others and then simply react. Our response is based on the *meaning we attach to their actions*. Our response creates symbols and signification to ascribe meaning to one another's actions. For example, if you are giving a presentation and someone is swaying their head slowly side to side during your speech, rather than simply interpreting that as a simple head movement or involuntary action, you ascribe a symbol, based on cultural norms, what you know of the person, and other factors, to surmise that the person is exhibiting the body language of subtle disapproval. You do not interpret the "real" reality of what the person is doing (simply moving their head) but instead, you construct meaning through the nonverbal communication, which you then juxtapose with social context and cultural norms. Your reality is shaped by your social understanding of another's actions, filtering through your perspective. You start to believe others did not approve of your speech, anxiety starts to generate, and you start to worry about a variety of other things related to your presentation. You don't exist in the physical space of reality, but in a "world" composed of your social understanding of the situation.

Premise 3: The meanings are handled in, and modified through, an interpretative process used by the person in dealing with the things he/she encounters.[17] Everyone has a different interpretive process. Mead referred to this as our inner conversation, or minding, to refer to the delay in our thought processes that result from taking time to interpret any given situation. That interpretation comes from our experiences, biology and a bevy of other factors, but most importantly, it is shaped by our language. Our language capability creates symbols, negotiated meanings, and our memories. Some child psychologists posit that the reason humans cannot remember anything from early childhood is that we lack the capacity of language to assign symbols to interactions, which in turn create memories. Language shapes our experience, is at the core of our memory, and drives meaning for our interpretations.

These premises and assumptions all lead to a central idea. *Each of us has a unique relationship with the world that is artificially created through our subjective experiences.* In essence, we live in an artificial simulation that we construct ourselves! That simulation is composed of our subjective understanding and interpretations of the communications we have with each other as humans. By relating on purpose with others, we can ensure that our communications and social interactions are pure, positively maximized and optimized to drive a pleasurable relationship with our unique reality. Joel Charon, a professor emeritus of sociology, wrote in his book *Symbolic Interactionism: An Introduction, An Interpretation, An Integration* about five central themes that embody symbolic interactionism. They are:[18]

> 1. The human being must be understood as a social person. It is the constant search for social interaction that leads us to do what we do. Instead of focusing on the individual and his or her personality, or on how the society or social situation causes human behavior, symbolic interactionism focuses on the activities that take place between actors. Interaction is the basic unit of study. Individuals are created through interaction; society too is created through social interaction. What we do depends on interaction with others earlier in our lifetimes, and it depends on our interaction right now. Social interaction is central to what we do. If we want to understand cause, focus on social interaction.
>
> 2. The human being must be understood as a thinking being. Human action is not only interaction among individuals but also interaction within the individual. It is not our ideas or attitudes or values that are as important as the constant active ongoing

process of thinking. We are not simply conditioned, we are not simply beings who are influenced by those around us, we are not simply products of society. We are, to our very core, thinking animals, always conversing with ourselves as we interact with others. If we want to understand cause, focus on human thinking.

3. Humans do not sense their environment directly, instead, humans define the situation they are in. An environment may actually exist, but it is our definition of it that is important. Definition does not simply randomly happen; instead, it results from ongoing social interaction and thinking.

4. The cause of human action is the result of what is occurring in our present situation. Cause unfolds in the present social interaction, present thinking, and present definition. It is not society's encounters with us in our past, that causes action nor is it our own past experience that does. It is, instead, social interaction, thinking, definition of the situation that takes place in the present. Our past enters into our actions primarily because we think about it and apply it to the definition of the present situation.

5. Human beings are described as active beings in relation to their environment. Words such as *conditioning, responding, controlled, imprisoned,* and *formed* are not used to describe the human being in symbolic interaction. In contrast to other social-scientific perspectives humans are not thought of as being passive in relation to their surroundings, but actively involved in what they do.

Essentially, our thinking creates our whole reality; shapes our entire existence. Inner Passivity, Inner Aggression, Locus of Control, Cognitive Distortion and Emotional Distortion all affect our ability to think on purpose. If our thought processes not only tether us to our sociality but shape our entire world view, developing an ability to think on purpose should be a priority above all else if we want to maximize our time here before we shuffle off this mortal coil.

The Looking Glass Self

Through symbolic interactionism, we know that our worldview is based upon our social understanding of reality. Researchers that sought to investigate the neural basis of social knowledge wrote in the *Annual Review of Psychology* that:[19]

> Social cognition within humans is distinguished by psychological processes that allow us to make inferences about what is going on inside other people – their intentions, feelings and thoughts. Some of these processes likely account for aspects of human social behavior that are unique, such as our culture and civilization. Most schemes divide social information processing into those processes that are relatively automatic and driven by the stimuli, versus those that are more deliberative and controlled, and sensitive to context and strategy. These distinctions are reflected in the neural structures that underlie social cognition, where there is a recent wealth of data primarily from functional neuroimaging.

Neurological evidence supports the idea that humans have a social brain, where certain mental functions of the brain are specifically dedicated to social interaction. In 1902, Charles Horton Cooley, an American sociologist who was a founding member of the American Sociological Association, developed the social psychological concept of the "looking glass self." He discovered that the part of the brain which allows humans to understand how other people think begins to develop in early childhood. From this, children develop an ability to think about how other people will think about them. This is known as "reflected appraisals" or "the looking glass self." Essentially, our view of ourselves is composed of how we think others view us. Cooley developed three main components of the looking glass self:

- We imagine how we must appear to others
- We imagine the judgment of that appearance
- We develop our self through the judgment of others

When developing the framework, Cooley said "the mind is mental" because the "human mind is social." Children begin to define themselves within the social construct of their surroundings. For example, a child learns that crying will produce a response from parents when they need food or when they want attention. Symbols carry the meaning.

Early philosophers embraced the concept of a symbolic relationship with reality. Some early instances of this type of thinking are present within Plato's

Allegory of the Cave. He described a group of people who lived chained to a rock inside of a cave all of their lives, facing a blank wall. The people can only see shadows projected onto the wall from objects passing in front of a fire that is behind them. These prisoners use the shadows to shape their reality, giving names to the symbols (shadows) they see on the wall. The symbolism of Plato's cave represents more broadly the notion that everyone lives within illusions of the world around us, within the shackles of our reality.

Dr. Phil McGraw, known more famously as Dr. Phil, is an American author and psychologist who also believes in the power of positive thinking over medication for the treatment of mental health. In a recent podcast, Dr. Phil describes what self-esteem is and where we get it:[20]

> Imagine that you work with someone for a couple of years and you observe that person showing up to work every day, 15 minutes early, coffee in place, and he's ready to go. You start to attribute certain traits and characteristics to him based on your observations. For example, you might start to think that he is dependable, based on his visible behaviors. That is exactly the way we form our own self-image. We watch ourselves go through life and watch ourselves overcome obstacles, such as passing the third grade or winning a little-league championship.

Essentially, we look at ourselves through other people's eyes to form our own self-image and level of self-worth. Our mental processes, especially the ones dedicated to social cognition, shape our entire existence. So, wouldn't it be nice if our thinking wasn't distorted? Thinking on purpose ensures that our mental processes are clear. Relating on purpose with others ensures that our social interactions are optimized, maximizing the clarity of our looking glass.

Why Marriages Begin

Marriages are a major part of social interaction as well. Matrimony itself is a socially or ritually recognized union between two spouses that has a romantic component to it, which is often called social attraction. Even though the social definition of marriage varies across religion and cultures, attraction is universal with respect to which mental processes engage when one person is attracted to another.

Psychologists that study marriage claim that expectations for today's relationships are higher than ever.[21] People are becoming pickier and holding out for the best possible mate. But what exactly does the modern person desire in a mate? Researchers wrote in the *Journal of Personality* an article titled

"Personality and mate preferences: five factors in mate selection and marital satisfaction," where they asked 300 heterosexual newlyweds and daters what traits they preferred in a spouse. Contrary to gendered stereotypes, the researchers discovered a lot of overlap between the lists of men and women. The top 10 are shown here:[22]

	By Women	By Men
1	Warm	Reliable
2	Reliable	Warm
3	Fair	Fair
4	Intelligent	Intelligent
5	Knowledgeable	Knowledgeable
6	Trusting	Conscientious
7	Secure	Trusting
8	Hardworking	Hardworking
9	Emotionally Stable	Secure
10	At Ease	At Ease

Notice anything? These are all traits which have subjective definitions that could vary from person to person. My definition of fair will differ from yours and your definition of warm might be different than mine. These traits are all based on having a shared social understanding of our culture. Our ability to then showcase that shared understanding of the trait then leads to a desirable interaction with potential mates. If you are lacking an ability to think on purpose, you will hinder your ability to attract potential mates because shared definitions of social constructs, which lead to what it means to exhibit these traits, will vary from person to person. You may think you are portraying traits of warmth and reliability but others may not think so. This generally serves as the basis for many forms of miscommunication. Notice how the term is normally referred to as miscommunication, not noncommunication (lack of communication in deteriorating relationships is normally a result of many instances of miscommunication first). When couples fight, it is because the actions or intent of one partner is understood or interpreted differently than intended by the other partner, creating a disconnect. This is the whole premise of Gary Chapman's famous book, *The Five Love Languages,* where he claims that everyone experiences love differently and interprets the same relationship behaviors differently. This is because the physical behaviors that both partners see can have differing social constructs laid on top of them. You may think you are the best husband in the world for doing the dishes, but she may view it as a nonfactor. The key is to have a single, shared understanding of those behaviors and actions.

There is a neurological component of attraction as well. A team of scientists[23] divided love into three categories and identified the hormones that stem from the brain during these love states:

Lust: Testosterone, Estrogen
Attraction: Dopamine, Norepinephrine, Serotonin
Attachment: Oxytocin, Vasopressin

With lust, the hypothalamus stimulates the production of testosterone and estrogen, driving up sexual motivation and libido. Attraction is closely related to lust but considered a distinct phenomenon. They often pair together but can be experienced individually. During attraction, the hypothalamus releases dopamine and norepinephrine, creating feelings of excitement and euphoria that most feel in new relationships. During attachment, oxytocin, known as the "cuddle hormone," develops feelings of trust and commitment to facilitate long-term bonding. Sounds great, right? Of course! But with most things, too much can be a bad thing.

Too much dopamine and oxytocin have been linked to binge eating, drug abuse, irrational behavior, jealousy, and adultery. Some researchers even posit that too much oxytocin leads to ethnocentrism, giving us a supreme love only for "our own people" since we have developed trust and connection with them over a long period of time and feel it would be difficult to develop that level of trust with others. Sexual arousal left unchecked has also been shown to "turn off regions in our brains that regulate critical thinking, self-awareness, and rational behavior, including parts of the prefrontal cortex...it deactivates a common set of regions associated with negative emotions, social judgment and 'mentalizing' that is, the assessment of other people's intentions and emotions."[24] I assume this is not a real revelation to most, but people do dumb things when in love. Humans engage in maladaptive behaviors when these hormones are overproduced because our rational brains are turned off. Thinking on purpose ensures that you can identify when these wonderful hormones have taken over and can then systematically reengage your prefrontal cortex to reignite critical thinking and rational behavior.

Why Marriages Fail

As of this writing, marriage dissolution in the United States has been on the decline for the first time in many decades. Philip Cohen, a research professor who identified this downward trend, looked at the divorce rate in the United States from the 1950s to present. He cites that starting in the 1950s, roughly 4 of every 100 marriages would end in divorce, raising to 10 of 100 by the 1980s, and to 25 of 100 by the mid-2000s. But between 2008 and 2016, he noticed that it dropped by 18 percent. What caused this drastic downward trend after 50 years of steady rise? He claims it is because of one reason alone – newlyweds are now waiting until they are older than 25 to get married.[25] He cites that those who wait until they are older are more highly educated, leading to better decisions in mate selection and higher maturity, which is true in part, but it doesn't tell the whole story. Higher-education is certainly important in terms of boosting logical thinking, but it has more to do with the age of the newlyweds itself. The age of 25 is the "new cut-off" point for adulthood according to many researchers since that is when the brain stops developing and maturing (remember that your prefrontal cortex is the last part of your brain to develop). Ever notice how you have to be 25 to rent a car or that your auto insurance drops drastically at age 25? That is a significant reason why. Actuaries who examine massive amounts of human behavior data in relation to automobile crashes have calculated that risky driving behavior drops dramatically after 25. You behave better when your rational brain is fully formed! With a fully functioning rational brain, you are able to fight the hormonal impulses that dominated your teenage behaviors and are better equipped to deal with the stresses of marriage. A fully formed rational brain enhances your ability to communicate, develop a shared social understanding, and not let anxiety or depression affect your ability to be present with your partner.

While enhanced cognition and rationality certainly play a major factor in a stronger marriage bond, researchers have recently discovered a genetic explanation to divorce as well. Researchers at Virginia Commonwealth University and Lund University in Sweden wrote a paper titled "Genetics, the Rearing Environment, and the Intergenerational Transmission of Divorce: A Swedish National Adoption Study," claiming that basic personality traits, such as negative emotionality and low levels of constraint, are major catalysts of divorce. The study authors claim:[26]

> For example, other research shows that people who are highly neurotic tend to perceive their partners as behaving more negatively than they objectively are [as rated by independent observers]...so, addressing these underlying, personality-driven cognitive distortions through cognitive-behavioral approaches may be a better strategy than trying to foster commitment.

Obviously, being a rational 25-year-old isn't the panacea for all marital woes. Many other factors play into whether two souls will spend eternity with each other. But having an ability to think on purpose ensures that a newlywed couple can respond to the constant changes of life and learn how to grow with each other as the years pass by.

Negative emotionality is a major relationship killer. In a recent study,[27] researchers wanted to get a general sense of what traits people saw as deal breakers. Surveying over 300 college students about what were the top relationship deal breakers, the researchers found that for long-term relationships, "anger issues" was atop the list. In a metanalysis[28] with over 6500 participants surveyed, researchers found that "undesirable personality traits" were the biggest long-term relationship deal breakers, ranking higher than "unhealthy lifestyles in sexual, romantic, and friendship contexts" and "divergent mating strategies in sexual and romantic contexts." However, the category of "undesirable personality traits" doesn't accurately represent the whole story. It isn't the personality traits themselves that kill relationships, it is the external behaviors that manifest from those personality traits that are undesirable. There is an important distinction between the two. Remember from the biological perspective, personality is inherited and doesn't change over time. We do not have any influence on our inherited genes and personality traits. But we do have an ability to rationally think about the negative behaviors that our personality traits drive us toward, shifting our emotionality toward more anodyne behaviors. Haidt says,[29] "genes are not blueprints specifying the structure of a person; they are better thought of as recipes for producing a person over many years." He cites how identical twins, who are created from the same recipe, can have different behaviors in similar situations. This is due to their independent thought processes that overlay their similar personality tendencies. When referring to happiness and relationships, Haidt says,[30] "conflicts in relationships – having an annoying office mate or roommate, or having chronic conflict with your spouse – is one of the surest ways to reduce your happiness. You never adapt to interpersonal conflict; it damages every day, even days when you don't see the other person but ruminate about the conflict nonetheless."

Low levels of constraint can also damage relationships. A committed relationship by definition suggests that both will be sacrificing a number of things in order to be with each other. The term "sacrificing" can be a bit bathetic when describing something like a joyous marriage, but constraint is good for a relationship, as well as overall society. Haidt writes:[31]

> Some constraint is good for us; absolute freedom is not. Durkheim, the sociologist who found that freedom from social ties is correlated with suicide also gave us the word "anomie" (normlessness). Anomie is the condition of a society in which there are no clear rules, norms or standards of value. In an anomic society, people can do as they please; but without any clear standards or respected social institutions to enforce those standards, it is harder for people to find things they want to do. Anomie breeds

feelings of rootlessness and anxiety and leads to an increase in amoral and antisocial behavior...one of the best predictors of the health of an American neighborhood is the degree to which adults respond to the misdeeds of other people's children. When community standards are enforced, there is constraint and cooperation.

If your natural tendencies encourage you to have low levels of constraint in regard to your relationships, unless that is a pre-existing arrangement you have with your partner, the relationship will not last long. Thinking on purpose gives you an ability to overcome detrimental personality characteristics which may affect your marital longevity.

In Sum

- Identity is the you that you know. Reputation is what the rest of the world sees when they look at you.
- How we relate to others is an essential factor of the human experience. Additionally, our own internal view of how our behaviors come across, or more specifically, how accurately our identity matches our reputation, is also one of the most important facets of the human condition. When our identity varies wildly from our reputation, that is referred to as a gap.
- "Interpersonal Relationships" is a core EI skill of the Bar-On model of emotional intelligence and is defined as the ability to develop and maintain mutually satisfying relationships.
- Researchers have discovered that social interaction itself has a direct correlation to enhanced mental functioning and that by associating with groups we each help bolster the intelligence of others.
- Microsociology is unique in that it is based on interpretative analysis, not an empirical observation, meaning that it aims to offer insights into how a given person, within a given context, interprets a phenomenon. This implies that two people can interpret the same event differently.
- Symbolic interactionists believe in our physical reality, meaning that the world we are experiencing does indeed exist, but also believe that humans cannot respond to this reality directly. According to symbolic interactionists, we can only respond to *the social understanding of reality*. According to the theory, there are three assumptions that frame symbolic interactionism:[32]

1. Individuals construct meaning via the communication process.
2. Self-concept is a motivation for behavior.
3. A unique relationship exists between the individual and society.

- Each one of us has a unique relationship with reality, due to our social understanding of reality.
- Charles Horton Cooley, an American sociologist who was a founding member of the American Sociological Association, developed the social psychological concept of the "looking glass self." He discovered that the part of the brain which allows humans to understand how other people think begins to develop in early childhood. From this, children develop an ability to think about how other people will think about them. This is known as "reflected appraisals" or "the looking glass self." Essentially, our view of our selves is composed of how we think others view us.
- The age of 25 is the "new cut-off" point for adulthood according to many researchers since that is when the brain stops developing and maturing (remember that your prefrontal cortex is the last part of your brain to develop).
- Constraint is good for a relationship, as well as overall society.

CHAPTER 16 | BEING ON PURPOSE

"What day is it?" asked Pooh. "It's today," squeaked Piglet. "My favorite day," said Pooh.

A. A. Milne, British Author

"Wherever you go, there you are."

JON KABAT-ZIN, Meditation teacher

The practice of meditation is one of the most ancient of human mental rituals, with many scholars debating its exact origins. Some believe that meditation began in Taoist China in the 6th century BCE, while others believe that the *Vedas* describes early forms of meditation all the way back in 1500 BCE. The Pāli Canon, traditionally described as the "Word of the Buddha," describes four rules which must be observed to achieve salvation: morality, contemplative concentration, knowledge, and liberation. Into the Common Era, the practice of meditation (contemplative concentration) is found in many religious texts, from Japanese Buddhism, Judaism, Christianity, and many others. While the physical practice of the art form has varied over the years and across the disciplines, the core concept remains the same. Meditation is used to calm thoughts and lower stress levels by forcing the mind to focus.

A modern form of meditation that has evolved into a range of secular therapies and courses is called mindfulness meditation. Mindfulness is the practice of being present and not focusing on anything except what is right in front of you. Not one minute, hour, or day into the past or the future, only right here, right now. Many researchers have found powerful connections between practicing mindfulness and reducing anxiety and depression. A recent study[1] found that after an eight-week mindfulness practice, the amygdala appears to shrink, according to MRI scans. The researchers claim that as the amygdala shrinks, the prefrontal cortex becomes thicker. The researchers state:[2]

> The picture we have is that mindfulness practice increases one's ability to recruit higher order, pre-frontal cortex

regions in order to down-regulate lower-order brain activity. Mindfulness, a psychological process reflecting attention and awareness to what is happening in the present moment, has been associated with increased well-being and decreased depression and anxiety in both healthy and patient populations. However, little research has explored underlying neural pathways. Recent work suggests that mindfulness (and mindfulness training interventions) may foster neuroplastic changes in cortico-limbic circuits responsible for stress and emotion regulation. Building on this work, we hypothesized that higher levels of dispositional mindfulness would be associated with decreased grey matter volume in the amygdala...volumetric analyses showed that higher dispositional mindfulness is associated with decreased grey matter volume in the right amygdala, and exploratory analyses revealed that higher dispositional mindfulness is also associated with decreased grey matter volume in the left caudate. Moreover, secondary analyses indicate that these amygdala and caudate volume associations persist after controlling for relevant demographic and individual difference factors (i.e., age, total grey matter volume, neuroticism, depression). Such volumetric differences may help explain why mindful individuals have reduced stress reactivity, and suggest new candidate structural neurobiological pathways linking mindfulness with mental and physical health outcomes.

Essentially, the researchers discovered that practicing mindfulness, a version of purposeful thinking, created positive neurological changes to the brain. Thinking on purpose comes from an ability to use the rational power of our prefrontal cortex to battle the emotional whims of the dominating amygdala. Practicing mindfulness provides a physical advantage in this battle because it bolsters the prefrontal cortex while simultaneously shrinking the emotional centers of the brain. Another recent study investigated how amygdala response increased within soldiers after military service. In an article titled "Human vulnerability to stress depends on amygdala's predisposition and hippocampal plasticity," researchers discovered that "over time, soldiers reported an increase in stress symptoms that was correlated with greater amygdala and hippocampus responsiveness to stress-related content."[3] Soldiers exhibit an increased stress response after being exposed to high-stress events, such as war. This led subsequent researchers to investigate if these effects could be reversed through various neuroplasticity techniques or meditation practices. In an article titled "Electrical fingerprint of the amygdala guides neurofeedback training for stress resilience," the authors highlight that a meditation method called *neurofeedback* is effective at reducing amygdala responses, referring to it as "a scalable non-pharmacological yet neuroscience-based training to prevent stress-induced psychopathology."[4] The researchers took 180 soldiers who were undergoing combat readiness training, divided them into two groups, and assigned one group to the amygdala neurofeedback training course. These soldiers watched a video of a hospital worker being berated by angry patients in a waiting room. The soldiers were asked to develop a mental strategy that would make the patients in the video calm down. A brain scanner behind the scenes monitored the brain activity of the soldiers as they were developing these mental models, searching for what the researchers referred to as an "electrical fingerprint" that was present when amygdala activity was suppressed by purposely thinking about calming strategies. The researchers found that during emotional regulation and rational decision-making, this electrical fingerprint was present in the brain, highlighting an increased connection between the amygdala and prefrontal cortex. The researchers continued the electroencephalography in subsequent studies and concluded that stronger connectivity between these two brain areas was present with the soldiers that practiced the neurofeedback than was present with the control group. Essentially, the circuit between the amygdala and prefrontal cortex was stronger within those that used purposeful thinking to come up with mental models to regulate emotional response. Thinking on purpose allowed soldiers who had developed hyper-sensitive emotional responses to reclaim their rationality and mental control. Practicing a version of mindfulness produced physiological and neurological changes that yielded powerful mental benefits. Other researchers have confirmed this phenomenon, citing in "Mindfulness and emotion regulation, an fMRI study," that:[5]

> Emotional dysregulation and maladaptive emotion regulation are major deficits in many psychiatric disorders, such as anxiety disorders or depression. Cognitive control strategies, such as the reappraisal of emotional situations or reality checking, are applied in psychotherapy to compensate these deficits. In the present study, a brief mindfulness intervention showed evidence of emotion-regulating effects on the neural level during an emotional expectation task. We found increased activation in brain regions associated with emotion regulation, along with reduced activation in brain regions involved in the processing of emotional valence and arousal. Mindfulness was associated with marked recruitment of brain structures involved in top–down emotion regulation, mainly in the

expectation of negative or potentially negative stimuli. During the perception of the negative stimuli, mindfulness attenuated activations in brain regions associated with emotion processing.

Mindfulness continues to show promising results in both psychotherapy and neurological treatment of brain disorders. The neuroplasticity benefits continue to be researched in various applications of mental health.

However, mindfulness as a category is extremely broad. There are multiple forms of mindfulness which have emerged recently, within them hundreds of different techniques that all lead to different desired outcomes. This chapter will focus on the proven mindfulness techniques that I have used with clients which align to purposeful cognition, giving you the specific strategies to keep your Inner Passivity, Inner Aggression, Locus of Control, Cognitive Distortion and Emotional Distortion under your control. These hand-selected mindfulness exercises have been used with various coaching clients as a way to specifically target each of these five domains. This chapter will give you the ability to *be* on purpose.

Break Free From Inner Passivity

In a paper titled "Mindful Emotion Regulation: Exploring the Neurocognitive Mechanisms behind Mindfulness," the authors describe how the maintenance of attention involves attentional switching and redirecting attentional drift back to the breath. "Mindfulness meditation requires that this switching and refocusing is conducted with an attitude that involves nonjudgment and openness to current experience, an accepting state of mind that has been referred to as intimate detachment."[6] Essentially, when we have trouble paying attention during a current task and our mind ventures off course, *those that practice mindfulness have an easier ability to stay on task and refocus attention.* There are many reasons why we venture off course or quickly turn toward another task. We may not be open to new experiences, have low impulse control, or have some form of a diagnosed condition like Attention-Deficit Disorder (ADD) or Attention-Deficit Hyperactivity Disorder (ADHD). Another culprit is our Inner Passivity. Remember, Inner Passivity is defined as an unconscious emotional element that limits the flow of our creativity or hinders our self-expression. We are only aware of the surface level symptoms of Inner Passivity. Inner Passivity can inhibit growth within relationships because it affects interrelationship decision making, creates confrontation avoidance, lessons assertiveness, and produces feelings of guilt and anxiety. Research has shown that humans can be addicted to unhappiness, due to psychic masochism and preferring negative emotionality to no emotionality. Inner Passivity is alluring because the human mind has a penchant for the negative, the lazy, and the anxious. When we have trouble focusing on a task, the tendency is to let our mind venture off down the rabbit hole, but not all the way toward ultimate boredom. We seek a state of passivity where our minds are minimally engaged in something trivial so that we can pass the time, hoping the boredom passes over us. Eliminating boredom has become a daily goal for us. One thing that makes this especially easy is digital technology. This is also extremely damaging to our ability to be creative and imaginative.

Psychologists have long studied how boredom affects the human mind. Many agree that being bored makes you much more creative; in both children and adults. In an article titled "How being bored out of your mind makes you more creative," the author writes:[7]

> Boredom might spark creativity because a restless mind hungers for stimulation. Maybe traversing an expanse of tedium creates a sort of cognitive forward motion. Boredom becomes a seeking state...what you're doing now is not satisfying. So you're seeking, you're engaged. A bored mind moves into a "daydreaming" state...parents will tell you that kids with "nothing to do" will eventually invent some weird, fun game to play—with a cardboard box, a light switch, whatever. Philosophers have intuited this for centuries; [Danish philosopher Søren Aabye Kierkegaard] described boredom as a prequel to creation: "The gods were bored; therefore they created human beings."

Psychologists worry that we no longer try to work through these slow moments, but instead look to eliminate them. We reach for our smartphones and mindlessly thumb through social media, boosting our Inner Passivity while attempting to eliminate our ennui and malaise. We waste precious time enslaved to our digital devices, feeding the phantom of our psyche; time that our brains can use to create new inventions and new ways of accomplishing work. Mindfulness can be used in this scenario to reclaim our creative space. We can practice the mindfulness technique of *taking a digital break*.

When we feel overwhelmed, our first instinct is to turn to our devices as a source of comfort. This excessive connectivity also feeds into our FOMO, or "fear of missing out," because we think we are missing something important if we are not constantly plugged in. But mindfully stepping away from your digital devices for short periods of time during your day creates more focus. Take a couple of mini digital breaks during your day for about ten to twenty minutes each. When you are feeling bored, do not reach for a device. This includes television or a tablet to read before bed. Sit and *be* bored. Be *really* bored. Many who honor the religious day of Sabbath (a period of rest between Friday sunset to Saturday sunset for some or all day Sunday for others) often will not use any digital technology during the whole time. It is commonly referred to as a favorite time of the week and time of immense creativity and family connection by those that honor the Sabbath. Taking a digital break will help you use mindfulness to eliminate your Inner Passivity.

Destroy Your Inner Aggression

Inner Aggression is an unconscious force within us that creates many self-defeating thoughts and behaviors on the conscious level. Inner Aggression is dynamic and represents a mental operating system that is constantly critical, defeating, and judgmental. Similar to how we identify Inner Passivity through the surface level manifestations that it creates, Inner Aggression is also identified in the same manner. Common conscious manifestations of Inner Aggression include an inner critic, self-defeating personality disorder, negative self-talk, lack of self-esteem and self-acceptance, and a variety of other self-destructive behaviors. Inner Aggression is the nagging voice that is always trying to bring you down, constantly ridiculing and berating your every move. Luckily, mindfulness can also be used to eliminate negative effects of our Inner Aggression, shifting the power dynamic back toward positivity. The mindfulness technique that is most effective at reducing the effects of our Inner Aggression is the practice of *self-affirmation.*

In a paper titled "Power Affects Performance When the Pressure Is On: Evidence for Low-Power Threat and High-Power Lift," researchers investigated different techniques that could shift power dynamics within various situations. The study authors created negotiation sequences with low-power-threats and high-power-effects, seeking to understand how role-based power affects overall negotiation outcomes. They found that a specific mindfulness technique – the practice of self-affirmation – reduced power differences in negotiations. "Buyers who completed the positive self-affirmation performed significantly better in negotiating a lower sale price for the biotechnology plant, effectively reducing the power differences between the buyer and seller." They concluded the study with "we link these outcomes conceptually to threat and lift effects by showing that...underperformance disappears when the low-power negotiator has an opportunity to self-affirm."[8] Inner Aggression represents a stark psychic power dynamic because your inner critic attempts to halt your progress and suppress your success through self-doubt and by attacking your self-integrity. The eldritch force within you is a powerhouse of negativity that preys on your worst fears. Research published in *Psychological Science* claims that self-affirmations increase our ability to deal with threats and unfavorable feedback (the two weapons of choice for our Inner Aggression). The study authors concluded that:[9]

Self-affirmation produces large effects: Even a simple reminder of one's core values reduces defensiveness against threatening information. But how, exactly, does self-affirmation work? We explored this question by examining the impact of self-affirmation on neurophysiological responses to threatening events. We hypothesized that because self-affirmation increases openness to threat and enhances approachability of unfavorable feedback, it should augment attention and emotional receptivity to performance errors. We further hypothesized that this augmentation could be assessed directly, at the level of the brain. We measured self-affirmed and nonaffirmed participants' electrophysiological responses to making errors on a task. As we anticipated, self-affirmation elicited greater error responsiveness than did nonaffirmation, as indexed by the error-related negativity, a neural signal of error monitoring. Self-affirmed participants also performed better on the task than did nonaffirmed participants.

Mindfulness, specifically the practice of self-affirming, not only increases our capacity to receive negative feedback but also helps shift the power from our Inner Aggression back to our rational brains. The mindfulness practice of self-affirmation that I have used with thousands of coaching clients is performed in the following manner:

1. Make a list of your negative qualities. This includes any criticism from external sources, like siblings, spouses, coworkers, or friends. Don't judge if they are accurate or not, simply write them down.
2. Write down positive affirmations. Now write down any positive aspects of your self-judgement. This can also include any positive remarks from others.
3. Speak out the affirmations out loud. Morning, day and night. As you get ready in the morning, eat lunch, or drive home after a long day, physically say the affirmations that you wrote down in step 2 out loud so that you can hear yourself saying them.
4. Anchor the affirmation. Notice what feels uncomfortable as you are saying your affirmations. Are you shifting in your chair? Does your stomach hurt? Focus on that specific negative feeling, that is seemingly random, as you positively affirm. Keep repeating the affirmation until that negative feeling goes away.
5. Externalize the affirmation. Have external sources, such as friends, coworkers, or loved ones, repeat the affirmations to you.

This is especially helpful before a big event, like a negotiation or job interview. This will bolster external voices, which help silence the inner critic.

There are many ways to self-affirm, and it may take some experimentation to discover what process, cadence, or intensity works for you. The main thing is that you do it, in some form or another. Not only will practicing mindful self-affirmation help restore your psychic power dynamic, but it will also lessen the intensity of your inner critic by giving you an ability to deal with negative or unsolicited internal feedback.

Regain Your Locus of Control

One is said to have an internal Locus of Control if an individual believes that her behaviors are guided by her personal efforts and decisions. One is said to have an external Locus of Control if she believes that her behavior is guided by fate, God, luck, or other external circumstances. If you remember from chapter 10, *positive thinking* about all events that happen is the key to developing an internal Locus of Control. Positive thinking is the most powerful tool you have in shifting your Locus of Control, because it creates new neural pathways, reduces anxiety, and ultimately drives positive behaviors. It's that simple. Luckily, the art of mindfulness is full of various techniques that can take advantage of positive thinking. The most powerful technique that I have used with coaching clients who are trying to regain an internal Locus of Control is the practice of *outcome-directed thinking*.

Outcome-directed thinking is the process of thinking about the end state or final solution to a problem instead of the problem itself. This is also referred to as a goal-oriented or solution-oriented mindset. Thinking about the outcome or end goal not only produces a positive outcome in your mind, but it also creates a variety of virtual paths to reach that goal with much more ease. Remember how you used to do a paper maze when you were younger, and it was considered cheating to start at the end of the maze and work backward? It's because that is a much easier way to complete the maze! That is the same as outcome-directed thinking. By starting with the end of the maze, you can more easily navigate the path forward (or backward, technically). This helps your Locus of Control by keeping your mindset on the positive. People succumb to an external locus if it feels like there is no solution or the problem is "just the way it is." Once you develop a solution to a problem, your mental state shifts toward the positive and toward an internal locus. Starting at the end of the maze, or using outcome-directed thinking, ensures you can see solutions more clearly.

Researchers who investigated the predictors of CBT techniques in relation to chronic pain discovered that goal-oriented thinking had immense physical and mental benefits. Chronic pain is a strong promoter of an external locus – after all, if you are experiencing chronic, ongoing pain, you may tend to think that it is out of your control. The researchers published findings in the *Journal of Pain*:[10]

> Psychological flexibility is the ability to be more aware, more focused on goals and more engaged. Another aspect of psychological flexibility pertinent to chronic pain, and supported by SAC (self-as-context, a therapeutic process that promotes psychological flexibility), is called committed action, which involves goal-directed, flexible persistence...greater psychological flexibility is associated with less pain-related anxiety and avoidance, less depression, less physical and psycho-social disability and other measures of patient function.

When the 412 participants of the study focused on goal-oriented outcomes, rather than on the pain they were feeling that stood in the way of their goals, they developed greater patient functioning. Outcome-directed thinking helped them regain their feelings of control, shifting the locus back to internal. You can use the mindfulness strategy of outcome-directed thinking to regain your internal locus, ultimately giving you the power to feel that your life is a consequence of your own actions and effort, not random luck or chance.

Starve Your Cognitive Distortion

Authors of *Mindfulness Workbook for OCD* claim that "cognitive distortions are the language of OCD," or obsessive-compulsive disorder. The National Institute of Mental Health defines OCD as "a common, chronic and long-lasting disorder in which a person has uncontrollable, reoccurring thoughts (obsessions) and behaviors (compulsions) that he or she feels the urge to repeat over and over."[11] If obsessions and compulsions are uncontrollable and are the language of Cognitive Distortion, is all hope lost? Recent research into memory and thought suppression seem to suggest otherwise.

Researchers at the University of Cambridge investigated the key chemicals within the brain that allow us to suppress unwanted thoughts and memories. The authors wrote:[12]

> Our ability to control our thoughts is fundamental to our well-being. When this capacity breaks down, it causes some of the most debilitating symptoms of psychiatric diseases: intrusive memories, images, hallucinations, ruminations,

and pathological and persistent worries. These are all key symptoms of mental illnesses such as PTSD, schizophrenia, depression, and anxiety.

The researchers discovered that a chemical named GABA (Gamma-Amino Butyric Acid) is the main inhibitory neurotransmitter in the brain. The test subjects with high levels of GABA had an ability to block the retrieval process and prevent thoughts from returning or occurring. The authors conclude:[13]

> The ability to disengage from unwanted thoughts is essential to mental health. Our results suggest that GABAergic inhibition of hippocampal retrieval processes enables such thoughts to be suppressed...these findings suggest that a functionally specific fronto-hippocampal inhibitory control pathway underlies the ability to suppress unwanted thoughts, and that the functional integrity of this pathway may depend on GABAergic interneuron networks local to the hippocampus.

This is the first time that a chemical has been identified as the neurotransmitter which can block the retrieval of unwanted thoughts. There is a two-pronged strategy that you can deploy to not only increase GABA levels naturally but also to naturally lessen the power of negative thoughts.

GABA, much like serotonin, is an inhibitory transmitter that has profound effects on the brain. Serotonin helps with impulse control, sleep, pain relief, and mood positivity, while GABA's main focus is to provide a calming and relaxing effect on the brain. As with most inhibitory transmitters, there are various ways to boost them naturally, without the need for chemicals or prescription drugs. In *30 Days to Everyday Anxiety Relief*, the author states that the vitamins Zinc, B6 and Magnesium improve GABA, as well as keeping blood-sugar levels stable and focusing on improving gut biome health.[14] However, the main way to increase GABA is to practice frequent, deep breathing. Mindfulness meditation incorporates deep breathing in many different exercises, meaning that a variety of different exercises can help you naturally boost GABA levels by focusing on deep, present, breathing. It's that simple. There is, however, a newly discovered non-natural way to increase GABA. Researchers[15] have found that hippocampal low-frequency stimulation (Hip-LFS) via an implanted brain electrode also increases GABA receptor expression. When researchers sought to inhibit amygdala stimulus-induced epileptic seizures in rats by shocking various parts of the brain with electricity, they found that certain types of shocks could also up-regulate GABA receptor expression. Call me crazy, but I'll take deep breathing over an implanted cattle prod.

The second prong of this two-part strategy is not to waste time trying to suppress thoughts at all. For example, don't think about pink elephants. Did that work? Chances are pink elephants are prancing around in your brain right now (you're welcome). Trying to suppress thoughts by thinking about suppressing thoughts doesn't work. Instead, trying to suppress thoughts by thinking about suppressing the thoughts labels them as unwanted. Unwanted and always occurring thoughts lead to OCD because we label the thoughts as "not our own," obsessive, or compulsive, because we do not want to have them, yet they continue to occur frequently. Many believe that mindfulness is a way to clear the mind, but this is a misconception. Mindfulness is about accepting your thoughts *non-judgmentally*. If you can accept your thoughts, they won't be obsessive or lead to compulsive behavior, ultimately blunting Cognitive Distortion. The mindfulness technique that helps you starve your Cognitive Distortion is the practice of *acceptance*. Accept everything that you think about. Not as good, nor as bad. Just as is. If you do not judge your thoughts, they can run free, eliminating any psychological weight you may ascribe to them which could eventually lead to negative rumination or compulsive thinking. Accept your thoughts the same way your skin accepts the wind blowing outside. The wind swirls all around you and just *is*. The wind may be a bit cold, but put on a coat and don't mind it anymore. You'll start to realize that the wind doesn't go away, but you simply don't notice it anymore.

Know Your Emotional Distortion

Remember back in chapter 12 where I discussed the last domain of Emotional Distortion. Emotional Distortion is the lack of emotional self-awareness, which ultimately drives errors in cognition and incorrect memory labeling. Lacking emotional self-awareness can produce a multitude of negative outcomes and developing this skill should be the cornerstone of any performance or mental health plan. Outside of developing core skills like emotional intelligence, mindfulness is a powerful way to eliminate Emotional Distortion. Researchers looked at how practicing mindfulness affected the brain and emotional regulation. In "Mindful Emotion Regulation: Exploring the Neurocognitive Mechanisms behind Mindfulness" the authors wrote:[16]

> Recent investigations...tested the skills of mindfulness meditators to reduce the emotional intensity they felt in response to an unpleasant image. The authors tested twelve long-time meditators and ten beginner meditators as they looked at pleasant, unpleasant, and neutral images, recording the task with fMRI. The results showed that both groups were able to experience reduced emotional reactions

on a subjective and neural level using mindfulness whilst looking at the images. Yet [the authors] further observed two different emotional regulation mechanisms that depend on the degree of experience of the meditator. In experienced meditators the medial prefrontal and posterior cingulate cortices were deactivated and did not influence brain regions involved in emotional reactivity during emotional processing. However, for beginner meditators, mindfulness induced a downregulation of the left amygdala during emotional processing. [Another] study with sound stimuli similarly found a negative correlation between the length of meditation hours and activation of the right amygdala while listening to unpleasant stimuli. These studies therefore suggest that practiced mindfulness skills lead to emotional regulation through accepting emotional states and enhancing present-moment awareness, whilst beginner mindfulness skills appear to rely on higher cortical brain regions to control low-level affective cerebral systems. The mechanism of self-regulation utilized during mindfulness therefore depends on the degree to which the meditator has practiced mindfulness.

Essentially, experienced mindfulness practitioners are able to completely shut off the portions of the brain that influence emotional reactivity and processing. Novice mindfulness practitioners are only able to suppress some amygdala activity, yielding some benefits right from the start. These findings suggest that mindfulness as a skill continues to develop and it creates neurological benefits in response to Emotional Distortion. One of the most powerful mindfulness techniques that I use with coaching clients who suffer from high levels of Emotional Distortion is to *awaken with gratitude.*

Gratitude is widely studied as a powerful, if not the most powerful, positivity-inducing psychological mechanism that yields immense benefit. Researchers have found that gratitude is the single most important ingredient in sustaining a healthy marriage[17] and romantic success,[18] is the key to happiness,[19] can win you new friends,[20] and can reduce impatience.[21] Within mindfulness, you can awaken with gratitude and train your mind to focus on the positive; to be thankful for everything that you have.

When we don't have gratitude for all that we have, we cheat the dreams of our younger self. Where you are today is where your younger self dreamed you would be (hopefully). Humans tend to dream about the places we will go, the things we will buy, and the activities that we will do. But many of us instantly move on to the next dream once we achieve or acquire what we used to dream about. Ever notice how you can spend years thinking about graduating college or getting a fancy sports car, only to reach that stage and then you instantly start thinking about something else? When we don't express gratitude for what we have, we continue to have anxiety about the future. We cheat the dreams of our younger selves. Take a moment to express gratitude. Even if you aren't where you thought you would be – you don't have the fancy car or you never graduated college – there are many things that you can be thankful for. Finding things to be thankful for, no matter how big or small, helps you eliminate the Emotional Distortion that is aligned to future rumination by forcing you to focus on the present. Gratitude aligns you with the present because it forces you to think about all of the good things that you have in your life.

In Sum

- Mindfulness is the practice of being present and not focusing on anything except what is right in front of you. Not one minute, hour, or day into the past or the future, only right here, right now. Many researchers have found powerful connections between practicing mindfulness and reducing anxiety and depression.
- We can practice the mindfulness technique of *taking a digital break* to battle Inner Passivity.
- The mindfulness technique that is most effective at reducing the effects of our Inner Aggression is the practice of *self-affirmation*.
- The most powerful technique to regain an internal Locus of Control is the practice of *outcome-directed thinking*.
- The mindfulness technique that helps you starve your Cognitive Distortion is the practice of *acceptance* and *deep breathing*.
- The most powerful mindfulness technique for those that suffer from high levels of Emotional Distortion is to *awaken with gratitude*.

CHAPTER 17 | PART III SUMMARY

"Keep your face to the sunshine and you cannot see a shadow."

HELEN KELLER

"Our minds influence the key activity of the brain, which influences everything; perception, cognition, thoughts and feelings, personal relationships; they're all a reflection of you."

DEEPAK CHOPRA, American-Indian Author

Part III centered on various real-world applications of thinking on purpose. Being a better leader, maximizing our relationships with others, or simply figuring out how to live in the present, are all areas that are affected by purposeful cognition. Our Inner Passivity, Inner Aggression, Locus of Control, Cognitive and Emotional Distortions rob us of our ability to lead organizations, have meaningful relationships with others and ourselves, and live the life that we deserve to live. Hopefully, by now, the research and content contained in this book successfully proselytize the idea that thinking on purpose is the key to everything. Our thoughts have a more profound impact on our entire human experience than anything else.

Leadership, relating to others, and mindfulness are all considered skills. They are skills we are not born with but develop over time. As with the acquisition of most skills, the environment and the processes we learn within have a profound impact on our ability to retain knowledge and later apply those skills. This is what the discipline of epistemology addresses.

Epistemology is the study of the nature, origin, and limits of human knowledge. The term is derived from the Greek *epistēmē* ("knowledge") and *logos* ("reason"), and accordingly, the field is sometimes referred to as the theory of knowledge. Aristotle first postulated that philosophy itself begins in a kind of puzzlement. Humans wish to comprehend the world that they live in and construct theories and symbols to help them do so. Epistemology is based on three conditions: truth, belief, and justification. Our ability to think on purpose can drastically affect these three conditions, meaning that our ability to learn vital life skills is dependent on our ability to clearly understand the world around us.

Take our vision for example. Many people believe what their eyes show them. But our vision can play tricks on us. Imagine a scenario where a stick is submerged in water and looks bent, even though it is not. Railroad tracks seem to merge in the distance, though they don't. We need to interpret our experiential phenomena through a cognitive filter to truly learn what is real. We need to think clearly to acquire the proper knowledge: the water doesn't bend the stick, water just appears to bend the stick through different light refraction. Essentially, epistemology refers to our knowledge acquisition and encompasses a construction of concepts and a validation of our senses. Aristotle posited that without logos (reason) humans would have no reason to believe in thoughts and actions. Our ability to reason and think about what our senses tell us is the difference between true and false knowledge.

Leadership, relationships, mindfulness, emotional intelligence, and many other life skills are acquired through our various senses. Our ability to think on purpose ensures that the acquisition of knowledge as we progress through life is pure and true.

Existentialism is another philosophical area which contains applications of purposeful thinking. According to existentialism, existence is always particular and individual, meaning that everyone has a unique existence. Humans *exist first* and then each individual spends a lifetime seeking knowledge to explain their individual existence or change their nature. Existentialism is concerned with finding oneself through free will, choice, and responsibility. Existentialists believe that through this pursuit, each of us creates a unique existence that is not able to be known by any other human being. This aligns with the "Problem of Other Minds," which is a philosophical problem that asks the question "given that I can only observe the outward behavior of others, how can I be sure that they have minds?" This philosophical position aligns with solipsism, which you should remember from chapter 15, is the notion that for any person, only one's own mind is known to exist. If each of us has a unique life experience, acquires knowledge differently, or is unsure that anyone else even has a mind, that means the world is a pretty lonely place! It also means that we can only be sure of our own mind and the power within it. Our mind shapes how we acquire knowledge and how we discover our true selves in this life. If we align with the philosophies of epistemology and existentialism, developing an ability to think on purpose is our only known way to clearly interpret the world around us. Purposeful cognition is not only a powerful tool in this quest, it is the only one we have.

CHAPTER 18 | CONCLUSION

"Now is not the end. It is not even the beginning of the end. But it is, perhaps, the end of the beginning."

WINSTON CHURCHILL

"Wisdom begins at the end."

DANIEL WEBSTER, American statesmen

In 2017, U.S. deaths from alcohol, drugs, and suicide hit the highest level since record-keeping began.[1] A newly released study from the National Safety Council found that Americans are now more likely to die from an opioid overdose than a car accident. For the first time in history, humans are self-medicating with drugs and alcohol as an attempt to battle our inner demons and it is killing us faster than anything else.

At the World Mental Health Day in 2017, the Duke of Cambridge spoke at Buckingham Palace about the increasing importance of mental health. He called for immediate action, asking the world to dedicate more resources than ever toward treating mental health. Ending with an impassioned peroration in which he declared, "we now accept that the health of our minds is as essential as the health of our bodies. Tonight, on the evening of World Mental Health Day, we celebrate that while there is more work to do, the walls of judgment and stigma around mental illness are finally falling." He was speaking about the emotional challenges of veterans, highlighting that overcoming emotional distress is as challenging, if not more so, than overcoming physical injuries. While the growing global focus of treating mental health is timely, more emphasis needs to be centered on psychological strategies to combat mental health issues that discourage sufferers from reaching for chemical solutions. The real-world consequences of self-medication which are affecting our friends, families, children, and loved ones are too profound and too permanent, often seeming indomitable. But this can be solved. We need to shift the collective mindset back inward, leaning on one of the most powerful forces this world has ever known – the human mind.

Humans will always have wavering levels of Inner Passivity and Inner Aggression. We will always believe on some varying level that some higher power is guiding our path and that our life's events aren't completely our own. Our brains will always distort events because the emotional centers of our brain are using an ancient mammalian language to communicate to our rational decision center.

But that is OK.

While eliminating these five psychological domains sounds enticing, it isn't feasible. We will always be wired to worry about danger, ruminate about the future, and succumb to fight or flight. That is a byproduct of the survival instinct which has kept the human race around for thousands of years. This is also a result of our emotional-rational communication pathway. A recent study[2] published in the *Journal of Scientific Reports* showed that researchers were able to predict decisions eleven seconds before people acted. In the study, the researchers used fMRI scans to monitor brain activity to recognize decision-making patterns before they became conscious in the brain. They were able to predict motor decisions eleven seconds before they were conscious and abstract decisions up to four seconds before they were conscious within the study participants. Our rational thinking centers will always be late to the party.

But that is OK.

The goal of mental health isn't about *achieving* a certain psychological state but in *pursuing* a better psychological state. Even body-builders, who are considered paragons of physical health, always strive to get stronger. They never achieve a state of perfection, rather they always seek to pursue it. Even the Founding Fathers of the United States of America, when writing the Declaration of Independence, wrote about "unalienable rights" which the Declaration says have been given to all humans by their creator, and which governments are created to protect. Those rights are "life, liberty and the pursuit of happiness." Notice how they didn't write life, liberty, and happiness? This is because happiness means something different to everyone and it is the *pursuit itself* that creates happiness as humans self-actualize. Much like happiness, mental health means something different to everyone. Some may suffer from high levels of Inner Passivity while others may have an inner critic that is overwhelmingly powerful. Some may agonize in distorted states while others simply allow life to happen to them. Everyone has a different definition of mental health and the elixirs that will deliver it, but each of us can embark on the same pursuit of it.

What affects our ability to think on purpose constantly shifts as well. The peripatetic nature of our inner demons makes it hard to pin down which domain, or combination of domains, is obstructing our ability to think on purpose. One day, Inner Passivity might be the culprit, while on another day, Inner Aggression may take over. The point is that we should not focus on obtaining a *state* of mental health but rather focus on the *pursuit* of it, through the practices outlined in this book.

Harold Percival authored a weighty tome in 1946 titled *Thinking and Destiny* where he proposed the notion that thinking creates karma and destiny. He offers a complete cosmology of the universe, conveying how to perfect our thinking and learn to think without creating thoughts. In chapter 14 of his thousand-page book, he writes:[3]

> By this system one may train himself to think without creating thoughts, that is, destiny; the system will aid him in knowing his Triune Self and, possibly, in becoming conscious of Consciousness. The system is concerned with training the feeling-mind and the desire-mind to control the body-mind; and, by control of the body-mind to control the senses, instead of allowing the senses to control the body-mind and thereby to control the minds of feeling-and-desire. By training oneself how to feel, what to desire, and how to think, the body will be trained at the same time. By this system one may locate and find the bearings of the portion of the doer dwelling in his body. If and while he does this, changes will be brought about in the body; diseases will disappear in their proper order, and the body will become sound and responsive and efficient...one who practices this system need not depend upon any other person than himself. His own thinker and knower will teach him as he gradually becomes conscious of them.

Percival was referring to thinking on purpose. He describes thinking on purpose as the key to knowing your true self, enhancing overall consciousness, and ridding the body of ailments. While Percival was able to link purposeful cognition to the cosmos, he wasn't able to uncover which psychological domains blocked purposeful thinking. The Purposeful Cognition Index is the first of its kind. The assessment measures levels of Inner Passivity, Inner Aggression, Locus of Control, Cognitive Distortion and Emotional Distortion, giving you a roadmap to help you on your pursuit of mental clarity.

At the beginning of this book, I mentioned that our most powerful drug available to us is our own mind. As the Buddha claimed, "our life is the creation of our mind." Our thoughts affect our mental and physical health, our relationships with others, and our entire worldly experience. The American Psychological Association states "the full public health benefits of such research will only be realized if behavioral, psychosocial and medical interventions for the prevention and treatment of mental and physical health conditions are evaluated individually and in combination. The Centers for

Disease Control and Prevention estimates that health behaviors account for at least 50 percent of all health problems and research indicates that health behaviors are related to 40 percent of premature deaths in the United States."

The time to act is now.

I hope that by learning of the psychological theories in this book, along with your new understanding of the five domains that block purposeful cognition, you have developed a new ability to think on purpose. I hope that your desire to combat mental stresses that arise in your life with chemicals or other self-administered medications is now diminished or completely eliminated. You have the power to own your thoughts, control your mind, and use purposeful thinking to create the life that you want. You are in control of the greatest superpower this universe has ever known – the human mind. Your thoughts guide your behaviors, which ultimately lead to your destiny. You now have the tools to harness its infinite power.

Now, let's see all that you can accomplish when you have fully developed your ability to think on purpose.

About the Purposeful Cognition Index

The Purposeful Cognition Index (PCI) was created with one goal in mind – to help you identify the psychological factors that are prohibiting you from thinking on purpose. Throughout all of psychological history, there have been hundreds of theories, ideas, and concepts that have been applied toward the betterment of mental health. Many of those theories that are still applicable today are organized into the five domains you have learned about in this book.

The ability to think on purpose ensures that you are in total control of your mental processes and the subsequent behaviors that follow. Thinking on purpose safeguards your memories, protects your perceptions, enhances your relationships and increases your social agility. Developing the ability to think on purpose is a cardinal aspect of mental health because it enables you to battle two of the most powerful emotions which have crippled humanity and created unhealthy dependencies on medications, drugs, and other detrimental coping mechanisms: anxiety and depression. By developing your ability to think on purpose, you will be able to understand and combat your levels of Inner Passivity and Inner Aggression, shift toward an internal Locus of Control, and eliminate both Cognitive and Emotional Distortion.

I developed the PCI after aggregating thousands of hours of coaching and therapy session notes into common themes and then I categorized them into the five domains. I reviewed the history of mental health treatment and much of the research aligned with psychological strategies that addressed these various domains. Early versions of the PCI were given to volunteers who had previously established being affected by one or more of the five domains. The assessment results verified accurately which of the five domains (and the degree within each domain) affected each participant.

Disclaimer about the PCI – All rights reserved. The PCI is not to be used to treat or diagnose any psychological condition, disease, ailment, or disorder. The results of your PCI assessment should be used for academic purposes only in order to develop an awareness of the concepts discussed in this book or to have meaningful conversations with your PCI certified coach. The PCI should not be used for any medical purposes. The intent of the author is only to offer information in a general nature to help you in your quest for emotional and spiritual well-being. Please seek a qualified professional if you suffer from any psychological or mental health disorders.

The PCI is currently available for you to take at www.Psyndesis.com/pci. I encourage you to take the assessment now so that you can determine which of the five domains affect your ability to think on purpose.

References

Adam, C. & Tannery, P. (1901). "La Recherche de la Vérité par La Lumiere Naturale." Oeuvres de Descartes, X, p. 535.

Admon, R. (2009). "Human vulnerability to stress depends on amygdala's predisposition and hippocampal plasticity." PNAS.

Aguilar, O. (2008). "Growing Environmental Stewards: The Overall Effect of a School Gardening Program on Environmental Attitudes and Environmental Locus of Control of Different Demographic Groups of Elementary School Children." *HortTechnology*.

Aczel, A. (2000). "The mystery of the Aleph: mathematics, the Kabbalah, and the search for infinity." New York: Four Walls Eight Windows.

Adolphs, R. (2009). The social brain: neural basis of social knowledge. *Annual review of psychology*, 60, 693-716.

Alexander, C. (1986). "Transcendental Consciousness: A Fourth State of consciousness beyond Sleep, Dream, and Waking."

Allais, M. (1953). "Le Comportement de l'Homme Rationnel devant le Risque: Critique des Postulats et Axiomes de l'Ecole Americaine."

Allione, T. (2008). "Feeding your demons: ancient wisdom for resolving inner conflict."

Anderson, J.R. (2010). *Cognitive Psychology and Its Implications*. New York, NY

"Autism and nutrition: The role of the gut-brain axis." Nutrition Research Reviews.

Ayalla, R. (2013). "When bad gets worse: the amplifying effect of materialism on traumatic stress and maladaptive consumption." *Journal of the Academy of Marketing Science*.

Balota, D.A. & Marsh, E.J. (2004). *Cognitive Psychology: Key Readings*. New York, NY: Psychology Press.

Bar-On, R. (1997). *BarOn Emotional Quotient Inventory*.

Beck, A. T. (1976). *Cognitive therapies and emotional disorders.* New York, NY, US: New American Library.

Beck, A.T. (1983). *Cognitive therapy of depression: New perspectives.* In P.J.

Bergland, C. (2017). "How do neuroplasticity and neurogenesis rewire your brain?" *Psychology Today.*

Bergler, E. (1952). *The Superego.* Madison, Connecticut.

Bergler, E. (1992). *Principles of Self-Damage.* Madison, Connecticut: International Universities Press.

Berkum, J. (2010). "Language in action. Mood and language comprehension."

Bested, A. (2013). "Intestinal microbiota, probiotics and mental health."

Blatt, S.J. (2008). "Polarities of experience: Relatedness and self-definition in personality, development, psychopathology, and the therapeutic process."

Blumer, H. (1969). *Symbolic interactionism: perspective and method.* Englewood Cliffs, N.J.: Prentice-Hall.

Botwin, M. D., Buss, D. M. and Shackelford, T. K. Personality and Mate Preferences: Five Factors In Mate Selection and Marital Satisfaction. Journal of Personality, 65: 107-136.

Bradberry, T. (2018). "9 Signs Your Perfectionism Is Out Of Control."

Brady, D. (2013). "Charles Manson's turning point: Dale Carnegie classes." *Business Week.*

Brown, B. (1999). *Soul without shame: a guide to liberating yourself from the judge within.* Boston: Shambhala Publications.

Brown, R. *A First Language.*

Bundrant, M. "Inner Passivity: How We Trick Ourselves into Helplessness."

Bryant, J., & Miron, D. (2003). "Excitation-transfer theory."

Bugental, J. (1964). "The third force in psychology." *Journal of Humanistic Psychology*.

Burns, D. D. (1980). *Feeling good: The new mood therapy*. New York, NY, US: New American Library.

Burns, D. D. (1989). *The feeling good handbook*. New York, NY, US: Morrow.

Burrow, A. & Rainone, N. (2016). "How many likes did I get?: Purpose moderates links between positive social media feedback and self-esteem." *Journal of Experimental Social Psychology*.

California Institute of Technology. (2010). "Gain and loss in optimistic versus pessimistic brains."

Campbell, J. (1971). "Hero with a thousand faces."

Carabotti, M. (2015). "The gut-brain axis: interactions between enteric microbiota, central and enteric nervous systems."

Carnegie, D. (1936). *How to Win Friends and Influence People*.

Carson, R. (2003). "Taming your gremlin: a surprisingly simple method for getting out of your own way."

Chan, R (2017). "Low-frequency hippocampal–cortical activity drives brain-wide resting-state functional MRI connectivity." *Proceedings of the National Academy of Sciences*.

Charon, J. (2004). *Symbolic Interactionism An Introduction, An Interpretation, An Integration*. Boston: Pearson.

Cherry, K. (2018). "The Role of the Biological Perspective in Psychology."

Cherry, K. (2018). "What is Biopsychology, Brain and Behavior?"

Chrousos, G. P. and Gold, P. W. (1992). "The concepts of stress and stress system disorders. Overview of physical and behavioral homeostasis." JAMA 267(Mar 4), 1244-52.

Clayton, J. "Treatment of Depression: Old Controversies and New Approaches." New York: Raven Press.

Cohen, P. N. (2018). The Coming Divorce Decline.

Cornell, A. (2005). "Radical gentleness: the inner critic transforms."

Cozzi, G. (2018). "Will a shrink make you richer? Gender differences in the effects of psychotherapy on labour efficiency." *European Economic Review*, Volume 109.

Crabtree, A. *Animal Magnetism, Early Hypnotism, and Psychical Research, 1766–1925 – An Annotated Bibliography.*

Crocq, M. A. (2015). "A history of anxiety: from Hippocrates to DSM." Dialogues in clinical neuroscience, 17(3), 319-25.

Damasio, A R. (1994). *Descartes' error : emotion, reason, and the human brain.* New York.

Debus, A. (1993). "Paracelsus and the medical revolution of the Renaissance."

Descartes, R. (1644). *Principia Philosophiae.*

Donald, D. (1995). *Lincoln.* New York: Simon and Schuster.

Dufresne, T. "Psychoanalysis Is Dead ... So How Does That Make You Feel?"

Earley, J. (2010). "Self-therapy for your inner critic: transforming self-criticism into self-confidence."

Eastwick, P. W., & Finkel, E. J. (2008). Sex differences in mate preferences revisited: Do people know what they initially desire in a romantic partner? *Journal of Personality and Social Psychology*, 94(2), 245-264.

Ezkurdia I. (2014). "Multiple evidence strands suggest that there may be as few as 19,000 human protein-coding genes." *Human Molecular Genetics.* 23 (22): 5866–78.

Ferguson, M. (2011). "You cannot leave it at the office: Spillover and crossover of coworker incivility." *Journal of Organizational Behavior.*

Ferster, C. B., & Skinner, B. F. (1957). *Schedules of reinforcement.*

Finkel, E. J. (2015). The Suffocation Model: Why Marriage in America Is Becoming an All-or-Nothing Institution. *Current Directions in Psychological Science*, 24(3), 238–244.

Firestone, R. (2002). "Conquer your critical inner voice: a revolutionary program to counter negative thoughts and live free from imagined limitations." Oakland, CA: New Harbinger Publications.

Firestone, L. (2018). *Conquer Your Critical Inner Voice.*

Fischer, S. (2013). *Hieronymus Bosch.* The Complete Works, Cologne.

Fitzgerald, K. "Error-related hyperactivity of the anterior cingulate cortex in obsessive-compulsive disorder." *Biological Psychiatry.*

Fotopoulou A. (2007). "Confabulation: Motivated reality monitoring." *Neuropsychologia.* 45 (10): 2180–90.

Franck, I. (1989). *Healers.* New York.

Freeman, J. (2011). "Integrated Emotions: Rethinking the way we evaluate our feelings."

Freeman, J. (2018). *"How to Improve Emotional Intelligence: 10 Tip for Increasing Self-Awareness."*

"Frequently Asked Questions About Lobotomies." (2005). NPR.

Freud, S. (1920). *Beyond the pleasure principle.*

Freud, S. (1923). *The ego and the id.*

Freud, S. and Rieff, P. (2008). *Three Case Histories.* New York, NY: Touchstone.

Friedrich, N. (1880). "The Wanderer and His Shadow."

Galen, P. (1986). "On bloodletting: a study of the origins, development, and validity of his opinions, with a translation of the three works." Cambridge University Press.

Garvin, D. (1993). "Building a Learning Organization." Harvard Business Review.

Geert-Jan, W. (2017). "Neural and computational processes underlying dynamic changes in self-esteem." *eLife*.

Gilpin, H. (2017). "Predictors of Treatment Outcome in Contextual Cognitive and Behavioral Therapies for Chronic Pain: A Systematic Review." *The Journal of Pain*.

Golding, J. (2018). "The relationship between parental Locus of Control and adolescent obesity: a longitudinal pre-birth cohort." *International Journal of Obesity*.

Green, C. (2001). *Classics in the History of Psychology*. York University, Toronto, Ontario. ISSN 1492-3713.

Greening, T. (2006). "Five basic postulates of humanistic psychology." *Journal of Humanistic Psychology*.

Grecucci, A. (2015). "Mindful Emotion Regulation: Exploring the Neurocognitive Mechanisms behind Mindfulness." *BioMed Research International*.

Griffin, D. (2014). "Locus of Control and Psychological Well-Being: Separating the Measurement of Internal and External Constructs -- A Pilot Study."

Haggerty, J. *History of Psychotherapy*.

Haidt, J. (2006). *The Happiness Hypothesis*.

Hamilton, J. (2015). "Depressive Rumination, the Default-Mode Network, and the Dark Matter of Clinical Neuroscience." *Biological Psychiatry*.

Hammer, G. (2018). *Hypnosis*. Encyclopedia Britannica.

Haque, A. (2004). "Psychology from Islamic Perspective: Contributions of Early Muslim Scholars and Challenges to Contemporary Muslim Psychologists." *Journal of Religion and Health*.

Heine, S. J. (2011). *Cultural Psychology*. New York: W. W. Norton & Company.

Hess, J.P. (2010). "The psychology of scary movies." Filmmaker IQ.

Hogan, R. (1990). "The Dark Side of Personality and Extreme Leader Behavior."

Hogan, R. (2015). "Reflections on the Dark Side."

Hogan, R. (2009). "Why Personality Matters."

Hollingham, R. (2008). *Blood and Guts: A History of Surgery*. New York: St Martin's Press.

Isgandarova, N. (2015). "Music in Islamic spiritual care: a review of classical sources." *Religious Studies and Theology*.

Jackson, S. W. (1999). *Care of the Psyche: A History of Psychological Healing*. Yale University Press.

Jackson, W. (2001). "A short guide to humoral medicine." *Trends in Pharmacological Sciences*.

Johansson, J. (2016). "Greater Fall Risk in Elderly Women Than in Men Is Associated With Increased Gait Variability During Multitasking."

Johnson & Scott. (1976). "The Weapon Effect on Eyewitness Testimonies."

Jonason, P. K. (2015). Relationship Dealbreakers: Traits People Avoid in Potential Mates. *Personality and Social Psychology Bulletin*, 41(12), 1697–1711 Joseph, S. (2017). *Authentic: How to be yourself and why it matters*.

Judge, T. A.; Locke, E. A.; Durham, C. C. (1997). "The dispositional causes of job satisfaction: A core evaluations approach." *Research in Organizational Behavior*. 19: 151–188.

Kahneman, D. (2011). *Thinking, fast and slow*.

Kass, F. (1987). "Self-Defeating Personality Disorder: An Empirical Study." *Journal of Personality Disorders*.

Keele University. "Humor styles and bullying in schools: Not a laughing matter." *ScienceDaily*.

Kellert, S. H. (1993). "In the Wake of Chaos: Unpredictable Order in Dynamical Systems." University of Chicago Press.

Kendon, A. (1975). *Organization of Behavior in Face-To-Face Interaction.*

Kenyon, J. (2019). "Electrical fingerprint of the amygdala guides neurofeedback training for stress resilience." *Nature Human Behavior.* 3, pages 63–73 (2019).

Kihlstrom, J. "Is Freud Still Alive? No, Not Really."

Kocaslan, G. (2014). "Quantum Interpretation to Decision Making Under Risk: The Observer Effect In Allais Paradox." *NeuroQuantology.*

Kok, B. "How Positive Emotions Build Physical Health: Perceived Positive Social Connections Account for the Upward Spiral Between Positive Emotions and Vagal Tone."

Kruglanski, & E. T. Higgins. *Handbook of theories of social psychology.* Thousand Oaks, CA: Sage Publications Ltd.

Larner, A. (2002). "Phineas Gage and the beginnings of neuropsychology." *Advances in Clinical Neuroscience and Rehabilitation.* 2 (3): 26

Leary, M. R. (2012). *Sociometer theory.*

Legault, L. (2012). "Preserving Integrity in the Face of Performance Threat: Self-Affirmation Enhances Neurophysiological Responsiveness to Errors." *Psychological Science.*

Lee, Y. (2015). "Psychological links between type of mobile phone user and stress." *Behaviour & Information Technology.*

Lewis, R. (1979). "Taking Chances, The Psychology of Losing and How to Profit From It."

Loftus E. (1992). "Is the unconscious smart or dumb?" *Am Psychol.*

Loh, K. K., & Kanai, R. (2014). "Higher media multi-tasking activity is associated with smaller gray-matter density in the anterior cingulate cortex." *PLOS ONE.*

Longe, O. (2010). "Having a word with yourself: Neural correlates of self-criticism and self-reassurance." *Neuroimage.*

Lutz, J. (2014). "Mindfulness and emotion regulation, an fMRI study." University of Switzerland.

Mader, S. S. (2000). *Human biology.* McGraw-Hill, New York.

Maslow, A. H. (1970). *Motivation and personality.* New York: Harper & Row.

Maslow, A. H. (1970). *Religions, values, and peak experiences.* New York: Penguin.

Maltby, D. (2007). "Personality, Individual Differences and Intelligence."

Matthews, R. "Freud: He Wasn't All Wrong."

McLeod, S. A. (2008). "Wilhelm Wundt."

McLeod, S. A. (2016). "Id, ego and superego."

McLeod, S. A. (2017). "Psychodynamic approach."

McLeod, S. A. (2018). "Skinner - operant conditioning."

McNally, L. (2012). "Cooperation and the evolution of intelligence." Proceedings of the Royal Society B: Biological Sciences.

Menon, S. (2014). "Interdisciplinary Perspectives on Consciousness and the Self."

Mikulovic, S. (2018). "Ventral hippocampal OLM cells control type 2 theta oscillations and response to predator odor." *Nature Communications.*

Miller, G. A. (1956). "The magical number seven, plus or minus two: Some limits on our capacity for processing information." *Psychological Review.*

Moisala. (2015). "Media multitasking is associated with distractibility and increased prefrontal activity in adolescents and young adults."

Moll, T. (2010). "Emotional contagion in soccer penalty shootouts: Celebration of individual success is associated with ultimate team success." *Journal of Sports Sciences.*

Morin, A. (2018). *13 Things Mentally Strong People Don't Do.*

Muhammad I. "The Reconstruction of Religious Thought in Islam. The Spirit of Muslim Culture."

Nguyen, L. (2018). "The impact of gratitude on adolescent materialism and generosity."

Normand, B. (2007). "Intellectual Self-Defense." Seven Stories Press.

Nummenmaa, L. (2014). "Bodily maps of emotions." *Proceedings of the National Academy of Sciences.*

O'Brien, L. (2013). "The curious appeal of horror movies: Why do we like to feel scared?" IGN.

Ohio University. "Dwelling on stressful events can increase inflammation in the body, study finds." *ScienceDaily.*

Palmer, D. (2006). "On Chomsky's Appraisal of Skinner's Verbal Behavior: A Half Century of Misunderstanding." *The Behavior analyst*, 29(2), 253-67.

Palombo, D. (2016). "Medial Temporal Lobe Contributions to Episodic Future Thinking: Scene Construction or Future Projection?" *Cerebral Cortex.*

Pashler, H. (2002). "Stevens' Handbook of Experimental Psychology." New York: Wiley.

Park, J. (2017). "Baroreflex dysfunction and augmented sympathetic nerve responses during mental stress in veterans with posttraumatic stress disorder (PTSD)." *The Journal of Physiology.*

Percival, H. (1947). *Thinking and Destiny.*

Pevnser, J. "Leonardo da Vinci's contributions to neuroscience." *Trends in Neuroscience*, Volume 25, Issue 4.

Plato, Phaedrus, trans. by Alexander Nehamas and Paul Woodruff. From Plato: Complete Works, ed. by John M. Cooper.

Plutchik, R. (1982). "A psychoevolutionary theory of emotions." *Social Science Information,* 21(4–5), 529–553.

Purdy, E. (2019). *30 Days to Everyday Anxiety Relief.*

Reinhart, R. (2014). "Causal Control of Medial-Frontal Cortex Governs Electrophysiological and Behavioral Indices of Performance Monitoring and Learning." *Journal of Neuroscience.*

Restak, R. (2000). "Fixing the Brain." Mysteries of the Mind. Washington, D.C.: National Geographic Society.

Revonsuo, A. (2010). *Consciousness: The Science of Subjectivity.*

Robert, K. (2019. "Decoding the contents and strength of imagery before volitional engagement." *Scientific Reports* 9, Article number: 3504

Robinson, H. (2003). "Dualism." The Stanford Encyclopedia of Philosophy.

Rogers, C. (1953). *Client-centered therapy: Its current practice, implications and theory.* London: Constable.

Rozin. (2001). "Negativity Bias, Negativity Dominance, and Contagion." *Personality and Social Psychology Review*, Vol. 5.

Sack, D. (2014). "Are you Addicted to Happiness?"

Salay, L. (2018). "A midline thalamic circuit determines reactions to visual threat." *Nature.*

Sana, F. (2013). "Laptop multitasking hinders classroom learning for both users and nearby peers."

Saphire-Bernstein, S. "Oxytocin receptor gene (OXTR) is related to psychological resources."

Sarkis, S.M. (2018). "Gaslighting: Recognize Manipulative and Emotionally Abusive People--and Break Free."

Schmitz, T. (2017). "Hippocampal GABA enables inhibitory control over unwanted thoughts." *Nature Communications* 8, Article number: 1311.

Schneider, K. (2015). *The Handbook of Humanistic Psychology: Theory, Research, and Practice.* Thousand Oaks: CA: SAGE Publications.

Seng, E. (2010). "Dynamics of Changes in Self-Efficacy and Locus of Control Expectancies in the Behavioral and Drug Treatment of Severe Migraine." *Annals of Behavioral Medicine.*

Shamdasani, S. (2005). "Psychotherapy: the invention of a word." History of the Human Sciences.

Sharon, K. (2016). "Our Relationship to the World: Anxiety." Center for Personal Development.

Shorter, E. (1997). *A History of Psychiatry: From the Era of the Asylum to the Age of Prozac*. John Wiley & Sons.

Shirako, A. (2015). "Power Affects Performance When the Pressure Is On: Evidence for Low-Power Threat and High-Power Lift." *Personality and Social Psychology Bulletin*.

Skinner, B.F. (1981). "Selection by Consequences." *Science*.

Smith, D. (1964). "Review of Parents Not Guilty of Their Children's Neuroses." United Press International.

Smith, T. (2015). "The Book of Human Emotions: An Encyclopedia of Feeling from Anger to Wanderlust."

Sperry, R.W. (1952). "Neurology and the mind-body problem." *American Scientist*. 40: 291–312.

Stein, S. (2011). *The EQ Edge*.

Stinckens, N. (2002). "The inner critic on the move: analysis of the change process in a case of short-term client-centered/experiential therapy." *Counselling and Psychotherapy Research*. 2 (1): 40–54.

Stone, H. (1993). *Embracing your inner critic: turning self-criticism into a creative asset*.

Stoney, B. (2015). "Does personal social media usage affect efficiency and well-being?" *Computers in Human Behavior*.

Suetonius. *The Lives of Twelve Caesars, Life of Caligula*.
Taren, A. (2013). Dispositional mindfulness co-varies with smaller amygdala and caudate volumes in community adults. PLOS ONE 22;8(5).

Taylor, S.F. (2006). "Medial frontal cortex activity and loss-related responses to errors." *The Journal of Neuroscience*, 26, 4063-4070.

Thompson, C. (2017). "How being bored out of your mind makes you more creative." *Wired* Magazine.

Torres-Marín, J. (2018). "Is the use of humor associated with anger management? The assessment of individual differences in humor styles in Spain." *Personality and Individual Differences.*

"Unconscious mind." (2016). *New World Encyclopedia.*

Uncapher, M. (2016). "Media multitasking and memory: Differences in working memory and long-term memory."

University of Granada. "Self-defeating humor promotes psychological well-being, study reveals." *ScienceDaily.*

University of New South Wales. "Brain Function And Negative Thinking Linked To Late-onset Depression." *ScienceDaily.*

Vasquez, E. "Rumination and the Displacement of Aggression in United Kingdom Gang-Affiliated Youth." *Aggressive Behavior*, Volume 38.

Veissière, S. (2018). "Hypernatural Monitoring: A Social Rehearsal Account of Smartphone Addiction." *Frontiers in Psychology.*

Virginia Commonwealth University. "Why does divorce run in families? The answer may be genetics." ScienceDaily.

Vorobyev, V. (2015). "Risk-Taking Behavior in a Computerized Driving Task: Brain Activation Correlates of Decision-Making, Outcome, and Peer Influence in Male Adolescents." *PLOS ONE.*

Wadsworth, T. (2013). "Sex and the Pursuit of Happiness: How Other People's Sex Lives are Related to our Sense of Well-Being." *Social Indicators Research.*

Warrell. (2017). "Is Negativity Bias Sabotaging Your Success?"

Watson, J. B. (1913). "Psychology as the behaviorist views it." *Psychological Review*, 101(2), 248-253.

Watson, J. B. (1924). *Behaviorism.* People's Institute. New York.

Welch, J. (2009). *Winning.*

West, R. *Introducing communication theory: analysis and application.* New York, NY.

Westen, D. "The Scientific Legacy of Sigmund Freud."

Wilcox, K. (2012). "Are Close Friends the Enemy? Online Social Networks, Self-Esteem, and Self-Control." *Journal of Consumer Research*

Wilkins, R. H. (1992). *Neurosurgical Classics* (2nd ed.). Park Ridge, Illinois: American Association of Neurological Surgeons.

Wolpert, S. (2012). "That Giant Tarantula is Terrifying, But I'll Touch It."
Wu, K. (2017). "Love, Actually: The Science Behind Lust, Attraction, and Companionship." Harvard Review.

Wu, G., Wang, L., Hong, Z., Ren, S., & Zhou, F. (2017). "Hippocampal low-frequency stimulation inhibits after discharge and increases GABA (A) receptor expression in amygdala-kindled pharmacoresistant epileptic rats. *Neurological Research*, 39(8), 733–743.

Ybarra, O., Burnstein, E., Winkielman, P., Keller, M. C., Manis, M., Chan, E., & Rodriguez, J. (2008). "Mental Exercising Through Simple Socializing: Social Interaction Promotes General Cognitive Functioning." *Personality and Social Psychology Bulletin*, 34(2), 248–259.

Zagorsky, J. (2007). "Do you have to be smart to be rich? The impact of IQ on wealth, income, and financial distress."

Zhang, R. (2016). "Loss of hypothalamic corticotropin-releasing hormone markedly reduces anxiety behaviors in mice." *Molecular Psychiatry*.

Zeki, S. (2007). "The Neurobiology of Love". FEBS Letters, Volume 581, Issue 14.

ABOUT THE AUTHOR

DAN GREEN is an industrial-organizational psychologist who helps leaders and organizations achieve positive change. A bestselling author, Green has performed leadership and team development workshops all over the world for Fortune 500 organizations, professional sports teams, and the Federal Government.

Discover more at www.Psyndesis.com.

INDEX

A

Allais paradox · 124, 125
amygdala · 107, 114, 115, 116, 117, 120, 125, 130, 136, 138, 139, 146, 147, 150, 155, 193, 194, 202, 204, 213, 220, 224, 226
anchoring bias · 135
antifragility · 68, 69, 71, 72, 74, 79
anxiety · 3, 4, 7, 8, 15, 19, 37, 48, 49, 54, 57, 62, 63, 66, 67, 69, 70, 71, 72, 73, 74, 79, 86, 95, 96, 103, 104, 108, 111, 115, 118, 132, 133, 134, 135, 152, 200, 216, 226
Aristotle · 1, 45, 65, 75, 76, 78
attention · 40, 41, 42, 43, 49, 53, 62, 95, 97, 114, 120, 136, 154, 155
authentic · 60, 87, 160, 170, 174, 176

B

Bar-On, Reuven · 28, 116, 136, 213
basal ganglia · 66, 116, 117, 118, 120, 130, 139, 141, 165
Beck, Aaron · 87, 110, 111, 135, 214
behavioral · 17, 19, 22, 25, 26, 38, 39, 43, 46, 48, 52, 104, 215
Behaviorism · *See* behavioral
Bergler, Edmund · 13, 15, 16, 17, 19, 20, 52, 60, 64, 65, 214
biological · 14, 15, 42, 45, 46, 47, 48, 49, 54, 86, 114
bright side · 1, 2, 86, 87, 153, 154

C

Caligula · 158, 224
CBT · *See* Cognitive Behavioral Therapy
change · 14, 27, 43, 53, 62, 68, 78, 92, 93, 94, 95, 101, 106, 107, 108, 109, 111, 113, 114, 120, 135, 136, 137, 159, 168, 169, 190, 207, 224
change management · iii
chunks · 39

cogito · 2, 231
cognitive · 3, 4, 16, 34, 35, 38, 39, 40, 41, 42, 43, 45, 47, 53, 87, 97, 102, 106, 110, 111, 118, 119, 122, 123, 125, 126, 132, 135, 151, 206
Cognitive Behavioral Therapy · 3, 19, 25, 63, 111, 127, 152
cognitive bias · 2, 122, 125, 135, 136
cognitive distortion · *See* cognitive distortions
Cognitive Distortion · iii, 3, 51, 53, 54, 60, 67, 116, 117, 122, 126, 128, 129, 130, 132, 148, 150, 160, 161, 162, 163, 164, 166, 167, 176, 184, 196, 201, 203, 205, 210
cognitive distortions · 2, 111, 116, 122, 127, 130, 132, 135, 136, 151, 152
common coding theory · 107, 109

D

dark side · 1, 2, 86, 87, 153, 154, 156
Darwin, Charles · 46
Descartes, René · 2, 45, 46, 126, 152, 153, 213, 216, 231

E

ego · 2, 13, 14, 15, 16, 18, 20, 49, 52, 65, 217, 221, 231
Emotional Distortion · iii, 3, 51, 54, 138, 140, 141, 143, 147, 149, 152, 160, 161, 162, 163, 164, 166, 167, 170, 175, 177, 184, 196, 203, 204, 205, 210, 212
emotional intelligence · 2, 4, 19, 28, 42, 66, 77, 78, 87, 108, 113, 114, 116, 118, 120, 121, 122, 126, 136, 137, 141, 165, 166, 173, 174, 177, 191, 203, 207
  Assertiveness · 78, 79, 122, 166, 196
  Empathy · 78, 121, 122, 180
  Interpersonal Relationships · 174, 191
  Self-Awareness · 68, 120, 138, 217
  Self-Expression · 138
  Stress Management · 138
epistemology · 40, 206, 207
Excitation Transfer Theory · 67
existentialism · 2, 153, 207

F

Fact or Opinion · 130
fatalism · 35, 42, 53, 100
five psychological perspectives · 2, 68
fMRI · 163, 195, 203, 209, 221
Freud, Sigmund · 10, 12, 13, 14, 15, 17, 18, 19, 20, 50, 51, 52, 65, 154, 156, 217, 220, 221, 226
Freudian slips · 13, 19, 20, 52

G

gaslighting · 61, 223
God · 13, 57, 72, 100, 102, 109, 151
gratitude · 72, 204, 205, 222
gut microbiome · 117, 120

H

heuristics · 122, 123, 136, 155
Hierarchy of Needs · 29, 30, 73
hippocampus · 138, 139, 140, 149, 194, 202
HPA axis · 62, 114
humanism · 4, 29, 34
Humanistic · *See* humanism

I

id · 2, 13, 14, 15, 18, 20, 49, 52, 93, 156, 217
identity · 92, 172, 173, 179, 191
Inner Aggression · iii, 3, 51, 53, 54, 79, 80, 82, 84, 85, 87, 91, 94, 98, 99, 151, 160, 161, 162, 163, 165, 168, 170, 175, 176, 177, 184, 196, 198, 199, 205, 206, 209, 210, 212
inner critic · 4, 42, 54, 60, 80, 81, 82, 87, 88, 90, 91, 92, 93, 98, 99, 198, 216, 224
Inner Passivity · iii, 3, 19, 20, 49, 51, 52, 53, 54, 56, 60, 61, 62, 63, 64, 65, 67, 68, 69, 75, 78, 79, 80, 87, 89, 98, 100, 102, 108, 109, 122, 151, 160, 161, 162, 163, 165, 168, 176, 184, 196, 197, 198, 205, 206, 209, 210, 212, 214

Intersubjectivity · 179
IQ · 49, 120, 121, 125, 126, 218, 226

J

Jung · 13, 15, 16, 20, 52, 65, 102, 156

K

Kahneman, Daniel · 125, 155, 156, 219
keeping up with the Joneses · 128

L

leaders · 3, 88, 97, 122, 141, 154, 158, 159, 161, 165, 168, 169, 170, 175
leadership · 137, 158, 159, 170, 206, 207
    Autocratic · 158
    Charismatic · 159
    Democratic · 159
    Laissez-Faire · 159
    Servant · 159
    Transformational · 159
lobotomy · 8, 10, 51
locus of control · 2, 3, 49, 54, 86, 87, 94, 98, 100, 101, 102, 103, 104, 107, 108, 109, 151, 200, 206, 218
Locus of Control · 3, 51, 52, 54, 100, 101, 102, 103, 104, 105, 108, 109, 151, 161, 163, 164, 166, 167, 168, 170, 176, 177, 184, 196, 200, 205, 210, 212, 213, 218, 223
looking glass self · 185, 192

M

magnetism · *See* mesmerism
Maslow, Abraham · 29, 30, 35, 50, 73, 221
materialism · 72, 74, 213, 222
meditation · 95, 193, 194, 196, 202, 204
mesmerism · 9
Michaelson, Peter · 56, 60, 68
mindfulness · 63, 193, 194, 195, 196, 197, 198, 199, 200, 201, 203, 204, 205, 206, 207, 224

mirror neurons · 105, 107, 108, 109
Myers-Briggs Type Indicator · 16

N

neuroplasticity · 105, 106, 107, 109, 214

O

Obsessive Compulsive Disorder · 63, 82
optimism · 166
oxytocin · 94, 95

P

Passive Externalization · 60
Pavlov · 22
Pavlov, Ivan · 21
perception · 10, 16, 38, 40, 41, 42, 43, 53, 107, 126, 128, 153
personality · 4, 8, 13, 14, 15, 16, 19, 20, 31, 44, 51, 65, 80, 82, 84, 87, 98, 100, 111, 125, 126, 137, 154, 156, 159, 173, 183, 189, 190, 191, 198, 214, 221
personality assessments · 16
pessimism · 25, 50, 166
phenomenology · 180, 181
prefrontal cortex · 84, 107, 115, 116, 117, 120, 125, 126, 136, 138, 139, 141, 142, 143, 146, 155, 165, 188, 189, 192, 193, 194
principle of charity · 70
psychic masochism · 16, 19, 20, 52, 64, 65, 66, 67, 69, 75, 79, 82, 98
psychoanalysis · 10, 12, 13, 15, 16
psychodynamic · 13, 17, 18, 19, 46, 51, 52, 68
psychosomatic disorders · 62, 79
psychotherapy · 1, 8, 9, 11, 13, 51, 63, 93, 216
Purposeful Cognition Index · 3, 34, 56, 67, 68, 80, 88, 102, 138, 140, 149, 156, 174, 210, 212

R

reputation · 155, 173, 177, 191
Rogers, Carl · 29, 31, 34, 50, 223
ruminating · 66, 70, 71, 85, 91, 108

S

schedules of reinforcement · 24
self-actualization · 2, 25, 28, 29, 30, 34, 35, 43, 53, 78, 87, 122
self-defeating personality disorder · 82, 98
self-esteem · 34, 54, 61, 77, 80, 86, 87, 93, 94, 95, 96, 97, 98, 99, 101, 102, 128, 129, 198, 215, 218
Self-Esteem · *See* self-esteem
Skinner, B.F. · 23, 24, 25, 40, 50, 52, 216, 221, 222, 224
social interaction · 94, 178, 179, 182, 183, 184, 185, 186, 191
   microsociology · 179, 191
social prediction · 95, 96, 97, 98
solipsism · 179, 207
Solipsism · 152
superego · 2, 13, 14, 15, 16, 18, 20, 49, 52, 65, 221
symbolic interactionism · 181, 182, 183, 185, 191

T

trepanation · *See* trepanning
trepanning · 6

V

vagus nerve · 118
via negativa · 72, 73, 74

W

Washington Capitals · 162
Watson, John · 21, 22, 23, 225
Wundt, William · 10, 17, 221

Z

Zahavian signal · 127, 128

zone of proximal development · 89, 90

ENDNOTES

INTRODUCTION | THE QUEST FOR PURPOSE

[1] Some attribute this quote to Frank Outlaw, Buddha, or Ralph Waldo Emmerson, though the version is attributed to Lao Tzu.
[2] Some literature claims that Marko Marulić, a Croatian humanist, first used the term 60 years earlier, but many scholars agree that Goclenius first published the term in his Lexicon Philosophicum.
[3] The oldest known surgical treatise whose author is unknown.
[4] see e.g., Everson, 1991; Green & Groff, 2003.
[5] The Dead Sea Scrolls were the library of the Essene, an ancient Jewish sect of the 2nd century.
[6] Medieval Muslim physicians also developed practices to treat patients suffering from a variety of "diseases of the mind."
[7] Descartes wrote this phrase only once, in a posthumously published lesser-known work. It appeared there mid-sentence, uncapitalized, and with a comma. (Commas were not used in classical Latin but were a regular feature of scholastic Latin. Most modern reference works show it with a comma, but it is often presented without a comma in academic work and in popular usage.) In the primary source, Descartes's *Principia Philosophiae*, the proposition appears as ego cogito, ergo sum.
[8] "Therefore, we are most likely in a simulation, because we exist." – Elon Musk
[9] The earliest known translation as "I am thinking, therefore I am" is from 1872 by Charles Porterfield Krauth.
[10] The *dubito* is often mistakenly attributed to Descartes.
[11] "Cogito." Oxford Dictionaries. Oxford University Press.

CHAPTER 1 | THE SEARCH FOR SANITY

[1] Little is known about Bosch's life except for that his works were widely copied, were especially macabre and contained nightmarish depictions of hell.
[2] Also known as "Cutting the Stone" or "The Cure of Folly."

³ Trepanning, also known as trepanation, trephination, trephining or making a burr hole (the verb trepan derives from Old French from Medieval Latin *trepanum* from Greek *trypanon*, literally "borer, auger").
⁴ Over 1500 trephined skulls from the Neolithic period have been uncovered throughout the world, from places such as China, America, Europe, Siberia, etc.
⁵ Restak, R. (2000). "Fixing the Brain." *Mysteries of the Mind.*
⁶ Shorter, Edward. *A History of Psychiatry.*
⁷ It is important to note that when the world was conquered by Christianity, insanity and mental illness went untreated. Treatment did not start again until the Early Middle Ages.
⁸ *Galen on Bloodletting.* Cambridge University Press.
⁹ Jackson, W. A. (2001). "A short guide to humoral medicine."
¹⁰ "Frequently Asked Questions About Lobotomies," NPR 2005
¹¹ See Cozzi, G. (2018). "Will a shrink make you richer? Gender differences in the effects of psychotherapy on labour efficiency."
¹² See Haggerty. "History of Psychotherapy."
¹³ The Medical Renaissance, from 1400 to 1700 CE, is the period of progress in European medical knowledge, and a renewed interest in the ideas of the ancient Greeks and Romans. Such medical discoveries during the Medical Renaissance are credited with paving the way for modern medicine.
¹⁴ See Jackson, S. *Care of the Psyche: A History of Psychological Healing.*
¹⁵ See Shamdasani, S. (2005) 'Psychotherapy': the invention of a word.
¹⁶ See Crabtree, A. Animal Magnetism, Early Hypnotism, and Psychical Research, 1766–1925
¹⁷ See Hypnosis, History and Early Research. Britannica.
¹⁸ See Hypnosis, History and Early Research. Britannica.
¹⁹ He was the first to refer to himself as a psychologist.
²⁰ See Pashler, H. Stevens' Handbook of Experimental Psychology.
²¹ See Heine, S. J. (2011). *Cultural Psychology.*
²² See McLeod, S. A. (2008). Wilhelm Wundt.

CHAPTER 2 | THE INNER DEPTHS OF THE MIND

¹ See Freud, S. and Rieff, P. (2008). "Three Case Histories."
² See Freud, S. and Rieff, P. (2008). "Three Case Histories."
³ See McLeod, S. A. (2017). Psychodynamic Approach.
⁴ See Alexander, C. "Transcendental Consciousness."
⁵ See Bergmann, S. (2013). *The Unconscious in Shakespeare's Plays.*
⁶ See Aczel. *The Mystery of the Aleph.*
⁷ See *Unconscious Mind*, New World Encyclopedia.
⁸ See Cherry, K. (2018). "The Conscious and Unconscious Mind."
⁹ See Freud, 1923, p.15
¹⁰ See Plato. *Phaedrus.* "The Charioteer represents intellect, reason, or the part of the soul that must guide the soul to truth; one horse represents rational or moral impulse or the positive part of passionate nature (e.g., righteous indignation); while the other represents the soul's irrational passions, appetites, or concupiscent nature. The

Charioteer directs the entire chariot/soul, trying to stop the horses from going different ways, and to proceed towards enlightenment."
[11] See Campbell. (1971). *Hero With a Thousand Faces.*
[12] See Bergler, E. (1952). *The Superego.*
[13] See Bergler, E. (1992). *Principles of Self-Damage.*
[14] See Lewis, R. *The Psychology of Losing and How to Profit From It.*
[15] See Kihlstrom, J. *Is Freud Still Alive? No, Not Really.*
[16] See Westen, "The Scientific Legacy of Sigmund Freud."
[17] See Loftus. (1992). "Is the unconscious smart or dumb?"
[18] See Westen, "The Scientific Legacy of Sigmund Freud."
[19] See McLeod, S. A. (2017). Psychodynamic Approach.

CHAPTER 3 | THERE WILL BE CONSEQUENCES

[1] See Watson, J. "Psychology as the Behaviorist Views It."
[2] See Watson, J. "Psychology as the Behaviorist Views It."
[3] See Watson, J. *Behaviorism.*
[4] See Skinner, B. F. "Selection by Consequences."
[5] See Ferster, C. & Skinner, B. *Schedules of Reinforcement.*
[6] See McLeod, S. A. "Skinner – Operant Conditioning."
[7] See McLeod, S. A. "Skinner – Operant Conditioning."

CHAPTER 4 | THE THIRD FORCE

[1] See Donald, D. *Lincoln.*
[2] See Bar-On, R. *Bar-On Emotional Quotient Inventory.*
[3] See Greening, T. "Five Basic Postulates of Humanistic Psychology."
[4] See Schneider, K. *The Handbook of Humanistic Psychology.*
[5] See Schneider, K. *The Handbook of Humanistic Psychology.*
[6] See Maslow, A. *Motivation and Personality.*
[7] See Rogers, C. *Client-Centered Therapy.*
[8] See Bugental, J. (1964). The third force in psychology.

CHAPTER 5 | THE REVOLUTION

[1] See Johnson & Scott. "The Weapon Effect on Eyewitness Testimonies."
[2] See Anderson, J.R. (2010). Cognitive Psychology and Its Implications.
[3] See Anderson, J.R. (2010). Cognitive Psychology and Its Implications.
[4] See Miller, G. A. (1956). "The magical number seven, plus or minus two: Some limits on our capacity for processing information."
[5] See Miller, G. A. (1956). "The magical number seven, plus or minus two: Some limits on our capacity for processing information."
[6] See Palmer D. C. (2006). On Chomsky's Appraisal of Skinner's Verbal Behavior: A Half Century of Misunderstanding.
[7] See Brown, R. *A First Language.*
[8] See Anderson, J.R. *Cognitive Psychology and Its Implications.*
[9] See Balota, D.A. & Marsh, E.J. *Cognitive Psychology: Key Readings.*

[10] See Berkum, J. "Language in action - Mood and language comprehension."

CHAPTER 6 | INVESTIGATION OF INHERITANCE

[1] See Larner, A; Leach, J. "Phineas Gage and the beginnings of neuropsychology."
[2] See Pevsner, J. "Leonardo da Vinci's contributions to neuroscience."
[3] See Robinson, H. "Dualism," The Stanford Encyclopedia of Philosophy.
[4] See Damasio, A. (1994). "Descartes' error: emotion, reason, and the human brain."
[5] See Cherry, K. (2018). "The Role of the Biological Perspective in Psychology."
[6] See Cherry, K. (2018). "What is Biopsychology, Brain and Behavior?"
[7] See Mader, S. S. (2000): Human biology.
[8] See Cherry, K. (2018). "What is Biopsychology, Brain and Behavior?"
[9] See Cherry, K. (2018). "What is Biopsychology, Brain and Behavior?"

CHAPTER 8 | INNER PASSIVITY

[1] See Michaelson, P. *Phantom of the Psyche.*
[2] See Michaelson, P. *Phantom of the Psyche.*
[3] See Michaelson, P. *Phantom of the Psyche.*
[4] See Michaelson, P. *Phantom of the Psyche.*
[5] See Michaelson, P. "When Life Becomes Unreal and Dream Like."
[6] See Sharon, K. "Our Relationship to the World: Anxiety."
[7] See Bundrant, M. "Inner Passivity: How We Trick Ourselves into Helplessness."
[8] See Michaelson, P. *Phantom of the Psyche.*
[9] See Michaelson, P. *Phantom of the Psyche.*
[10] See Michaelson, P. *Phantom of the Psyche.*
[11] A great book on this is *Gaslighting: Recognize Manipulative and Emotionally Abusive People--and Break Free*, by Stephanie Moulton Sarkis.
[12] See Michaelson, P. *Phantom of the Psyche.*
[13] See Cannon, W. *The Mechanical Factors of Digestion.*
[14] See Chrousos, G. (1992). The concepts of stress and stress system disorders.
[15] See Michaelson, P. *Phantom of the Psyche.*
[16] Some literature refers to this as 'chosen sadness.'
[17] See "Choosing Sadness: The Irony of Depression."
[18] See "Choosing Sadness: The Irony of Depression."
[19] See "Are you Addicted to Happiness?"
[20] See "Are you Addicted to Happiness?"
[21] See Bergler, E. (1952). *The Superego.*
[22] See Bergler, E. (1992). *Principles of Self-Damage.*
[23] See *"Why Do We Like Watching Scary Films"?*
[24] See Haidt, J., McCauley, C., & Rozin, P. (1994). Individual differences in sensitivity to disgust: A scale sampling seven domains of disgust elicitors.
[25] This is the concept behind the saying "birds of a feather flock together."
[26] See Hess. (2010). "The Psychology of Scary Movies."
[27] See O'Brien. (2013). "The curious appeal of horror movies."
[28] Bergler's "basic neurosis" is a good place to dive deep into this subject.
[29] See Bryant, J., & Miron, D. (2003). "Excitation-transfer theory."

30 See Michaelson, P. *Phantom of the Psyche*.
31 See Michaelson, P. *Phantom of the Psyche*.
32 See Taleb. (2012). *Antifragile*.
33 Antifragility has also been applied in physics, risk analysis, molecular biology, transportation planning, engineering, Aerospace (NASA), megaproject management, and computer science.
34 See Wolff's law, developed by the German anatomist and surgeon Julius Wolff (1836–1902) in the 19th century, states that bone in a healthy person or animal will adapt to the loads under which it is placed. If loading on a particular bone increases, the bone will remodel itself over time to become stronger to resist that sort of loading.
35 For a deeper dive into this concept, read *Antifragile*, by Taleb.
36 See Kellert, S. (1993). *In the Wake of Chaos: Unpredictable Order in Dynamical Systems*.
37 See Loh, K. K., & Kanai, R. (2014). "Higher media multi-tasking activity is associated with smaller gray-matter density in the anterior cingulate cortex."
38 See Uncapher, M. (2016). "Media multitasking and memory: Differences in working memory and long-term memory."
39 See Moisala et al. (2015). "Media multitasking is associated with distractibility and increased prefrontal activity in adolescents and young adults."
40 See Sana, F. (2013). "Laptop multitasking hinders classroom learning for both users and nearby peers."
41 See Brooks, S. (2015). "Does personal social media usage affect efficiency and well-being?"
42 See Johansson, J. (2016). "Greater Fall Risk in Elderly Women Than in Men Is Associated With Increased Gait Variability During Multitasking."
43 See Baillargeon, N. *Intellectual Self-Defense*.
44 Research by Jonathan Haidt in *The Coddling of the American Mind* has suggested that a common humanity approach is needed to rebuild America's moral foundations and political divides.
45 The other themes are Skin in the Game, Lindy Effect, Barbell Strategy, and Green Lumber Fallacy.
46 See Nguyen, L. (2018). "The impact of gratitude on adolescent materialism and generosity."
47 See Haidt, J. (2018). *The Coddling of the American Mind*. p151.
48 See Ruvio. (2013). When bad gets worse: the amplifying effect of materialism on traumatic stress and maladaptive consumption.
49 See Ruvio. (2013). When bad gets worse: the amplifying effect of materialism on traumatic stress and maladaptive consumption.
50 See Taleb. (2012). *Antifragile*.
51 See Grant, A. (2011). "Too Much of a Good Thing."
52 See Grant, A. (2011). "Too Much of a Good Thing."
53 This is one of the core themes of Malcolm Gladwell's book, *David and Goliath*.
54 Grant does posit that some virtues have a true definable midpoint, such as pride being the intermediate between humility and vanity.
55 See Bradberry, T. (2018). "9 Signs Your Perfectionism Is Out Of Control."

CHAPTER 9 | INNER AGGRESSION

[1] See Stinckens, N. (2002). "The inner critic on the move: analysis of the change process in a case of short-term client-centered/experiential therapy."
[2] Reinhart, R. "Causal Control of Medial-Frontal Cortex Governs Electrophysiological and Behavioral Indices of Performance Monitoring and Learning."
[3] See Taylor, S. "Medial frontal cortex activity and loss-related responses to errors."
[4] See Fitzgerald, K. "Error-related hyperactivity of the anterior cingulate cortex in obsessive-compulsive disorder."
[5] It is important to note that SD-PD is not officially listed in the Diagnostic and Statistical Manual of Mental Disorders (DSM-5), but rather referred to as Personality Disorder-Trait Specified.
[6] See Kass, F. (1987). "Self-Defeating Personality Disorder: An Empirical Study." *Journal of Personality Disorders.*
[7] See Torres-Marin. (2018). "Is the use of humor associated with anger management? The assessment of individual differences in humor styles in Spain."
[8] See University of Granada. "Self-defeating humor promotes psychological well-being." ScienceDaily. ScienceDaily, 8 February 2018.
[9] See Keele University. "Humor styles and bullying in schools: Not a laughing matter."
[10] See J. Paul Hamilton. "Depressive Rumination, the Default-Mode Network, and the Dark Matter of Clinical Neuroscience."
[11] See J. Paul Hamilton. "Depressive Rumination, the Default-Mode Network, and the Dark Matter of Clinical Neuroscience."
[12] See Judge, T. A. (1997). "The dispositional causes of job satisfaction: A core evaluations approach."
[13] See Marsh, H.W. (1990). "Causal ordering of academic self-concept and academic achievement: A multiwave, longitudinal path analysis."
[14] See Baumeister, R. F.(2003). "Does High Self-Esteem Cause Better Performance, Interpersonal Success, Happiness, or Healthier Lifestyles?"
[15] See Orth U. (2014). "The development of self-esteem."
[16] See Orth U. (2014). "The development of self-esteem."
[17] See Blatt, S.J. (2008). Polarities of experience: Relatedness and self-definition in personality, development, psychopathology, and the therapeutic process.
[18] See Beck, A.T. (1983). Cognitive therapy of depression: New perspectives.
[19] See Longe O. (2010). Having a word with yourself: Neural correlates of self-criticism and self-reassurance.
[20] See Zone of proximal development. (2009). In Penguin dictionary of psychology.
[21] Scaffolding consists of enabling a child to solve a task or achieve a goal that would be beyond his unassisted efforts.
[22] See Firestone, L. (2018). *Conquer Your Critical Inner Voice.*
[23] See Morin, A. (2018). *13 Things Mentally Strong People Don't Do.*
[24] See Eduardo A. Vasquez, Sarah Osman and Jane L. Wood, School of Psychology, University of Kent. Rumination and the Displacement of Aggression in United Kingdom Gang-Affiliated Youth. Aggressive Behavior, Volume 38
[25] See University of New South Wales. "Brain Function And Negative Thinking Linked To Late-onset Depression." ScienceDaily. ScienceDaily, 23 June 2006.

[26] See Ohio University. "Dwelling on stressful events can increase inflammation in the body, study finds." ScienceDaily. ScienceDaily, 13 March 2013.

[27] See Brown, B. (1999). *Soul without shame: a guide to liberating yourself from the judge within.*

[28] See Firestone, R. (2002). *Conquer your critical inner voice: a revolutionary program to counter negative thoughts and live free from imagined limitations.*

[29] See Carson, R. (2003) [1983]. *Taming your gremlin: a surprisingly simple method for getting out of your own way.*

[30] See Stone, H.(1993). *Embracing your inner critic: turning self-criticism into a creative asset.*

[31] See Earley, J. (2010). *Self-therapy for your inner critic: transforming self-criticism into self-confidence.*

[32] See Cornell, A. (2005). "Radical gentleness: the inner critic transforms."

[33] See Allione, T. (2008). *Feeding your demons: ancient wisdom for resolving inner conflict.*

[34] See S. Saphire-Bernstein, B. M. Oxytocin receptor gene (OXTR) is related to psychological resources.

[35] "At a particular location, the oxytocin receptor gene has two versions: an "A" (adenine) variant and a "G" (guanine) variant. Several studies have suggested that people with at least one "A" variant have an increased sensitivity to stress, poorer social skills and worse mental health outcomes. The researchers found that people who have either two "A" nucleotides or one "A" and one "G" at this specific location on the oxytocin receptor gene have substantially lower levels of optimism, self-esteem and mastery and significantly higher levels of depressive symptoms than people with two "G" nucleotides." See S. Saphire-Bernstein, B. M. Oxytocin receptor gene (OXTR) is related to psychological resources.

[36] See Zak, P. *The Morale Molecule.*

[37] See Geert-Jan W. (2017). "Neural and computational processes underlying dynamic changes in self-esteem."

[38] See Geert-Jan W. (2017). "Neural and computational processes underlying dynamic changes in self-esteem."

[39] See Leary, M. R. (2012). Sociometer theory.

[40] See Rozin. (2001). "Negativity Bias, Negativity Dominance, and Contagion."

[41] See Warrell. (2017). "Is Negativity Bias Sabotaging Your Success?"

CHAPTER 10 | LOCUS OF CONTROL

[1] See Rotter, J. *Psychological Monographs.*

[2] He later published his famous I-E scale (a scale that measures internal vs. external Locus of Control) in the Journal *Psychological Monographs* as a way to assess internal vs. external Locus of Control within the assessment taker.

[3] Sub-categories to this philosophy are nature vs. nurture, biological determinism, and behaviorism.

[4] See Nietzsche, *The Wanderer and His Shadow.*

[5] See Mamlin, Harris, & Case. "A Methodological Analysis of Research on Locus of Control and Learning Disabilities: Rethinking a Common Assumption."

[6] See Griffin, D. "Locus of Control and Psychological Well-Being."

[7] See Maltby, Day & Macaskill, 2007

[8] See Mamlin, Harris, & Case. "A Methodological Analysis of Research on Locus of Control and Learning Disabilities: Rethinking a Common Assumption."

[9] See Judge, T. A.; Locke, E. A.; Durham, C. C. (1997). "The dispositional causes of job satisfaction: A core evaluations approach."

[10] See Golding, J. The relationship between parental Locus of Control and adolescent obesity: a longitudinal pre-birth cohort.

[11] See Yu-Kang Lee. "Helpful-stressful cycle? Psychological links between type of mobile phone user and stress."

[12] See Elizabeth K. Seng. "Dynamics of Changes in Self-Efficacy and Locus of Control Expectancies in the Behavioral and Drug Treatment of Severe Migraine."

[13] See Merideth Ferguson. "You cannot leave it at the office: Spillover and crossover of coworker incivility."

[14] See Aguilar, O.M., Growing Environmental Stewards: The Overall Effect of a School Gardening Program on Environmental Attitudes and Environmental Locus of Control of Different Demographic Groups of Elementary School Children.

[15] See R Zhang, M. (2016). Loss of hypothalamic corticotropin-releasing hormone markedly reduces anxiety behaviors in mice.

[16] See R Zhang, M. (2016). Loss of hypothalamic corticotropin-releasing hormone markedly reduces anxiety behaviors in mice.

[17] See Jeanie Park. (2017). Baroreflex dysfunction and augmented sympathetic nerve responses during mental stress in veterans with posttraumatic stress disorder (PTSD).

[18] See https://www.endocrineweb.com/endocrinology/overview-hypothalamus

[19] See Ezkurdia, I. (2014). "Multiple evidence strands suggest that there may be as few as 19,000 human protein-coding genes." *Human Molecular Genetics.*

[20] See Bergland (2017). How do neuroplasticity and neurogenesis rewire your brain?

[21] There are many books on this subject alone. If this subject interests you, I suggest the following: *The Brain's Way of Healing: Remarkable Discoveries and Recoveries from the Frontiers of Neuroplasticity* by Norman Doidge, *Neuroplasticity* by Moheb Costandi, *Switch on Your Brain: The Key to Peak Happiness, Thinking, and Health* by Dr. Caroline Leaf, *The Power of Neuroplasticity* by Shad Helmstetter, *The Stress-Proof Brain: Master Your Emotional Response to Stress Using Mindfulness & Neuroplasticity* by Melanie Greenberg, *The Brain That Changes Itself: Stories of Personal Triumph from the Frontiers of Brain Science* by Norman Doidge, *My Stroke of Insight: A Brain Scientist's Personal Journey* by Jill Bolte Taylor, *The Mind and the Brain: Neuroplasticity and the Power of Mental Force* by Jeffrey M. Schwartz and Sharon Begley, *Breaking the Habit of Being Yourself: How to Lose Your Mind and Create a New One* by Dr. Joe Dispenza

[22] See Sperry, R.W. (1952). "Neurology and the mind-body problem." American Scientist. 40: 291–312.

CHAPTER 11 | COGNITIVE DISTORTION

[1] See Beck, Aaron (1996). "The Past and the future of Cognitive Therapy."

[2] See Beck, A. T. (1976). *Cognitive therapies and emotional disorders.*

[3] See Burns, D. D. (1980). *Feeling good: The new mood therapy.*

[4] See Burns, D. D. (1989). *The feeling good handbook.*

[5] See Haidt, J. (2006). *The Happiness Hypothesis.*

[6] See Bradberry, T. (2007). *Emotional Intelligence 2.0.*

[7] Some research puts the success rate at a whopping 90%!

[8] See Bested, A. (2013). "Intestinal microbiota, probiotics and mental health."
[9] See Bested, A. (2013). "Intestinal microbiota, probiotics and mental health."
[10] See Carabotti, M. (2015). The gut-brain axis: interactions between enteric microbiota, central and enteric nervous systems.
[11] See Kok, B. "How Positive Emotions Build Physical Health: Perceived Positive Social Connections Account for the Upward Spiral Between Positive Emotions and Vagal Tone."
[12] See Carabotti, M. (2015). The gut-brain axis: interactions between enteric microbiota, central and enteric nervous systems.
[13] See Autism and nutrition: "The role of the gut-brain axis." Nutrition Research Reviews
[14] Approximately 70%.
[15] See Pistollato, F. (2016). "Role of gut microbiota and nutrients in amyloid formation and pathogenesis of Alzheimer disease."
[16] See Bradberry, T. (2007). *Emotional Intelligence 2.0.*
[17] See Zagorsky, J. (2007). "Do you have to be smart to be rich? The impact of IQ on wealth, income, and financial distress."
[18] See Allais, M. (1953). "Le Comportement de l'Homme Rationnel devant le Risque: Critique des Postulats et Axiomes de l'Ecole Americaine."
[19] See Koçaslan, Gelengül. "Quantum Interpretation to Decision Making Under Risk: The Observer Effect In Allais Paradox."
[20] Cognitive dissonance is defined as the state of having inconsistent thoughts, beliefs, or attitudes, especially as relating to behavioral decisions and attitude change.
[21] This has also been referred to as pronking or pronging
[22] See Wadsworth. (2013). "Sex and the Pursuit of Happiness: How Other People's Sex Lives are Related to our Sense of Well-Being."
[23] See Keith Wilcox, Andrew T. Stephen. "Are Close Friends the Enemy? Online Social Networks, Self-Esteem, and Self-Control."
[24] See Anthony L. Burrow, Nicolette Rainone. How many likes did I get?: Purpose moderates links between positive social media feedback and self-esteem.
[25] The research on this varies. I have seen numbers as low as 50,000 and as high as 100,000 per day.
[26] See Crocq M. A. (2015). A history of anxiety: from Hippocrates to DSM.
[27] See the *Diagnostic and Statistical Manual of Mental Disorders*, Fifth Edition.

CHAPTER 12 | EMOTIONAL DISTORTION

[1] Reuven Bar-On uses this definition in the Bar-On model of EI.
[2] See the Bar-On Concept of EI, found at his personal website http://www.reuvenbaron.org
[3] See Bradberry, T. (2007). *Emotional Intelligence 2.0.*
[4] The names of the pillars vary across the different EI models but these are the general categories.
[5] See Fotopoulou A. (2007). "Confabulation: Motivated reality monitoring." *Neuropsychologia.* 45 (10): 2180–90.
[6] See Palombo, D. (2016). "Medial Temporal Lobe Contributions to Episodic Future Thinking: Scene Construction or Future Projection?" *Cerebral Cortex.*

[7] See Chan, R (2017). "Low-frequency hippocampal–cortical activity drives brain-wide resting-state functional MRI connectivity." *Proceedings of the National Academy of Sciences.*

[8] See Mikulovic, S. (2018). "Ventral hippocampal OLM cells control type 2 theta oscillations and response to predator odor." *Nature Communications.*

[9] See Nummenmaa, L. (2014). "Bodily maps of emotions." *Proceedings of the National Academy of Sciences.*

[10] See Nummenmaa, L. (2014). "Bodily maps of emotions." *Proceedings of the National Academy of Sciences.*

[11] See Plutchik, R. (1982). A psychoevolutionary theory of emotions. *Social Science Information,* 21(4–5), 529–553.

[12] See Plutchik, R. (1982). A psychoevolutionary theory of emotions. *Social Science Information,* 21(4–5), 529–553.

[13] See Plutchik, R. (1982). A psychoevolutionary theory of emotions. *Social Science Information,* 21(4–5), 529–553.

[14] See Smith, T. (2015). "The Book of Human Emotions: An Encyclopedia of Feeling from Anger to Wanderlust."

[15] See Wolpert, S. (2012). "That Giant Tarantula is Terrifying, But I'll Touch It."

[16] See Wolpert, S. (2012). "That Giant Tarantula is Terrifying, But I'll Touch It."

[17] See Lieberman, M. D. (2007). "Putting Feelings Into Words." *Psychological Science.*

[18] See Lieberman, M. D. (2007). "Putting Feelings Into Words." *Psychological Science.*

[19] See Freeman, J. (2018). *"How to Improve Emotional Intelligence: 10 Tip for Increasing Self-Awareness."*

[20] Taken directly from Freeman, J. (2011). "Integrated Emotions: Rethinking the way we evaluate our feelings."

CHAPTER 13 | PART II SUMMARY

[1] See Haidt, J. (2006). *The Happiness Hypothesis.*
[2] See Revonsuo, A. (2010). Consciousness: The Science of Subjectivity.
[3] Side note, I truly do think we live in a simulation!
[4] See Hogan, R. (1990). "The Dark Side of Personality and Extreme Leader Behavior."
[5] See Hogan, R. (2015). "Reflections on the Dark Side."
[6] See Kahneman, Daniel (2011). *Thinking, fast and slow.*
[7] See Haidt, J. (2006). *The Happiness Hypothesis.*
[8] See Jung, C.G. (1938). "Psychology and Religion."

CHAPTER 14 | LEADING ON PURPOSE

[1] See Suetonius, *The Lives of Twelve Caesars.* Life of Caligula.
[2] Most of the research claims either five, seven, or twelve total styles.
[3] See Joseph, S. (2017). *Authentic: How to be yourself and why it matters.*
[4] See Welch, J. (2009). *Winning.*
[5] See Welch, J. (2009). *Winning.*
[6] See California Institute of Technology. (2010). "Gain and loss in optimistic versus pessimistic brains."

[7] See Welch, J. (2009). *Winning*.
[8] See Salay, L. (2018). "A midline thalamic circuit determines reactions to visual threat." *Nature*.
[9] This is research done by BCUOMA, the British Columbia Used Oil Management Association.
[10] See Vorobyev, V. (2015) "Risk-Taking Behavior in a Computerized Driving Task: Brain Activation Correlates of Decision-Making, Outcome, and Peer Influence in Male Adolescents." *PLOS ONE*.
[11] See Vorobyev, V. (2015) "Risk-Taking Behavior in a Computerized Driving Task: Brain Activation Correlates of Decision-Making, Outcome, and Peer Influence in Male Adolescents." *PLOS ONE*.
[12] See Garvin, D. (1993). "Building a Learning Organization." *Harvard Business Review*.
[13] See Moll, T. (2010). "Emotional contagion in soccer penalty shootouts: Celebration of individual success is associated with ultimate team success." *Journal of Sports Sciences*.
[14] See Moll, T. (2010). "Emotional contagion in soccer penalty shootouts: Celebration of individual success is associated with ultimate team success." *Journal of Sports Sciences*.

CHAPTER 15 | RELATING ON PURPOSE

[1] See Brady, D. (2013). "Charles Manson's turning point: Dale Carnegie classes." *Business Week*.
[2] See Hogan, R. (2009). "Why Personality Matters."
[3] See Hogan, R. (2009). "Why Personality Matters."
[4] See Stein, S. (2011). *The EQ Edge*.
[5] See Carnegie, D. (1936). *How to Win Friends and Influence People*.
[6] See Haidt, J. (2006). *The Happiness Hypothesis*.
[7] See McNally, L. (2012). "Cooperation and the evolution of intelligence." Proceedings of the Royal Society B: Biological Sciences.
[8] See Ybarra, O., Burnstein, E., Winkielman, P., Keller, M. C., Manis, M., Chan, E., & Rodriguez, J. (2008). "Mental Exercising Through Simple Socializing: Social Interaction Promotes General Cognitive Functioning." *Personality and Social Psychology Bulletin*, 34(2), 248–259.
[9] See Veissière, S. (2018). "Hypernatural Monitoring: A Social Rehearsal Account of Smartphone Addiction." *Frontiers in Psychology*.
[10] See Kendon, A. (1975). *Organization of Behavior in Face-To-Face Interaction*.
[11] See Menon, S. (2014). "Interdisciplinary Perspectives on Consciousness and the Self."
[12] See Menon, S. (2014). "Interdisciplinary Perspectives on Consciousness and the Self."
[13] Taken directly from the Encyclopedia of Phenomenology.
[14] See West, R. *Introducing communication theory: analysis and application*. New York, NY.
[15] See Blumer, H. (1969). *Symbolic interactionism: perspective and method*. Englewood Cliffs, N.J.: Prentice-Hall.
[16] See Blumer, H. (1969). *Symbolic interactionism: perspective and method*. Englewood Cliffs, N.J.: Prentice-Hall.

[17] See Blumer, H. (1969). *Symbolic interactionism: perspective and method.* Englewood Cliffs, N.J.: Prentice-Hall.
[18] Taken directly from Charon, J. (2004). *Symbolic Interactionism An Introduction, An Interpretation, An Integration.* Boston: Pearson.
[19] See Adolphs, R. (2009). The social brain: neural basis of social knowledge. *Annual review of psychology*, 60, 693-716.
[20] Paraphrased from Dr. Phil's conversation with Joe Rogan on podcast #1254
[21] See Finkel, E. J. (2015). The Suffocation Model: Why Marriage in America Is Becoming an All-or-Nothing Institution. *Current Directions in Psychological Science*, 24(3), 238–244.
[22] Taken from Botwin, M. D., Buss, D. M. and Shackelford, T. K. Personality and Mate Preferences: Five Factors In Mate Selection and Marital Satisfaction. Journal of Personality, 65: 107-136.
[23] See Wu, K. (2017). "Love, Actually: The Science Behind Lust, Attraction, and Companionship." Harvard Review.
[24] See Zeki, S. (2007). "The Neurobiology of Love." FEBS Letters, Volume 581, Issue 14.
[25] See Cohen, P. N. (2018). The Coming Divorce Decline.
[26] See Virginia Commonwealth University. "Why does divorce run in families? The answer may be genetics." ScienceDaily.
[27] See Eastwick, P. W., & Finkel, E. J. (2008). Sex differences in mate preferences revisited: Do people know what they initially desire in a romantic partner? *Journal of Personality and Social Psychology*, 94(2), 245-264.
[28] See Jonason, P. K. (2015). Relationship Dealbreakers: Traits People Avoid in Potential Mates. *Personality and Social Psychology Bulletin*, 41(12), 1697–1711.
[29] See Haidt, J. (2006). *The Happiness Hypothesis.*
[30] See Haidt, J. (2006). *The Happiness Hypothesis.*
[31] See Haidt, J. (2006). *The Happiness Hypothesis.*
[32] See West, R. *Introducing communication theory: analysis and application.* New York, NY.

CHAPTER 16 | BEING ON PURPOSE

[1] See Taren, A. (2013). Dispositional mindfulness co-varies with smaller amygdala and caudate volumes in community adults. PLOS ONE 22;8(5).
[2] See Taren, A. (2013). Dispositional mindfulness co-varies with smaller amygdala and caudate volumes in community adults. PLOS ONE 22;8(5).
[3] See Admon, R. (2009). "Human vulnerability to stress depends on amygdala's predisposition and hippocampal plasticity." PNAS.
[4] See Kenyon, J. (2019). "Electrical fingerprint of the amygdala guides neurofeedback training for stress resilience." *Nature Human Behavior.* 3, pages 63–73 (2019).
[5] See Lutz, J. (2014). "Mindfulness and emotion regulation, an fMRI study." University of Switzerland.
[6] See Grecucci, A. (2015). "Mindful Emotion Regulation: Exploring the Neurocognitive Mechanisms behind Mindfulness." *BioMed Research International.*
[7] See Thompson, C. (2017). "How being bored out of your mind makes you more creative." *Wired* Magazine.

[8] See Shirako, A. (2015). "Power Affects Performance When the Pressure Is On: Evidence for Low-Power Threat and High-Power Lift." *Personality and Social Psychology Bulletin.*
[9] See Legault, L. (2012). "Preserving Integrity in the Face of Performance Threat: Self-Affirmation Enhances Neurophysiological Responsiveness to Errors." *Psychological Science.*
[10] See Gilpin, H. (2017). "Predictors of Treatment Outcome in Contextual Cognitive and Behavioral Therapies for Chronic Pain: A Systematic Review." *The Journal of Pain.*
[11] See https://www.nimh.nih.gov/health/topics/obsessive-compulsive-disorder-ocd/index.shtml
[12] Taken directly from University of Cambridge. "Scientists identify mechanism that helps us inhibit unwanted thoughts." ScienceDaily. ScienceDaily, 3 November 2017.
[13] See Schmitz, T. (2017). "Hippocampal GABA enables inhibitory control over unwanted thoughts." *Nature Communications* 8, Article number: 1311.
[14] See Purdy, E. (2019). *30 Days to Everyday Anxiety Relief.*
[15] See Wu, G., Wang, L., Hong, Z., Ren, S., & Zhou, F. (2017). "Hippocampal low-frequency stimulation inhibits after discharge and increases GABA (A) receptor expression in amygdala-kindled pharmacoresistant epileptic rats. *Neurological Research*, 39(8), 733–743.
[16] See Grecucci, A. (2015). "Mindful Emotion Regulation: Exploring the Neurocognitive Mechanisms behind Mindfulness." *BioMed Research International.*
[17] See Barton, A. (2015). "Linking financial distress to marital quality: The intermediary roles of demand/withdraw and spousal gratitude expressions." *Personal Relationships,* 2015; 22 (3): 536.
[18] See Algoe, S. (2010). "It's the Little Things: Everyday Gratitude as a Booster Shot for Romantic Relationships." *Personal Relationships.*
[19] See George Mason University. (2009). "Key To Happiness Is Gratitude, And Men May Be Locked Out." *ScienceDaily.*
[20] See Williams, L. (2015). "Warm Thanks: Gratitude Expression Facilitates Social Affiliation in New Relationships via Perceived Warmth." *Emotion.*
[21] See Northeastern University College of Science. (2014). "Can gratitude reduce costly impatience?." *ScienceDaily.*

CHAPTER 18 | CONCLUSION

[1] Analysis of data from National Center for Health Statistics, CDC.
[2] See Robert, K. (2019. "Decoding the contents and strength of imagery before volitional engagement." *Scientific Reports* 9, Article number: 3504
[3] See Percival, H. (1947). *Thinking and Destiny.*

CPSIA information can be obtained
at www.ICGtesting.com
Printed in the USA
LVHW110959050919
630033LV00001B/17/P